amazon.com

Other books by Robert Spector

The Nordstrom Way
Lessons from The Nordstrom Way

amazon.com

Get Big Fast

Robert Spector

HarperBusiness
An Imprint of HarperCollins*Publishers*

Grateful acknowledgment is made to reprint excerpts from *Architects of the Web* by Robert Reid. Copyright © 1997 by Robert Reid. Reprinted by permission of John Wiley & Sons, Inc.

HarperCollins books may be purchased for educational, business, or sales promotional use. For information please write: Special Markets Department, HarperCollins Publishers Inc., 10 East 53rd Street, New York, NY 10022.

FIRST EDITION

Designed by Jeannette Jacobs

Printed on acid-free paper

Library of Congress Cataloging-in-Publication Data

Spector, Robert, 1947–
Amazon.com: get big fast/[Robert Spector].
p. cm.
ISBN 0-06-662041-4
1. Amazon.com—History 2. Internet bookstores—United States—History—20th century. 3. Electronic commerce—United States—History—20th century. I. Title
Z473.A485 S64 2000
381'.45002'02854678—dc21 99-087599

00 01 02 03 04 ❖/RRD 10 9 8 7 6 5 4 3 2 1

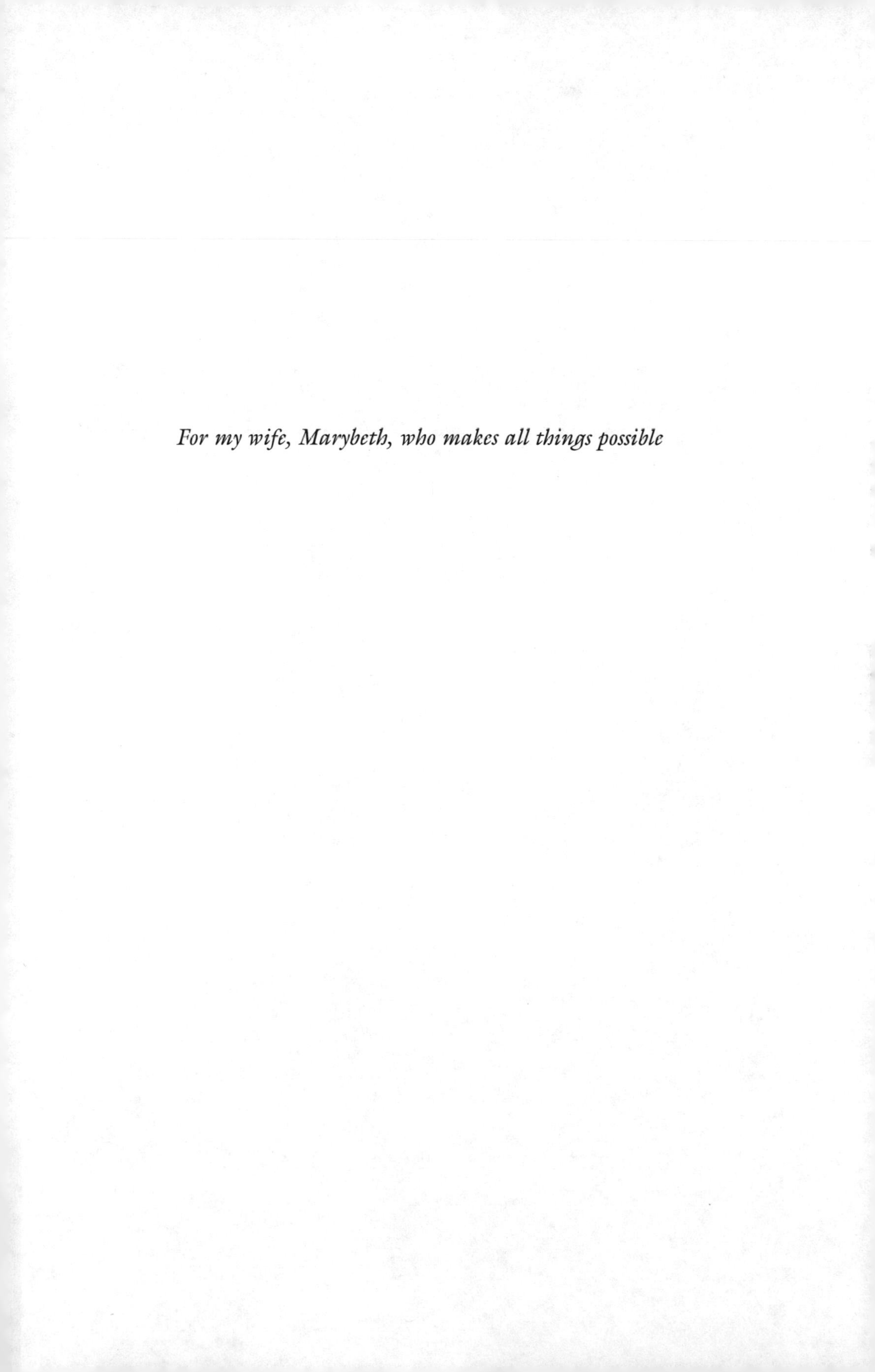

For my wife, Marybeth, who makes all things possible

Tossing aside just about every experience-honed
tenet of business to build business in a
methodical fashion, Internet businesses have adopted
a grow-at-any-cost, without-any-revenue,
claim-as-much-market-real-estate-before-anyone-moves-in
approach to business. This mentality has come to be
known as "Get Big Fast."

—Robert Reid, *Architects of the Web*

contents

acknowledgments

This book could not have been written without the contributions of many, many people.

First and foremost is my agent, Elizabeth Wales, who was with me every step of the way, reading and rereading the manuscript, and making astute suggestions, including the title for this book. And thanks to Nancy Shawn of Wales Literary Agency.

To my editor, David Conti: Thank you for believing in this project and my ability to pull it off. And thanks to Devi Pillai.

Thanks to Paul Andrews for hooking me up with Glenn Fleishman, who in turn connected me with former Amazonians, who hooked me up with others, including Paul Barton-Davis, Nicholas Lovejoy, Scott Lipsky, Dana Brown, Nils Nordal, Gina Meyers, Maire Masco, E. Heath Merriwether, and Lauralee Smith.

Much appreciation to Tom Alberg, Nick Hanauer, and Eric Dillon for their generous insights into how Amazon.com became Amazon.com.

Also thanks to Brian Bailey, Petyr Beck, Maureen Bell, Brian Bershad, Henry Blodget, Grace Chichilnisky, Jack Covert, Christina Crawford, Craig Danuloff, John Decker, Dan Doernberg, Avin Mark Domnitz, Roy Goldman, Alex Gove, Albert N. Greco, Bill Heston, Harvey Hirsch, Richard Howorth, Barry Lafer, Ed Lazowska, Cheryl Lewy, Brian Marsh, Jennifer McCord, Jim McDowell, John Miller, Tim O'Reilly, Mike Parks, Vito Perillo, Philip Pfeffer, Michael Powell, Barry Provorse, Ramanan Raghavendran, Jeffrey Rayport, Jennifer Risko, Chuck Robinson,

David Rogelberg, Paul Saffo, Bernie Schroeder, David Siegel, Bob Spitz, Barbara Theroux, Rachel Unkefer, Alberto Vitale, Charles Waltner, Ursula Werner, Ryan Winter, Perry Woo, and Dennis Zook.

A special thank-you to Professor Jeffrey F. Rayport of Harvard Business School for the use of his 1997 study on Amazon.com, which was prepared by research associate Dickson L. Louie.

Finally, I could not have retained my sanity without the love, affection, steadfastness, and support of my wife, Marybeth Spector.

Robert Spector
Seattle, Washington

preface

Writing this first book about how Amazon.com became Amazon.com was, in a word, challenging. When the proposal for this book was written and accepted in the late fall of 1998, it centered on the publishing and bookselling business. That's where my research began. Months later, the scope of the story extended to the retail business. Still later, it became obvious that the rise of Amazon.com has had a profound influence on virtually every sector of business in the world. No wonder Jeff Bezos's dog, Kamala, is named for a metamorph that appeared in an episode of *Star Trek: The Next Generation*; Amazon.com is in a constant state of metamorphosis.

That was at least one of the reasons why Jeff Bezos and Amazon.com declined to participate in this project. The company's official position was that it was too early for a book. Although Mr. Bezos neither encouraged nor discouraged people from speaking with me, no current employees agreed to be interviewed on or off the record. Amazon.com remains a secretive organization. (I did conduct one interview with Jeff Bezos on November 17, 1998, but that was for another book, which I later put aside to write this book. The material from that interview is included in these pages.)

I did receive the cooperation of several people who witnessed the creation of the company, particularly Nicholas Hanauer, Eric Dillon, and Thomas Alberg, who have been part of an ex officio board of advisors since the beginning. Mr. Alberg currently serves on the Amazon.com board of directors. They were invaluable in telling the story, as were Paul Barton-Davis, employee Number 2, and Nicholas Lovejoy, employee Number 5.

This is the first in-depth look at Amazon.com, but it certainly won't be the last. I'm looking forward to Jeff Bezos's memoir somewhere down the road. In the meantime, the following pages will tell you what he did and how he did it.

introduction

Hammering Man, a 48-foot tall, seven-inch thick, black silhouette sculpture, stands resolutely, left leg in front of right leg, near the decorative marble-arched entrance to the Seattle Art Museum, the site of the annual shareholders' meeting of Amazon.com. The date is May 20, 1999. Covered in jet black automotive paint, the 13-ton, fabricated steel figure, created by artist Jonathan Borofsky as a tribute to American workers, gets its name from the sculpted hammer that is an extension of a silent motorized left hand. The left arm moves four times per minute from over the statue's head down to a 75-degree angle where it meets the motionless right arm, which holds a flat object that is "hammered."

Hammering Man's life in Seattle has not been without incident. In 1991, as it was elevated from a flatbed truck by a crane, the lifting strap snapped when it was a foot off the ground and the 26,000-pound piece crashed to the pavement, its feet gashing two gigantic footprints in the sidewalk at First Avenue and Seneca Street. "It was like reality," an onlooker told the *Seattle Times*. "Life doesn't always go smoothly and sometimes you fall down." After a year of repairs, Hammering Man returned to Seattle, this time without incident; but it's been a target for political statements and whimsy ever since. A group of guerrilla performance artists once fastened a 700-pound steel ball-and-chain to the right leg; on one dark Christmas night, some mischievous elves used a weather balloon to drop a red and white Santa's cap (the size of a ship's sail) atop his head.

On this sunny May morning, the crowd of some 350 eager shareholders mill about the lobby of the Robert Venturi–designed Seattle Art Museum, sipping freshly brewed Starbucks coffee and munching on tiny bagels with cream cheese, waiting in anticipation to hear from their *own* Hammering Man, Jeffrey P. Bezos—part business genius, part class cutup—who has methodically and resolutely pounded out a new business model for the Internet Age. And like Hammering Man, Bezos has been the target of admiration and envy ("Why him—and not you?" asked *Wired*) as well as scorn ("Amazon.toast," derided Internet pundit George Colony in 1997; "Amazon.bomb," proclaimed *Barron's* in 1999). But this is a day for affection. Some shareholders are positively giddy with anticipation at the prospect of seeing and hearing from the man who has helped to make them money—in some cases, *lots* of money.

For the most part, the Amazon.com shareholders look very much like the kind of people one sees at any annual meeting—lots of retired people with white hair and plenty of time to look after their interests; a thirtysomething dad from Allentown, Pennsylvania, explaining the procedure of the meeting to his nine-year-old son, who proudly wears a Seattle Mariners baseball cap. But this being Seattle, there is also in attendance a tattooed, body-pierced, purple-haired Gen-X former Amazon.com employee, who's made more money than he ever dreamed of, thanks to the oft-split stock that's risen 5,600 percent (yes, *5,600* percent) in the mere two years since the company went public on May 15, 1997. Also wending his way through the crowd is the legendary L. John Doerr, the highly visible partner in the venture capital company Kleiner Perkins Caufield & Byers, dressed professorially in blue blazer, gray slacks, striped shirt, no tie. The wily, wiry Doerr is a director of the company and personally holds 1,011,561 shares, worth on this particular day about $131 million. And over there is another member of the board, the similarly dressed Scott Cook, cofounder of Intuit, Inc., a leading personal finance, tax, and accounting software and web services company. (He's also a director of Amazon.com's auction rival, eBay, Inc.). Paul Saffo, director of the

Institute for the Future, who knows both Cook and Bezos, observes that, "Scott and Jeff are very similar people in terms of the methodicalness of their strategy," and considers each man an "extraordinarily thoughtful strategist."

And it's strategy the investors want to hear as, precisely at the scheduled hour of 10 a.m., they quickly file into the gray-walled auditorium of the museum. An anticipatory buzz is in the air. From out of the multitude, down one of the aisles, springs Bezos, who bounds up the stairs of the tiny stage dressed very much like John Doerr—dark blazer and pants, and a white shirt, open at the collar, sans tie. Looking like your favorite high school science teacher who's trying to quickly bring the student assembly to order, Bezos good-naturedly directs the last few stragglers to unoccupied seats: "There are a few seats down here," he points out, then gliding across the stage, "and a couple more over here."

After quickly dispensing with the formal part of the meeting—the procedural review, introduction of directors, voting on proposals, etc.—Bezos, planted behind a lectern, prepares to talk to the shareholders about the state of their company, and the progress they've made in the year since the last shareholders' meeting. They all know that over the past 12 months, Jeff Bezos and Amazon.com have been all over the media—features on PBS's *NewsHour* and CBS's *60 Minutes II*; cover stories in *Business Week*, *Fortune*, *Forbes*, *Wired*, and the *New York Times Magazine*—which has crowned Amazon.com the poster child of the Internet and Bezos a pioneer of the new economy. In the past year, "Amazon" entered the business lexicon as a verb when the *Wall Street Journal* wrote about established offline companies facing the threat of being "amazoned," i.e., "forfeiting business to an Internet newcomer." *Forbes* proclaimed that "Youbet.com wants to be the Amazon.com of horse racing." *Fortune* (which is particularly fond of the analogy) called Babycenter.com "the Amazon of cyberbabies" and Sportsite.com (which sells Zambonis) the "Amazon.com of icemakers on wheels," and asked, "Who'll be the Amazon.com of the $1 Trillion

Car Biz?" Finally, *Fortune* columnist Stewart Alsop wondered, "Is There an Amazon.com for Every Industry?" (With its significant minority investments in drugstore.com, HomeGrocer.com, Pets.com, and Gear.com, Bezos seems to think so.)

Boasting a brand name recognized by 55 percent of the conscious population, the word "Amazon.com" has become a part of the popular culture. To prove the point, Bezos proudly serves up to the shareholders several video-clip references to Amazon.com from several television shows: *Tonight Show* (Leno: "Bill Clinton thought Amazon.com was Janet Reno's e-mail address"), *3rd Rock from the Sun*, and *Hollywood Squares.* He then shows the comic strip *Sherman's Lagoon*, which has one of its characters walking through a jungle saying, "So, this is the Amazon. Very cool. I've heard so much about it. Look, there's a parrot. Listen to the birds. The insects. The monkeys. Smell the tropical flowers. The Amazon sure is cool. It's nothing like their website." The audience laughs and applauds with approval.

In the past year, virtually everyone in the business media has wanted to hear what rising star Jeff Bezos has to say, not just about the direction of Amazon.com but also on a variety of other subjects, including his favorite books (*The Remains of the Day* by Kazuo Ishiguro and *Dune* by Frank Herbert) and even more personal things such as his spending habits and his sleeping habits. As for the former, he offers the shareholders a peek at some of the items he has recently personally purchased from Amazon.com's auction website. Assembled in a display on a table next to the podium are: an autographed photograph of Albert Einstein, a five-pound porcelain bust of *Star Wars* character Boba Fett, and a Bozo the Clown light-switch plate. "When I was a kid, people kidded me, because my name Bezos was close to Bozo," he jokes. (Thankfully, he neglected to bring the skeleton of an Ice Age cave bear for which he paid $40,000.) As for his patterns of slumber, for a *Wall Street Journal* feature story entitled "Sleep: The New Status Symbol," he revealed, "I need eight [hours] and I get it almost every night. . . . No matter how much I've got on my mind, about five minutes after I turn out the light, I'm asleep." (By contrast, Donald Trump replied in the same article: "I get my ultimate sleep when I'm in the company of a beautiful woman.")

Also in the past year, Bezos had spoken at the World Economic Forum's annual meeting in Davos, Switzerland, and was among the 100 corporate leaders invited to Bill Gates's annual CEO Summit, which attracted the likes of Warren Buffett of Berkshire-Hathaway, Michael Eisner of the Walt Disney Company, and Jack Welch of General Electric to the Microsoft headquarters in nearby Redmond, Washington. Jeff and his wife, Mackenzie, had moved out of their rented 900-square-foot apartment in downtown Seattle's trendy Belltown neighborhood and were now nestled in their new $10 million home (7,000 square feet; five bedrooms)—formerly owned by a scion of the Weyerhaeuser timber dynasty—in exclusive Medina on Lake Washington's "Gold Coast," where the affluent population of 3,085 includes Chairman Gates and Nathan Myhrvold, the former chief technical officer for Microsoft. Oh, yes, Bezos's net worth was about $10 billion—or more than the entire gross domestic product of Iceland.

The next hour and fifteen minutes become, in essence, "The Jeff Bezos Show," as he discusses a range of subjects including the efficiency of Amazon.com's business model; the company's understanding and development of the "customer experience"; its newest offerings (at the time, auctions and electronic greeting cards); and its latest investments, before taking a long series of questions from the shareholders that cover everything from credit-card privacy issues, to the volatility of the stock, to the decision to offer a 50 percent discount on all books on the *New York Times* bestseller list. Bezos smoothly metamorphoses from one persona to another. Sometimes he's a green-eyeshade account: "The dollar number of net margins is what we're trying to optimize; not the percentage of that margin. So as we move forward, if we believe that by having lower percentage net margins we can have a more than compensatory higher top line, that change to our business plan would be an advantageous move for us to make for shareholders." Later, he's a jokester: Asked if he's worried about online shoppers' having ready access to information that lets them compare prices among all retailers, he answers with a deadpan, "It's a concern in one sense, but it's a concern the way that gravity is a concern for Boeing." (The line gets a laugh.) Then, in the next sentence, he's a cool visionary: "It's the way of e-commerce. Customers are going to have near-perfect information. The merchants who don't understand this, and don't build their business plans on that basis, are, I think, going to have the most problems."

Suddenly, one question stops the show. A young Asian-American shareholder raises his hand and politely asks: "When is the company expected to earn a profit?"

Most of the audience members laugh; a few applaud. Bezos is unruffled. He's expecting it. He's answered this one before.

"I should say a couple of things about this, because sometimes it's misunderstood," he says, leaning toward the crowd. "For any of you who have any doubt about this (a smile slowly appears): Amazon.com believes that it is *very* important that *one* day . . . we *will* be profitable." (More laughter.) Modulating to a sober tone, he adds, "We don't subscribe to any kind of new math or anything like that. Long term, all companies will trade on a reasonable [price/earnings] multiple. That's how this works. Your market cap has to reflect the current and present value of your future cash flows."

As he speaks, it's obvious that Bezos senses an opportunity to drive home the essence of the Amazon.com strategy, to explain to shareholders and journalists alike why losses continue—and will continue—to mount up before any profit is on the horizon: "What we're doing now is focusing on investing in all of the 'insurmountable opportunities' [John Doerr's phrase about the Internet] that we see. Our U.S. book business was profitable in the month of December [1998], which is a seasonably strange month [because shopping activity is so high]. I believe that if we had been better able to organize ourselves, we shouldn't have had that business be profitable in the month of December. [More audience laughter.] A rational set of shareholders would penalize the management team of a company for being unable to figure out how to better allocate the capital in order to invest more aggressively in this critical category-formation time. Look," he adds, with the conviction of a true believer, "there's *so much* Internet opportunity, that *now* is the time to invest. We're trying to make all of our decisions in a long-term context."

Although he didn't utter these specific words, Bezos's intent was clear: At this stage of its development, Amazon.com's strategy was to *get big fast*—by investing aggressively in new product categories and new businesses, by spending money on brand awareness and getting new customers; by doing whatever it takes to make sure that Amazon.com will be one of the survivors.

As the meeting winds down, a shareholder asks Bezos if he's at all concerned about whether the companies in which Amazon.com recently has invested (drugstore.com, HomeGrocer.com, and Pets.com, all of which are hyperlinked from the Amazon.com site) will be able to deliver the same kind of customer-service experience that Amazon.com has tried to create. While expressing confidence that the management of these companies will do a good job, he readily concedes. "You do enough of these things and you're going to bet wrong." On the other hand, he tells the shareholders, if the people running Amazon.com "don't make some significant mistakes in our investments . . . then we won't be doing a good job for our shareholders because we won't be swinging for the fences. You should *expect* mistakes.

"And I think that's actually a really great question to end on. Thank you very much. It was a pleasure to see you."

After finishing their applause, the shareholders briskly exit the art museum and head out into the light of the noonday sun. The sight of Hammering Man prompts at least one onlooker to wonder whether Amazon.com will continue to tower over the competition. Or will it one day collapse of the weight of its expectations (and debt) with all the sound and fury of a 13-ton sculpture crashing to the ground? Many observers believe that the bubble will ultimately burst and that Amazon.com will be just another chapter in the history of electronic commerce. They may be right. On the other hand, most people who know Jeff Bezos believe that the prospect of failure is virtually incomprehensible; almost every one of them says that Bezos is one of the two or three smartest people they have ever met. In one form or another, they echo this opinion of him, as expressed by Graciella Chichilnisky, Jeff's first employer: "In the knowledge sector, the key issues are rate of innovation and depth of penetration. He will anticipate the changes. I bet on Jeff Bezos's brain."

chapter one

who is jeffrey bezos?

Presently the younger generation will come knocking at my door.
—Henrik Ibsen, *The Master Builder*

Operation Pedro Pan ("Peter Pan") was one of the most massive political rescue missions of young people in history. Masterminded and organized by Father Bryan O. Walsh of the Catholic Welfare Bureau in Miami, Florida, this dramatic humanitarian effort began the day after Christmas 1960 and ran until October 1962, when the United States and the USSR were facing off over Soviet-supplied ballistic-missile installations in Cuba. On October 22, when President John F. Kennedy announced a naval blockade of Cuba to prevent the delivery of more missiles, Cuban president Fidel Castro responded by terminating all flights from Havana to Miami. By the time Operation Pedro Pan was brought to a halt, more than 14,000 boys and girls, ages 6 to 17, had landed on U.S. shores. Once the unaccompanied children arrived, they were placed into foster care through the Cuban Children's Program, another humanitarian project created by Fr. Walsh and financed by influential south Florida businessmen.

One of the oldest of the group was 17-year-old Miguel Bezos, whom everyone called Mike. Bezos (pronounced BAY-zoes—Spanish for "kisses") quickly mastered English and was able to graduate from high school in Delaware, where he shared quarters in a Catholic mission with 15 other refugees. Diploma in hand, he headed west to New Mexico, where he enrolled at the University of Albuquerque. In 1963 he took a job in a local bank, where he met another employee, 17-year-old Jacklyn "Jackie" Gise Jorgensen, a newly married, attractive native of Cotulla, Texas. Although the two young people came from dramatically different backgrounds, both of their fates were influenced in some way by America's cold war battles with the Soviet Union and the worldwide communist threat. For Mike, it was the escape from Cuba; for Jackie, it was part of her father's job. Lawrence Preston Gise (whom everyone called Preston) had just been appointed by the Congress of the United States to be manager of the Atomic Energy Commission's (AEC) western region. Operating out of headquarters in Albuquerque, he supervised the region's 26,000 employees at the Sandia, Los Alamos, and Lawrence Livermore laboratories.

Before joining the AEC, Gise (rhymes with "dice"), who hailed from Valley Wells, Texas, had worked on space technology and missile defense systems for the Defense Advanced Research Projects Agency (DARPA), the research and development arm of the Department of Defense that was created in 1958 as the first response by the U.S. government to the Soviet launching of the *Sputnik I* satellite in 1957. Intended to be a creative counterbalance to conventional military thinking in research and development, DARPA was formed, according to its official mission statement, "to assure that the United States maintains a lead in applying state-of-the-art technology for military capabilities and to prevent technological surprise from her adversaries." In 1970, DARPA's engineers created a model for a powerful communications network for the U.S. military that could still function even if a nuclear attack demolished conventional lines of communication. The system, dubbed ARPAnet, was the foundation of what would eventually become the Internet. (But we're getting ahead of the story. More about ARPAnet later.)

When Mike and Jackie met, she was already pregnant, and on January 12, 1964, she gave birth to a boy, named Jeffrey Preston, who Mike would later legally adopt after he and Jackie married in 1968. Five years after Jeff's birth, his half sister Christina, was born, and the following year, half brother Mark completed the family. Jeff has said that he has no memory of his biological father. "But the reality, as far as I'm concerned, is that my dad [Mike Bezos] is my natural father," he has said. "The only time I ever think about it, genuinely, is when a doctor asks me to fill out a form." He added, "It's a fine truth to have out there. I'm not embarrassed by it." In fact, Bezos has claimed that when he turned 10 years old and his parents informed him that he was adopted, he wasn't particularly concerned. On the other hand, when his parents broke the news that he needed to wear glasses, "*That*," he recalled, "made me cry."

After earning his college degree, Mike Bezos went to work at Exxon as a petroleum engineer, a job that eventually took him, Jackie, and Jeff to Houston, Texas—the first of many moves in the life of the Bezos family.

In Houston, Jeff showed his precociousness early. At age three, he and his mother were embroiled in a battle of wills over his sleeping accommodations—he wanted a real bed; she thought he hadn't outgrown his crib. One day, Jackie walked into Jeff's bedroom and saw him trying to fashion himself a bed by tearing apart the crib with a screwdriver; she knew that she had met her match. At his Montessori school, he would become so absorbed in whatever task he was doing that teachers could get him to move on to the next activity only by lifting him up while he was still *in* his chair, carrying him across the room, and planting him at the next work spot.

To satisfy Jeff's intellect and curiosity, Jackie often brought home little electronic gadgets from Radio Shack. While attending Houston's River Oaks Elementary School, he became devoted to playing with an Infinity Cube, a device with motorized mirrors that allowed the user to stare into "infinity." But when Jeff wanted an Infinity Cube of his own, Jackie balked at the $20 price tag. Undaunted, Jeff purchased separately all the necessary pieces (which were cheaper than the toy itself) and built his own Infinity Cube because, he said at the time, "You have to be able to think . . . for yourself." This story was included in a 1977 book, published locally in the Houston area, entitled *Turning on Bright Minds: A Parent Looks at Gifted Education in Texas.* Written by Julie Ray, the book follows Jeff (renamed Tim) through a typical school day at River Oaks, a magnet public school that was part of a citywide voluntary integration program. Ray described the 12-year-old (who commuted 40 miles round-trip every day) as "friendly but serious," as well as "courtly," and "possessed of general intellectual excellence." Nevertheless, his elementary school teachers evaluated the young man as "not particularly gifted in leadership."

But other grown-ups who came in contact with Jeff saw something in him that those teachers obviously missed. His parents signed him up for youth league football, which is a rite of passage in the pigskin-obsessed state of Texas, even though his mother feared her slightly built son—who barely made the minimum weight requirement—would surely be steamrolled by the bigger boys. She was pleasantly surprised when her fiercely competitive son was tapped by the coach to be *captain* of the defensive team. It wasn't so much Jeff's physical prowess as it was his ability to remember not only his assignment on every play, but everyone else's as well.

An addition to his father, the other strong male figure in Jeff's life was his grandfather, Preston Gise, the former regional manager for the Atomic Energy Commission. In 1968, he retired to his ranch, the Lazy G, in Cotulla (pronounced *kuh-TOO-luh*), Texas (population 3,600), located near the northeast Mexican border about 90 miles west of San Antonio, and 90 miles east of Laredo in LaSalle County. Cotulla, a prime territory for the trophy hunting of whitetail deer, was where Jeff spent his summers, from age 4 to 16, under the watchful eye of Preston Gise. Maureen Bell, whose mother married Preston after his first wife (Jeff's grandmother, Mattie Louise Strait), passed away, remembered "Pop" Gise as "a delightful man. Very, very intelligent. He researched everything that he did." Technically oriented, Gise encouraged and nurtured his grandson's interest in science and gadgetry. No wonder Jeff's garage at home was always filled with curiosities, such as Heathkit amateur radios, an open umbrella spine wrapped in aluminum foil (used for solar cooking), and an old Hoover vacuum cleaner that was converted into a hovercraft.

"There was always something going on in our garage," said Jackie Bezos. "His projects became more complex with age but unfortunately, the garage never got any bigger."

His grandfather also taught Jeff how to fix windmills (not to tilt at them), lay pipe, and repair pumps—as well as brand, vaccinate, and castrate cattle (certainly valuable tools for a future master of the Internet). "We all do that around here; it's survival for us," said Maureen Bell.

Jackie Bezos believed that the ranching experience taught her son the necessity of becoming self-sufficient when working with the land. "One of the things [Jeff] learned is that there really aren't any problems without solutions. Obstacles are only obstacles if you think they're obstacles. Otherwise, they're opportunities."

Ursula Werner, a high school friend, recalled, "Jeff would speak of his grandfather with great love. It was clear the strength of the love that he had for this man. I hadn't heard him speak of anyone in that way. It made me realize what a profound bond there must have been between them. I got the sense that he gave Jeff a lot of freedom, which is what grandparents do, and encouraged Jeff to be who he ultimately has become."

The Bezoses moved to Pensacola, Florida, and then to a solid, upper-middle-class neighborhood in Miami, for part of Jeff's high school years. Mike Bezos's return to Miami as a successful Exxon executive was a far cry from his first visit to the city as a poor refugee from Cuba.

Werner remembered the close-knit Bezos family as "a largely happy, easygoing household. Jeff's mother is an incredibly strong, very loving woman. If drive and devotion are genetically passed along, that's where those qualities come from." Jeff flashed his drive to his fellow classmates at Palmetto High School when he announced his intention of becoming the valedictorian of the class of 1982. According to a former classmate, the rest of the class—already intimidated by his intellect, competitiveness, and confidence—didn't doubt him. He not only graduated number one out of 680 students, but he also won his school's Best Science Student award in his sophomore, junior, and senior years and the Best Math Student award in his junior and senior years. In addition, he was one of three members of his graduating class to win the science prize in the prestigious Silver Knight competition for south Florida high school students. Entrants in the competition, which is sponsored by the *Miami Herald* (a newspaper in the Knight-Ridder syndicate), are judged on academic achievement, written essays, and a rigorous interview process in front of a panel.

As a high school student, Jeff thought about becoming an astronaut or a physicist. He won a trip to NASA's Marshall Space Flight Center in Huntsville, Alabama, for writing a paper entitled "The Effect of Zero Gravity on the Aging Rate of the Common Housefly," as part of a NASA-sponsored student competition. He made no secret that he wanted to build a commercial space station because, he believed, the future of the human race was not on Earth; the planet might be struck by a foreign object from outer space. In his graduation valedictory speech, he argued for the colonization of space as a way to secure the future of the human race. In a 1982 *Miami Herald* feature story on all the high school valedictorians in South Dade County, Jeff was described as hoping to one day build space hotels, amusements parks, yachts, and colonies for 2 or 3 million people orbiting the planet. "The whole idea is to preserve the Earth," he told the *Herald*, who wrote that Bezos's ultimate objective was "to get all people off the Earth and see it turned into a huge national park." He wasn't kidding; building a space station was a very serious dream. "Jeff had many dreams and very big ideas, and space was where a lot of those dreams were focused," said his high school friend, Ursula Werner. "He believed that we, as a species, had to explore space because this was a very fragile world, and we weren't taking good enough care of it. He was not so focused on the ecology side—that we need to worry about our Earth more—but more about taking a long-term view of the Earth as a finite place to live. His was the classic *Star Trek* approach of the 'final frontier.' We had the capability to explore space, all we needed to do was to pour money into it and then it would be explored. A space station was an obvious first step for that. His level of dreaming was so creative that you felt, gosh, this is more than just fantasy. This is a drive of some kind." Today, Werner believes Bezos's ultimate goal for Amazon.com is to amass enough of a personal fortune to build his own space station, and to be able to change the future.

Werner was a senior at Palmetto when she first met Jeff, who back in those days looked like a teenage version of the actor Martin Short—slightly built, hair parted down the middle. "I think it might have been a party or it may have been through National Honor Society. We overlapped in some of the same circles," said Ursula, who was a year ahead of Jeff and was valedictorian of her class. "I was taken with him probably from the moment I met him. He's an incredibly charming man. He has an infectious personality and draws you in very quickly. He is very focused on people when he's with them. He has one of the most wonderful senses of humor of almost anyone I've met. But unlike some people who have a terrific sense of humor, he can appreciate someone else's sense of humor. I love the way he laughs. It's something I will always remember about him."

Jeff Bezos has always been a meticulous long-range planner. Werner recalled the elaborate lengths he went to in order to create a scavenger hunt to celebrate her eighteenth birthday on March 11, 1981. He spent several days leading up to the birthday to plant clues all over the city of Miami. At the beginning of the scavenger hunt, Jeff and Ursula got into his car, with Jeff behind the wheel. Exactly where they would go next depended on how well Ursula played the game. He gave her the first clue, and, she recalled, "I had to sit there and try to figure out what he was talking about. He would not give me any indication of whether I was right or wrong. He would say, 'Where do you think I should drive?' and I would take a guess. To give you an indication of how much trouble he went to, he hid one clue under a railroad tie on an old part of the railroad track on South Dixie Highway. He hid a clue under a toilet bowl lid on the sales floor of Home Depot. He had gone to a teller at one of the banks (one clue involved the teller's name) and told her: 'When someone comes in on March 11, she will ask you for a million dollars in one dollar bills, give her this clue.' It was amazing. Aside from the birth of my three children, I can't ever remember when I've had such an exhausting experience. The world around Jeff Bezos is filled with terrific stories like that because he has such a creative and playful mind."

In his first major entrepreneurial enterprise, Jeff teamed up with Ursula in the summer of 1982, to create a summer-education camp called the DREAM Institute (DREAM stood for Directed REAsoning Methods). They were able to sign up five kids in the fourth, fifth, or sixth grades, including Jeff's brother Mark and sister Christina. Bezos and Werner charged $150 for the two-week session, which ran from 9 a.m. to 12 noon in Jeff's carpeted bedroom at the house on 13720 SW 73rd Avenue in Miami.

In what would be very much the Bezos modus operandi, the program was an amalgam of science and literature, past and future. Ursula picked out the literature and social science books—*Watership Down*, *Black Beauty*, *Gulliver's Travels*, *Treasure Island*, and *David Copperfield*, and the Thornton Wilder plays *Our Town* and *The Matchmaker*—and Jeff selected the science fiction and fantasy—*The Once and Future King*, *Stranger in a Strange Land*, *The Lord of the Rings*, and *Dune*. The curriculum covered topics as diverse as fossil fuels and fission, space colonies and interstellar travel, black holes and electric currents; nuclear arms limitation talks and how to operate a camera. The program, as Jeff and Ursula wrote on a flyer to the students' parents, "emphasizes the use of new ways of thinking in old areas." In an interview that summer of 1982 with the *Miami Herald*, Jeff explained, "We don't just teach them something. We ask them to apply it."

To this day, Jeff considers Ursula his first business partner. After Werner went off to Duke University and Bezos to Princeton, the couple eventually split up, but remain friends. "My mother loves Jeff," said Werner. "They had a very close relationship when Jeff and I were going out—to the point that Jeff and I had a huge fight once, and she went over to take care of *him* (his parents were in Norway at the time) and see how *he* was doing." Werner is now an attorney in the antitrust division of the United States Justice Department in Washington, D.C.

PRINCETON

Jeff entered Princeton in the fall of 1982. For someone who describes his youth as a socially awkward time, he was active and popular. He was elected president of Tau Beta Pi fraternity, and was a member of the 160-member Quadrangle Club (one of the 12 co-ed eating clubs on campus) and a member of Students for the Exploration and Development of Space. His classmates in the class of 1986 included Phil Goldman, now general manager at WebTV; Katherine Betts, the editor of *Harper's Bazaar* magazine; and David Risher, a vice president at Amazon.com.

During his college summers, he was able to find some useful and interesting jobs. In 1984, the Bezos family was living in Norway, where Mike had been transferred by Exxon. That year, Jeff worked for Exxon in the town of Stavanger, as a programmer/analyst. According to his resume, that summer he developed a financial model for calculating oil royalties using the nonprocedural software language IFPS on an IBM 4341 computer. The following summer, he worked for IBM's Santa Teresa Research Labs in San Jose, California, where, as he wrote in his resume, "In three days, [I] completed a project allocated four weeks for completion, re-implementing an IBM software productivity tool user interface by writing exec routine to automatically and selectively change the productivity tool."

At Princeton, his intention was to study electrical engineering and business administration, but, for a time, he entertained thoughts of a career in theoretical physics. Unfortunately, he found that despite ranking among the top 25 students in his honors physics program, "it was clear to me that there were three people in the class who were much, much better at it than I was, and it was much, much easier for them. It was really sort of a startling insight, that there were these people whose brains were wired differently," he told *Wired*, which described the revelation as Jeff's first intellectual disappointment. Nevertheless, he wasn't too intellectually scarred by the disappointment. He graduated summa cum laude in 1986 with a B.S.E. in electrical engineering and computer science, with a grade point average in his department of 4.2 out of 4.0 (Princeton gives a 4.3 for an A+) and a 3.9 overall GPA, and was elected to Phi Beta Kappa. For his thesis, he designed and built a special purpose computer for calculating DNA edit distances.

Armed with a Princeton degree, brimming with self-confidence, and believing in the inevitability of his own success, Jeff Bezos was ready to take the next step. His determination was revealed in this Ray Bradbury quote, which appeared next to his picture in the yearbook:

> The Universe says No to us.
>
> We in answer fire a broadside of flesh at it and cry Yes!

TAKEAWAYS

At the risk of reading too much into how the events of Jeff Bezos's youth influenced the creation of Amazon.com, it's obvious that he displayed evidence of success at an early age, and continually added to that evidence as he walked through the door of the business world.

Bezos was precocious as an adolescent, willful, focused, and confident. As a youth league leader on the football field, he could remember his assignment and everybody else's as well. When his mother wouldn't buy him an Infinity Cube, he made his own. When he mapped out the scavenger hunt for his girlfriend's birthday, he demonstrated the kind of strategizing and long-term thinking that would form the direction of Amazon.com.

- Focus on the task at hand.
- Understand that there are no problems without solutions.
- View the inevitable obstacles as nothing more than opportunities.
- Think long term.

chapter two

i'll take manhattan

What we have to learn to do, we learn by doing.

—Aristotle

Every move Jeffrey Bezos made in his professional career—and every bit of experience and knowledge he gained—was a building block in the eventual creation of Amazon.com.

Based on his record at Princeton, Bezos was wooed by a variety of established companies, including Intel, Bell Labs, and Andersen Consulting. But reading the *Daily Princetonian* student newspaper one day, his eyes stopped at an intriguing full-page advertisement for Fitel, a start-up financial telecommunications firm based in Manhattan that, according to the ad copy, was searching for Princeton's "best computer science graduates."

In May 1986, right after graduation, he became employee Number Eleven at Fitel, which was the creation of professors Graciella Chichilnisky and Jeffrey Heal, colleagues in the Economics Department at Columbia University in New York. As manager of administration and development, Bezos oversaw an international telecommunications network that used computerized programs to simplify the complicated transfer of equity and data from one country to another. The process involved the interconnection of an intricate web of buyers, sellers, brokers, and assorted intermediary banks. This specialized global communications network was a bit of a mini-Internet and was a precursor of financial trading websites such as E*Trade Securities.

Promoted to associate director of technology and business development in February 1987, Bezos developed and marketed Equinet, a network designed by Professor Chichilnisky to link brokers, investors, and banks and provide them with the information required for the cross-border trades. Chichilnisky recalled that Bezos was so adept at improving computer protocols (the sets of rules that enable computers to communicate with each other) that he saved Fitel about 30 percent in communication costs. At the same time, the 23-year-old managed a combined 12 programmers and analysts in the firm's London and New York operations (he commuted between the two offices every week), overseeing design, programming, and testing; and managed relationships with major clients such as Salomon Brothers, the investment bank that was Fitel's largest account. He also managed customer support groups in North America, the Far East, and Australia, and opened Fitel's Tokyo office.

Looking back on this period of Bezos's career path, Chichilnisky believes the experience of dealing with global networks enabled Bezos to learn the basics of international communications and their value to a growing business. While Fitel was a specialized and market-specific company, Amazon.com is not, because, Chichilnisky speculated, Jeff "wanted a business that was nonspecialized because it would have more rapid penetration into markets."

In April 1988, he moved on to Bankers Trust Company, where he was named assistant vice president for Global Fiduciary Services; 10 months later, at the age of 26, he became the youngest vice president in the history of Bankers Trust. His primary contribution was overseeing a six-person programming department that designed and developed a communications network called BTWorld. BTWorld was a software program that was installed in computers in the offices of more than a hundred *Fortune* 500 companies whose pension and profit-sharing plans (representing $250 billion in assets) were managed and invested by Bankers Trust. The computerized system enabled the bank's clients to check periodically on the performance of their investments—rates of return on assets, transactions, interest earned, dividends paid, etc.—without having to wait for a hard copy of the standardized report that Bankers Trust regularly supplied to clients.

Although such handy access to research is commonplace today, it was groundbreaking in the late 1980s. In fact, many of the old guard at Bankers Trust felt that, "this was something that couldn't be done, shouldn't be done, and that the traditional way of delivering this information in hard copy was better," recalled Harvey Hirsch, who was Bezos's boss back then. "The feeling was: Why change? Why make the investment?" Previously, the data that went into the hard copy reports had been maintained and manipulated on large mainframe computers. While Bezos was an outspoken advocate for the power of personal computers, a number of people at BT were convinced that the tracking and manipulating of the pension and profit-sharing data couldn't be done on a PC, which they felt lacked sufficient memory or power.

"A lot of corporate types—far less entrepreneurial than Jeff—were vehemently opposed to what he was proposing," added Hirsch, a former vice president at Bankers Trust. "We're talking about defenders of the old technology." Although the opposition was a source of frustration because it slowed everything down, Bezos persevered. "Jeff has a way of stripping away the extraneous and focusing on what's really important. He sees different ways of doing things and better ways of doing things. He told the naysayers, 'I believe in this new technology and I'm going to show you how it's going to work'—and he did. At the end of the day, he proved them all wrong. He has no trouble puncturing someone's balloon if he thinks that they're proposing to do something the wrong way or in an inappropriate way. He'll argue his point of view very persuasively. That doesn't mean that he didn't break some eggs in the process because he proved people wrong, but I don't think he ever did it in a way that angered or infuriated people. It was all very professional."

Bezos also found time to dabble in projects away from Bankers

Trust. In 1990, he met Halsey Minor, an investment-banking analyst at Merrill Lynch in New York. At the time, Minor was working on an idea for a system that would disseminate information and training material over Merrill's internal network using hyperlinks, animation, and graphics—in other words, an *intranet* that was created several years before the term was coined. With Merrill's financial backing, Minor formed a small company with an ambitious name—Global Publishing Corporation—and began to create the infrastructure for the network. Pleased with the initial results, Merrill backed Minor on a more ambitious project that would enable news feeds to be personalized for subscribers based on their individual interests and needs. Bezos and Minor, then 26 and 25 respectively, signed a three-year contract with Merrill, and began working on the project.

But just a few weeks later, Bezos and Minor were in Minor's office when someone from Merrill Lynch called with word: Merrill had changed its mind about the project and was pulling the plug on the funding.

Two years later, Minor went on to become founder, chairman, and chief executive officer of San Francisco–based CNET Inc., which today is the leading Internet technology news and information company. Turn the clock ahead a few more years, and there are Bezos and Minor on the cover of the July 27, 1998, issue of *Forbes*, along with 11 other Internet impresarios, including Jerry Yang of Yahoo! and Rob Glaser of RealNetworks, under the headline "Masters of the New Universe."

Reflecting on his memories of working with Bezos, Minor said that, "Outside of Bill Gates, I think there are few other people who share Jeff's deep technical understanding and combine it with highly refined strategic and tactical instincts." Minor recalled that Bezos was a greater admirer of Gates as well as the lesser-known Alan Kay, who invented the graphical user interface at Xerox. "Jeff is one of the few hard-core developers who can do other things," said Minor. "He always had the dream of starting his own company."

In 1990, Bezos was not yet ready to start his own company, but he *was* ready to leave Bankers Trust after two years, and to get out of the financial services business. He told corporate headhunters that he was looking to hook up with a technology company, where he could chase his real passion—"second-phase" automation. Bezos has described second-phase automation as "the common theme that has run through my life. The first phase of automation is when you use technology to do the same old business processes, but just faster and more efficiently." A typical first phase of automation in the e-commerce field would be barcode scanners and point-of-sale systems. With the Internet, "you're doing the same process you've always done, but just more efficiently." He described the second phase of automation as "when you can fundamentally change the underlying business process and do things in a completely new way. So it's more of a revolution instead of an evolution."

D. E. SHAW

D. E. Shaw & Co. was that kind of "second-phase" company, and David E. Shaw, the founder, chairman, and chief executive officer, was the sort of boss that could stimulate Jeff's intellect and drive. Although Jeff had little desire to stay in the financial community, a headhunter convinced him that D. E. Shaw was something different and, indeed, it was. In the early 1980s, David Shaw, a Ph.D. in computer science from Stanford University, had run a successful computer software company called Stanford Systems Corporation, and had rubbed shoulders (and egos) at Stanford University with the likes of Leonard Bosack, cofounder of Cisco Systems; Andreas Bechtolsheim, cofounder of Sun Microsystems (and now at Cisco); and Jim Clark, founder of Silicon Graphics, Inc. and later chairman of Netscape. He served on the faculty of the Department of Computer Science at Columbia University before joining the stock brokerage firm Morgan Stanley & Co. in 1986 as vice president in charge of automated analytical trading technology.

In 1988, with $28 million in start-up capital, he founded D. E. Shaw & Co. as a quantitative hedge fund. The trick to making money in this arcane discipline was to employ techniques such as statistical arbitrage, which uses complex algorithms (programmed sets of mathematical formulas designed for a computer to perform a specific function) to track—and ultimately to capitalize on—tiny discrepancies in shares of traded stock. For example, if shares of Microsoft trade for $99.50 in New York and $100 in Tokyo, the fund would simultaneously buy the share in New York and sell it in Tokyo for a guaranteed profit of 50 cents per share (less the costs of the transaction). "Traditionally, quantitative hedge funds had built sophisticated, computer-based tools to help traders make trading decisions," said Bezos. "What D. E. Shaw & Co. did was invert that whole model. Computer programmers would program the machines and teach the machines financing. The machines would actually make all of the trading decisions. That really was a completely different model of the world."

Investment Dealer's Digest agreed, calling D. E. Shaw & Co. "arguably the most cutting-edge trading firm on Wall Street." The *Wall Street Journal* placed the company "in the vanguard of computerized selling." *Fortune* claimed it was "the most intriguing and mysterious force on Wall Street today. . . . A well-funded research lab in the sky—a place where the avant garde meets arbitrage, and intellectualism and profit-seeking mix harmoniously." The magazine concluded that D. E. Shaw was "the answer you'll get if you ask the question, What's the most technologically sophisticated firm on the Street?" Although it was (metaphorically) *on* Wall Street, the company didn't consider itself *of* Wall Street. "We don't want this to seem like a regular Wall Street firm, because it isn't," Shaw told *Fortune* in a rare interview. The offices were so handsomely appointed that photos of it were displayed in a design show at the Museum of Modern Art in New York. The company eschewed both a rigid dress code and a formal vacation policy; if you needed a vacation, you took one.

Fortune wrote that, "Given his reputation as an amalgam of Einstein, Midas, and Rasputin, Shaw in person turns out to be surprisingly unpretentious." To Bezos, Shaw was a kindred spirit and an intellectual equal. "David Shaw is a very smart guy," said Bezos. "He's one of the few people I know who has a fully developed left brain and a fully developed right brain." Plus, D. E. Shaw & Co. was extraordinarily selective in its hiring, claiming to employ only one candidate for every hundred of the mathematicians, computer scientists, researchers, and traders who applied for a position. A good portion of the company's time and money was spent recruiting the best brains and talent they could attract. "David Shaw defined a very unique culture," recalled Brian Marsh, who joined the company in 1994. "It was a very open and creative environment; almost academic in flavor. David Shaw is very charismatic in much the same way that Jeff is. When I first met David, I thought, 'God, here's a guy I want to work for.' "

In December 1990, Jeff was hired as a vice president at D. E. Shaw & Co., and two years later, at the age of 28, became the firm's youngest senior vice president. As one of four managers, he initiated, developed, and led a 24-person unit that was responsible for exploring new markets. Bezos's department was the largest in the company. Brian Marsh, who worked briefly for Bezos, recalled that "Jeff had a really good handle on his business. He understood how to talk about what he was doing, so that he could get people excited about it. Leadership involves, among other things, the ability to really articulate what is exciting about what everybody is working on, so that you can get everybody on board. He really understands how to do that."

Jeff's social life was busy but without a steady girlfriend. "I didn't really date much until my last year of college," he said. "I had a formal plan to date. I had all my friends set me up on blind dates. None of them worked out very well." When he moved to New York, he became a self-described "professional dater." As with most everything else in his life, he sought to devise a system that would ultimately yield the desired result; in this case, a meaningful relationship. He called his system, "women flow," a turn on the Wall Street term "deal flow," where bankers set a minimum amount on the size of deals they would invest in. "The number one criterion was that I wanted a woman who could get me out of a Third World prison," he said, tongue only partly in cheek. In other words, he was looking for someone resourceful because, "Life's too short to hang out with people who aren't resourceful."

As it turned out, he found the woman he was looking for right there at D. E. Shaw. Her name was Mackenzie Tuttle, a thin, attractive brunette, who was a research associate on Jeff's staff. Mackenzie was a graduate of the Hotchkiss School, the prestigious independent boarding school located in rural Lakeville, Connecticut, and a 1992 graduate of Princeton, Jeff's alma mater. While at Princeton, Mackenzie, an aspiring writer, was a research assistant to Toni Morrison when the Princeton professor and novelist was writing "Jazz." The couple were married in 1993, and started a comfortable life on the Upper West Side of Manhattan.

THE WORLD BEGINS TO CHANGE: A BRIEF HISTORY OF THE INTERNET

The same year the Bezoses were married, 1993, was essentially the birth of what we know as the World Wide Web. The seeds for the Web—or more precisely the Internet—were planted in 1959 in the wake of the Soviet Union's successful launching of the *Sputnik* satellite and the growing cold war fear of potential nuclear attack. A department of defense agency—the Defense Agency Research Projects Administration (known as DARPA, which was the agency that employed Bezos's grandfather for many years)—was given the task of creating a U.S. military communications network that could continue to function even after a nuclear attack. Unlike the centralized standard telephone network that existed at that time, this network would be *decentralized* at strategically placed sites, in order to enable any computer to communicate with any other computer through units of information called "packets." Each consecutively numbered packet would dart from computer to computer until it arrived at its destination computer, where all the separate packets would be combined back into the correct order into the original message. In the event of a nuclear attack, each packet would keep moving and searching until it found a route that was still functioning. ARPAnet, which is what the experimental system was called, debuted in September 1969, with interconnected computer hosts at three universities in California and one in Utah. Over time, several research universities joined in the development of the burgeoning network and eventually were wired to the system. In the 1970s, NSFnet, a related computer network of researchers that was sponsored and funded by the National Science Foundation (NSF) rapidly connected even more universities in the United States and abroad, and enabled participants to communicate via the new medium of electronic mail (e-mail).

Although NSFnet was established for academic ends, the first traces of commercial possibilities began to be seen in the 1980s. As graduating engineering students began migrating to private sector companies such as Hewlett-Packard and IBM, they took with them their e-mail addresses, which made it easier to stay in touch with friends and colleagues. Now that the *corporate* world was connected to the Net, it wasn't long before users moved from business correspondence to discussions of books, movies, and politics, to personal/business correspondence such as "I've got a Honda Accord that I want to sell" or "I'm looking for a roommate." In 1990, the NSF established an acceptable-use policy for commerce on the Internet, which paved the way for entrepreneurial engineers to become Internet service providers (ISPs). ISPs helped users and businesses connect to the Internet through existing telephone lines. When the primary ISPs—UUNET, PSInet, NETCOM, BBN, and MCI—set up and operated their own separate transcontinental trunk lines, they created what we recognize today as the Internet.

During this period of the late 1980s and early 1990s, the most popular bookstore chain in Silicon Valley was Computer Literacy Bookshops, Inc. (CLB) which had been doing business in Sunnyvale, California, since 1983, catering to computer engineers and scientists. The *Whole Earth Software Review* once described the store as "a civilized haven in a savage landscape." Soon after opening its doors, CLB was mailing computer books to customers all over the world.

"Our core audience was computer professionals and technical people," recalled Dan Doernberg, who, with his wife, Rachel Unkefer, co-owned the chain, which eventually expanded to four stores. "One of the key audiences we were serving was the data communications networking people—the people who were at companies like Sun Microsystems—who were building the Internet and doing these developments. They were not just using the technology; they were *creating* the technology. We were heavily tied in with the people who were making the key developments in the Internet and in many, many cases we were serving those people as their book supplier. We had a real firsthand view of the Internet as opposed to being a business that used the Net."

Eventually, Unkefer recalled, "Lots of customers would ask, 'Why don't you guys have e-mail? I needed to call you to find out something at one o'clock in the morning and you weren't open.' They wanted an easy way to get their hands on this technical material we carried, so they pushed us in that direction. One of our customers worked at NASA [National Aeronautics and Space Administration] Ames Research Center in Mountain View, California. He had a friend who was a systems administrator who agreed to allow us to connect our UNIX [-based] computer over the phone lines to their Internet servers. Then, anybody in the world who wanted to e-mail a question could do that." (AT&T's UNIX operating system was preferred by techies and academics because of its power.)

On August 25, 1991, Computer Literacy registered its domain name—clbooks.com—making it the *first* bookseller to be found on the Internet. "But we didn't widely publicize it, because at that time, it was not permissible to do business on the Internet, and we didn't want to offend people," said Unkefer, who today appreciates the irony of that statement. Of course, this was not an electronic buying system, but rather an e-mail-based system, which was a step up from mail order via telephone. A very large percentage of that e-mail business was international.

Because of security concerns and the prohibition of commerce on the net, "we did not want customers sending their credit card numbers in e-mail, so we set up a preregistration system," Unkefer said. "The customer would fill out a form, including credit card number and signature, and they'd fax or snail-mail the form to us. As soon as we received it, we'd set them up as an e-mail account and allow them to order books via e-mail using just the e-mail address as the account authorization. There were no passwords. At that point, you could counterfeit an e-mail address, so we would ship only to the address on the registration, which we felt was reasonably secure. The e-mail was no different from getting a fax or a phone call. You still had to do the same manual order-taking."

Within a year or so, two more bookstores registered their domain names—Cleveland, Ohio–based BookStacks Unlimited's *books.com*, on October 9, 1992, and Cambridge, Massachusetts–based Wordsworth's *wordsworth.com* on December 23, 1992. (Amazon.com would not be officially registered until November 1, 1994.)

Literally all of Computer Literacy's Internet customers were certified techies. The Internet was not yet ready for prime time because it was virtually impossible for a nontechie to navigate its puzzling programs, to locate all the research and discussion groups, and to manipulate the information once found. There were no ways to link to other websites. But in 1993, Tim Berners-Lee, a researcher at the Conseil Européen pour la Recherche Nucléaire atomic research center in Switzerland, introduced software and networking protocols (the series of commands and sequences computers use to communicate over a network) that enabled the user to browse documents and navigate the Internet with point-and-click commands that were relatively easy to understand. Navigation was made possible with the use of highlighted words or symbols, called "hyperlinks," which, when clicked on, instantly linked the computer to another site. This was the birth of the World Wide Web, which has been called "the Rosetta Stone of the Internet," because it unlocked the power of the system for the nontechies of the world and created an omnipresent network that was simple to use and beneficial for everyone.

Still, while the Internet was a fascinating tool, it was serving only a select audience, and as a text-based, artless, colorless, and silent medium, it was hardly a compelling draw for computer neophytes.

But these circumstances were rapidly changing. In October 1993, a small, tightly knit group of University of Illinois students led by Marc Andreessen brought the Web to the masses. Working out of the National Center for Supercomputer Application (NCSA), an institute located on the University of Illinois campus, the students introduced Web browser software, called Mosaic, which was designed to retrieve information anywhere on the Web, with the use of graphics. Within a few months, a hundred thousand users had downloaded the UNIX version of Mosaic that was posted on the NCSA's servers. These new wonders were still essentially the domain of the hard-core computer cognoscenti who were sitting in front of their UNIX workstations. The real breakthrough came when Andreessen and crew created software to be run on the Apple Macintosh as well as Microsoft Windows operating system, which was used on most of the world's personal and commercial computers. By the mid-1990s, NSFnet officials, recognizing the shift from academic to commercial use, closed NSFnet. (ARPAnet had shut down a couple of years earlier.) The Internet, where no one yet had made money, was about to become the worldwide marketplace for both ideas and stuff. And Jeff Bezos found himself in the right place at the right time.

THE IDEA

Most experts pinpoint the moment in history when the Internet went mainstream in the period between September 1993 and March 1994. It was a time when corporations began putting up sites that were less for transactions and more for posting static information such as annual reports, product literature and technical specifications, press releases, and regional offices and phone numbers. But the Web was quickly growing. As Robert H. Reid explained in *Architects of the Web*:

> Because unlike the telephone network, whose architects had to lay lines, hire operators, manufacture telephones, and invent all manner of complex switchery, the Web rode upon an infrastructure that was largely in place before it took root. By the time Mosaic was released, desktop computers had become commonplace in offices and homes for years. Modem penetration was also surging, as communications hardware had become standard in most new PC configurations. Internet connections were already installed in thousands of companies and institutions. And computers in offices everywhere were by then networked in Local Area Networks [computer networks limited to an immediate area, usually one building or one floor of a single building]. . . . All of sudden in '93 and '94 people just started realizing that these networks could do very interesting things. Specifically, they could look outward, bringing the content and resources of the broader world into the enterprise.

None of this was lost on David Shaw, who decided to make a play on the Internet. In 1994, a year when most hedge funds either lost money or barely broke even, D. E. Shaw boasted a return of 26 percent. That same year, Shaw assigned Bezos the job of investigating Internet business possibilities. (Shaw would later claim that one of Bezos's primary duties in his last couple of years with his firm was researching these commercial opportunities, and that much of Bezos's significant findings for what would eventually become

Amazon.com were discovered under Shaw's direction—and on Shaw's dime.) That spring, Bezos's research for Shaw revealed an astonishing fact: Web usage was growing at a staggering clip of *2,300* percent a year, thanks to the availability of the Mosaic browser to users of Macs and Windows-based PCs. "You have to keep in mind that human beings aren't good at understanding exponential growth," Bezos said. "It's just not something we see in our everyday life. But things don't grow this fast outside of petri dishes. It just doesn't happen." Something that is growing 2,300 percent a year "is invisible today and ubiquitous tomorrow."

Looking for the best product that could be sold on the Web, Bezos compiled a list of 20 possibilities, including computer software, office supplies, apparel, and music.

In the course of his research, he was surprised to find that books rocketed from being almost at the bottom of the list to the very top, with music following in second place. Music was eliminated because of the way the industry was set up. With only six major record companies dominating the business and controlling distribution, Bezos feared that those companies had the leverage to freeze out an opportunistic outsider who wanted to challenge traditional bricks-and-mortar stores. That was unlikely to happen in the book business, which was already involved in a high-profile antitrust lawsuit between several publishing houses and the American Booksellers Association (which represents the interests of booksellers) over whether publishers gave better deals and terms to chain booksellers. Another factor in favor of books was the fact there were only 300,000 active music CDs, compared with more than 3 million different books active and in print around the world in all languages.

Furthermore, bookselling was large and fragmented, with no dominant 800-pound gorillas. The U.S. industry had tens of thousands of publishers, many of them with only a title or two to their credit. Random House, which was the biggest consumer publisher, accounted for less than 10 percent of the market. The combined sales of the two biggest bookselling chains, Barnes & Noble and Borders Group Inc., made up less than 25 percent of the approximately $30 billion total sales of all consumer adult books in 1994. Neither one of them had established themselves as a prominent global brand. Nonbookstore outlets—from mail-order to book clubs to warehouse stores—accounted for 54.3 percents; and independent stores 21.4 percent, according to the Consumer Research Study on Book Purchasing. U.S. book sales had been growing steadily since the early 1990s, reaching a peak of 513 million copies in 1994, which was an increase of 6.3 percent over the previous year, according to the Book Industry Study Group, a nonprofit research organization. That year, 17 titles sold more than 1 million copies and 83 titles sold in excess of 400,000 copies. The top-selling fiction book was *The Chamber* by John Grisham and the top-selling nonfiction title was *In the Kitchen with Rosie* by Rosie Daley, Oprah Winfrey's chef. The worldwide book industry—which was also large, growing, and fragmented—was projected to generate sales of $82 billion in 1996.

The book industry was already in the midst of a shift in its sales channels. In the 1980s, Crown Books revolutionized the industry overnight by opening up hundreds of discount stores, forcing other bookstores into some form of discounting books, which they hadn't done before. Also during that period, Barnes & Noble and Borders were expanding into shopping malls all over the country until there were few malls left without the presence of one or the other of those chains. By the first half of the 1990s, Barnes & Noble and Borders were closing their smaller shopping mall stores and replacing them with massive superstores (60,000-square-foot-and-larger structures that were often converted from bowling alleys and movie theatres). These stores carried on-site up to 175,000 titles—an impressive number but still less than 10 percent of the estimated 1.5 million English-language books in print. With rare exception, the thousands of independent bookstores carried dramatically fewer titles in small selling spaces. Furthermore, a physical store represented costly investments in inventory, real estate, and personnel. Consequently, Bezos saw that, "With that huge diversity of products, you could build a store online that simply could not exist in any other way. You could build a true superstore with exhaustive selection; and customers value selection."

An online bookstore would place virtually no limits on the number of books available to a consumer; and the World Wide Web's search and retrieval interface technology would make it easy for customers to surf the entire database of books in print. Buying decisions could be made easier for consumers by providing them with more and better information such as synopses, excerpts, and reviews. By serving a vast, international market from a centralized ordering and distribution location, an online bookseller could be run more economically than even the largest bricks-and-mortar bookseller. Despite its limitless reach, an online bookseller could be programmed to provide an inexpensive personalized shopping experience for its customers, and, even more important for the online bookseller, the information that could be collected on the individual customer's personal preferences and buying habits could create possibilities for direct marketing and personalized services. Bezos saw that because of these advantages over traditional retailers, online retailers had the potential to build large, global customer bases quickly and to achieve superior economic returns over the long term.

Another advantage to selling online books was availability. Books could easily be acquired either directly from publishers or from a network of distributors that carried up to about 400,000 titles in their inventories. Distribution was (and continues to be) dominated by two companies, Ingram Book Group, a division of Ingram Industries, Inc., which is based in LaVergne, Tennessee, and Baker & Taylor Books, based in Charlotte, North Carolina. Ingram had seven warehouses placed strategically around the country; Baker & Taylor had four. For many years, both of these companies sent out their inventory lists to their customers on microfiche, but in the late 1980s, they and others in the business switched to a digital format. These distributors are also, in effect, warehouses for bookstores, particularly small independent booksellers. When a customer asks for a book that is not in stock, the bookseller orders it, most likely, from either Ingram or Baker & Taylor.

Book publishing and bookselling are the two sides of an inefficient business where publishers, suppliers, and retailers are involved in conflicting intentions. Months before they produce a book, publishers must determine how many copies to print, but they can't come up with a number until they pitch the title to booksellers. To convince booksellers to stock plenty of copies and display them conspicuously, publishers give their retail accounts permission to return unsold books for credit. Once he became a bookseller, Bezos called it "not a rational business. The publisher takes all the return risk and the retailer makes the demand predictions."

Not surprisingly, one of the major inefficiencies in bookselling were the number of unsold books returned to the publisher, which in 1994 was a staggering 35 percent of the 460 million books shipped. (The generous return policy was a relic from the Depression when it was used as an enticement by publishers to encourage orders from booksellers.) In recent years, the substantial additional costs of returns played havoc with publishers' bottom lines. Bezos figured that an online bookseller could greatly reduce the number of returns, thereby making a virtual bookstore more efficient.

Mail order was a small but growing part of the book business, thanks to the consumer's increasing demand for convenience, coupled with the greater popularity of credit cards, 24-hour customer-service telephone lines, and overnight delivery services. Many stores, large and small, began to issue book catalogs, as did catalog-only companies, who catered to readers with special interests, such as science fiction, mystery, cooking, travel, gay issues, and religion. Catalogs also generated sales among readers who simply preferred to shop at home, or who were living overseas or in remote locations where there were few or no good bookstores. Mail-order business was also generated through membership clubs, such as Book-of-the-Month Club. In a small way, catalogs anticipated online bookstores. One noteworthy effort was "The Reader's Catalog," cocreated in 1989 by Jason Epstein, the editorial director of the Random House adult trade division, and Geoffrey O'Brien, the poet, author, and editor. "The Reader's Catalog" inventoried 40,000 titles from various publishers in dozens and dozens of categories—from Eastern religion to quantum physics, along with capsule reviews of the books. Although the catalog was intended to motivate readers to visit a bookstore, some booksellers felt it threatened their very existence. (In 1998, "The Reader's Catalog" database was acquired by barnesandnoble.com.)

As for the Internet, the competition was already there, in the presence of Computer Literacy's clbooks.com, and books.com, the brainchild of Charles Stack, a lawyer-turned-software developer from Cleveland, Ohio. In 1991 and 1992 respectively, each company began hooking up with book buyers via a bulletin board system (BBS), a network where people could communicate, make announcements, and upload and download files, without everyone having to be connected to the computer at the same time. In 1993, books.com established a connection to the Internet with a software service called Telnet, which enabled a user to log in to a remote computer on the Internet and easily search a database of available titles as if they were in the user's own computer. When books.com launched its website on the Web in 1994, the company offered 400,000 titles.

Finally, another major reason why books had to be the first product that Bezos would sell on the Internet was that *everybody understands what a book is.* You didn't have to explain product specifications; the book you'd buy on the Internet would be the same book you could buy at a bricks-and-mortar store. By contrast, if Bezos wanted to sell electronics on the Internet, he would have had to show side-by-side comparisons of the models, product reviews, comments from other users, etc. (For Amazon.com and other Internet retailers, this would all come later.) And the people who were already using the Internet were obviously computer-savvy, affluent, and, most importantly, frequent buyers of books.

Bezos recommended to David Shaw that D. E. Shaw's first Internet play should be selling books. To Bezos's surprise, the idea was rejected.

But Jeff couldn't let go of the idea; all he could see was that figure of 2,300 percent annual growth on the Internet and a huge, potentially wasted opportunity. A short time later, Bezos told Shaw that he had made a decision; he was going to resign from the company and "do this crazy thing"—start his own Internet bookselling company. As Bezos recalled, Shaw's immediate reaction was to suggest the two of them go for a walk. They ended up strolling through Central Park for two hours. Shaw told his young, ambitious senior vice president that he thought online bookselling was actually a great idea. But, he quickly added, it would be a *better* idea for somebody who didn't already have a good job. "That was actually a compelling argument to me," Bezos recalled. Although Shaw conceded that he himself had left an established business to pursue his own entrepreneurial desires, he emphasized that Bezos would be giving up financial security as well as a significant role in the present and future of D. E. Shaw & Co. "I saw the wisdom of that and he convinced me to think about it for another 48 hours."

For Bezos, it was difficult to make a final decision until he came upon the right context in which to make that decision. What this self-avowed nerd came up with was what he called "a regret-minimization framework"—in other words, he wanted to decrease the number of decisions in his life that he would eventually rue. "A lot of people live their lives this way," he said. "Very few are nerdy and dorky enough to call it a 'regret-minimization framework,' but that is what I came up with." So, he projected himself into the future, when he was eighty years old and reflecting on the choices he had made in his life.

"I knew that when I was eighty there was no chance that I would regret having walked away from my 1994 Wall Street bonus in the middle of the year. I wouldn't even have *remembered* that. But I did think there was a chance that I might regret significantly not participating in this thing called the Internet, that I believed passionately in. I also knew that if I had tried and failed, I wouldn't regret that. So, once I thought about it that way, it became incredibly easy to make that decision."

Shaw did tell Jeff that at some point down the road, they might be in competition with each other. As much as he admired David Shaw, Jeff Bezos was willing to live with that.

TAKEAWAYS

Rather than go to work for a large corporation immediately after graduating college, Jeff Bezos chose to go with a start-up firm where he was given an enormous amount of responsibility at a young age. He quickly became adept at computer protocols and communications networks, managing a department, dealing with Fortune 500 clients, working with billions of dollars of cash and assets, and gaining invaluable experience in international expansion. He saw firsthand how a creative company run by a charismatic, iconoclastic leader can succeed in its chosen field.

- Be extraordinarily selective in hiring.
- Hire people who are open, creative, and able to think for themselves.
- Be a leader by clearly articulating your excitement about your business, and, just as important, be able to convey that excitement to your employees.
- Find a business where there is no perceived leader and/or where the barriers for entry are low.
- Offer a product or service that is easily understandable. Bezos didn't have to explain the concept of a book to anyone.
- Follow your heart. If you feel you will one day regret not taking a chance, then take that chance. Bezos calls that regret-minimization. As he said: "I knew that if I had tried and failed, I wouldn't regret that."

chapter three

seattle

GEORGE: "Everybody's moving to Seattle."
JERRY: "It's the pesto of cities."

—*Seinfeld*

"When something is growing 2,300 percent a year, you have to move fast," Bezos said. "A sense of urgency becomes your most valuable asset."

Now that he knew what he wanted to do and how he wanted to do it, the question was: *Where* was he going to do it? In his methodical, analytical way, Bezos came up with three criteria for the location of his new business. First of all, it had to be in an area with a large pool of technical talent. Second, it had to be in a state with a relatively small population because only the residents of that state would be charged state sales tax for the books they ordered. That eliminated Silicon Valley. Finally, the city had to be near a major book wholesaler in order to insure timely delivery of books—first to Amazon and then to the consumer. After gathering statistics ranging from sales taxes to the number of daily flights out of the local airport, Bezos narrowed down the list to four cities in the West—Portland, Oregon; Boulder, Colorado; Lake Tahoe, Nevada; and Seattle, Washington—before ultimately settling on Seattle. Of the four states, Washington was the most populous with 5.6 million, compared to Nevada with 1.6 million, Oregon with 3.2 million, and Colorado with 3.9 million.

Why Seattle? It was certainly a Mecca for top-flight programming talent, thanks to the likes of Microsoft, Nintendo, Progressive

Networks (which later changed its name to RealNetworks), WRQ, Adobe, and hundreds of other software companies. It was the home of the University of Washington and its top-flight, nationally ranked computer science department, which was potentially a handy source for programmers. Plus, the city of Nordstrom, Starbucks, Costco, and Eddie Bauer (some pretty good retail models) was on everybody's short list of top places in America to do business, and thanks to its reputation for coffee, grunge music, and Mt. Rainier, Seattle had a buzz that the others didn't. And Seattle was about a six-hour drive from Roseburg, Oregon, where Ingram Book Group ran the largest book distribution center in the United States.

But above and beyond those quantifiable reasons, Seattle also had one other thing going for it. It was the home of a friend of Bezos's named Nicholas J. Hanauer. The then 34-year-old Nick Hanauer was the senior vice president of sales and marketing for his family business, Pacific Coast Feather Co., which is the nation's leading supplier of feathers for high-end down pillows, comforters, and mattress pads. With sales of almost $200 million a year, Pacific Coast Feather's customers include Eddie Bauer, Land's End, and Bed Bath & Beyond. The black-haired Hanauer, a dead ringer for Michael Dell, the chairman and CEO of Dell Computer, once posed in his pajamas for a national advertising campaign. Luxuriating on a down comforter, his smiling face was featured in a two-page color print ad for software developer SAP, which appeared in magazines such as *Forbes*, *Fortune*, and *Business Week*. (The ad promoted Pacific Coast Feather's use of SAP's inventory-tracking and operations software.)

Back in 1993, a mutual friend from Seattle, who was then working with Bezos at D. E. Shaw & Co., brought Hanauer and Bezos together for lunch in New York, and "we became instant friends," said Hanauer. "We stayed in touch, although not closely. We had dinner once or twice again with other people from D. E. Shaw. Then I heard through the grapevine that Jeff was interested in starting an Internet business, and at that time, I was interested in participating in e-commerce."

In a telephone call, Hanauer told Bezos two things: One, that he wanted to invest in Bezos's idea; and two, Bezos had to set up the business in Seattle. "I told him that Seattle was—and I continue to believe is—the center of the universe. I told him that he would have a wonderful life here, that it was a place that was attracting fabulous, talented people, that it was easy to get good people to come to work for him. I sold him hard on being able to ski on one weekend and sail on the next. I sold him hard that I would help him." Even after all that, Hanauer conceded, "At the end of the day, I'm not sure what finally swayed him. I'm not even sure if *he* knows."

In the summer of 1994, Jeff and Mackenzie gave up their apartment on the Upper West Side of Manhattan, packed up their belongings and watched the men from Moishe's Moving & Storage load up their things on a moving truck. Asked by the movers where to take the stuff, Bezos told them to start driving west, call him the next day from the road and he would have an answer. The couple, who did not own a car, flew to Texas (where his parents were then living) and his father, Mike, donated a 1988 Chevy Blazer for their trip west. "This is a car that *Consumer Reports* says not to buy used—under *any* circumstances at *any* price," said Jeff. "However, they say nothing about accepting one for *free*." The next day, Bezos called the movers and told them to head for Seattle. Hanauer recalled that, "When he ultimately decided to come, it was quite last minute. I got a call when he was on the road. He said, 'We're coming. Can we store our stuff at your house?' A big bunch of stuff soon arrived, and a week later, Jeff and Mackenzie arrived."

Picking up and leaving a place was second nature for Jeff, whose family had lived in various parts of the world. "Moves always invigorate me," he told a colleague. "There's really something very cleansing about it. Every move is an opportunity for spring cleaning." He later said that the journey to Seattle "was easy for me because my wife was supportive and also, thankfully, she's not geographically tied to a particular area, so we were able to pick up and move to the best place to do Amazon.com, which turned out to be Seattle." As the legend goes, as Mackenzie drove the Blazer toward the West Coast, Jeff sat in the passenger seat, tapping out the first draft of the business plan on his laptop. It's a nice story—oft-repeated in newspaper and magazine stories—but probably, like all myths, somewhat romanticized. Some people who later worked for Amazon.com say the business plan was hardly a finished document even a year after Jeff had arrived in Seattle.

Hanauer hooked up Bezos with a Seattle attorney named Todd Tarbert to take care of establishing bank accounts and other official business. When Bezos called Tarbert from the road about incorporating the company in the state of Washington, Tarbert naturally asked what the name of the new company was going to be. Bezos had already thought of the name.

"Cadabra, Inc.," he said over the cell phone. "Like Abracadabra."

To which Tarbert replied "Did you say, *Cadaver*?"

The company was indeed incorporated in the state of Washington on July 5, 1994, as Cadabra, Inc., but Bezos knew that he would eventually have to change the name. He preferred that the new appellation begin with the first letter of the alphabet because online websites were listed in alphabetical order—rather like a company listing itself in the Yellow Pages under AAA Auto Repair. (Amazon.com would later have a small online competitor line called A1 Books.) After perusing the entire "A" section of the dictionary, Bezos decided upon Amazon.com. (Another option was the Dutch "aard." It was too obscure, but it was an alphabetical winner.) "Jeff was really excited about the fact that here was a river that was 10 times larger than the next biggest river. It's not just big, it's so much bigger than its next nearest competitor," recalled Paul Barton-Davis, an early company employee. The company was renamed Amazon.com, and reregistered as a Delaware corporation on February 9, 1995. "He started with a brand name that was an empty vessel—that was very smart," said Hanauer. "Amazon.com could be anything we decided to make it. Jeff has always specifically called the company 'Amazon.com'; he never refers to the company as just plain 'Amazon.'" Nicholas Lovejoy, who was the fifth employee hired, recalled being involved in "a huge discussion about whether the company should be called Amazon or Amazon.com in terms of marketing, PR, letters, etc. Obviously, the website was Amazon.com. Jeff was adamant that it should be '.com.' I think everybody else who had a strong opinion thought the '.com' was stupid. With hindsight, that was brilliant. Today, we all talk about '.coms.' Amazon.com was the first. Nobody else was marketing the concept of being a '.com' company. That differentiated Amazon.com in terms of the branding."

Five days after showing up on Nick Hanauer's doorstep in July 1994, Mackenzie and Jeff rented a three-bedroom, 1690-square-foot ranch house in a middle-class neighborhood in Bellevue, the suburban city east of Lake Washington across from Seattle. At a monthly rent of $890, the drab, white 50-year-old house with a brown roof was nothing to write home about, but it did have one thing that Jeff *had* to have: a *garage*. This had symbolic importance to Jeff because he wanted to be able to say that he started his business in a garage, just like Messrs. Hewlett and Packard, and all the entrepreneurs who came after them. But the room in the Bellevue house wasn't a garage anymore—it had been converted into a family recreation room with a linoleum floor. Although, Jeff quipped, the converted garage, "wasn't fully legitimate," he did consider it "somewhat legitimate because it wasn't insulated." A big potbellied stove in the center of the room provided the heat.

SHEL KAPHAN

Before heading up to Seattle, MacKenzie and Jeff Bezos stopped off in northern California to interview three software programmers who had been recommended to him by a colleague at D. E. Shaw. He was looking to fill the position of vice president of research and development, "which was sort of the long pole in the tent," he said. From among this trio, "I found the perfect person."

That person was Sheldon J. "Shel" Kaphan. Then in his early forties, Kaphan was well known around Silicon Valley. "If somebody said, 'I want a guy who knows how to build very fast databases,' Shel's name would have come up," said a former colleague. "Depending on what circles you were connected into, you would end up running into Shel's name somewhere or other." A native of Santa Cruz, Kaphan received his B.A. in mathematics from the University of California, Santa Cruz. "Shel has an intuitive idea of how things work," said the former colleague. "He's not really willing to accept other people's say-so." Kaphan had done some work with a company called Frox, which had aspired to be the first computer-controlled media center. The Frox device featured digital processing of video and audio, a full-featured content browser, and a CD jukebox.

In the two years before he met Bezos, Kaphan had been working as a senior engineer at Kaleida Labs, Inc., a multimedia joint venture between Apple Computer Inc. and International Business Machines Corporation. As a product of two powerful, deep-pocketed, but very different corporations, Kaleida was a much ballyhooed curiosity in the programming community. Its original purpose was to create a cross-platform multimedia handheld player that was similar to a Personal Digital Assistant, but would play a compact disc. Kaphan was part of the original software engineering team that wrote a programming language called ScriptX, which would run on the multimedia player as well as on Macintosh, Windows, IBM OS2, and UNIX systems. By the time he met with Bezos, it was obvious that the Kaleida experiment wasn't working. (In fact, in the following year, 1995, Kaleida Labs was folded into Apple's operations.)

It took Bezos three months to convince Kaphan to join him in Seattle. "One reason [for Kaphan's reticence] is that he had been involved in a lot of start-ups and had seen a lot of them fail," said his former colleague, who worked with Kaphan at Kaleida Labs. "You end up being fairly world wise about what to do and what not to do in a start-up. Typically, those that do survive have a fair quotient of people who had been through lots of start-ups before. By the time Shel got to Kaleida, he pretty much knew what it was going to take for a start-up to succeed." His colleague said that before he hooked up with Bezos, Kaphan had been playing what's known in the Valley as the "Silicon Valley game." What is the Silicon Valley game? It's the optimal strategy for surviving in the Valley and actually coming out winning—or at least giving yourself a better than even chance of winning. "You figure that a start-up in Silicon Valley will have a lifetime of two to five years, and only one in twenty make it," said Kaphan's colleague. "So, from an engineer's point of view, if you want to become a millionaire, you don't want to stay with one company for 10 to 20 years because the company is likely to go belly up. What you want to do is find the new start-ups, get vested in with them, and stay with them for three or four years. You figure a working life of 30 years, you're likely to run through 10 companies. That actually gives you a good chance of succeeding at one of those companies."

Shel Kaphan was not only employee number one, but was also the second most important person in the creation of Amazon.com. In a few years, he would win the Silicon Valley game big time.

NAVIGATING SEATTLE

Bezos didn't waste any time getting to know people in the Seattle technology community. Before he had left D. E. Shaw and Co., his colleague Brian Marsh gave him the name of a college friend named Brian Bershad, who was a professor at the University of Washington Computer Science & Engineering Department. The UW CS&E department is ranked in the top 10 in the United States, with a nationally recognized 40-person faculty. Many of the students are eventually hired by the likes of Intel and Microsoft. In August 1994, Marsh called Bershad and told him that a friend of his, Jeff Bezos, was moving out to Seattle to start up a company and asked Bershad if he would meet with Jeff.

"I had dinner with Jeff and he gave me the pitch. Like everybody else, I didn't get it," recalled Bershad, who had the impression at that first meeting that Bezos was not yet fully sold on Seattle as the best place to start his company. To determine whether Seattle would work, Bezos knew that he needed to cultivate local contacts and to learn about potential sources for technological help. "He was talking to me because he was looking for connections to the University," said Bershad. "We generate 200 potential employees a year at the undergraduate level and a hundred potential employees a year at the graduate level in computer science. The availability of that kind of farm team was just one of the things that Jeff was looking at." (As it turned out, many of the early engineers at Amazon.com did come from the UW program. Part of the reason is that most of the early resumes Amazon.com was receiving were from the locals.)

Soon after that meeting, Bershad spent a day sightseeing in Seattle with Jeff and Mackenzie to show them some of his favorite parts of the city. The Bezoses quickly discovered what a lot of people have found: It's hard not to fall in love with Seattle on a beautiful summer's day.

After his meeting with Bezos, Bershad circulated an e-mail around the UW CS&E department with a brief description of what Bezos was looking for in a programmer. One of the people who responded was Paul Barton-Davis, who was a staff programmer in the department, and one of Bershad's squash partners. The 30-year-old British citizen had graduated from Portsmouth Polytechnic in the United Kingdom, with a B.S. in biomolecular science. His senior year research work on "Information Theory & DNA Sequence Analysis" must have caught the attention of Bezos, whose own senior thesis consisted of designing and building a special purpose computer for calculating DNA edit distances. After dropping out of a Ph.D. program in Germany, Barton-Davis switched from research in molecular biology to software engineering. In 1989, he moved to Seattle, where he got a job as an engineer and technical manager for a company called ScenicSoft, Inc. His duties included designing and writing a UNIX software code for automating the typesetting of real estate "multiple listing" books. In the fall of 1993, Barton-Davis became the webmaster of the first open World Wide Web site in the Pacific Northwest at the UW's Computer Science & Engineering Department. In the summer of 1994, Barton-Davis was a technical consultant and programmer for a Seattle Internet company called USPAN, which provided public information on the entertainment and leisure industries in the Pacific Northwest and private services to talent casting agents. With that background, among the people in the UW's CS&E department, Barton-Davis was considered "the Web guy."

When Barton-Davis read Bershad's message about Jeff Bezos, "My initial response was 'Why would I want to go do this?' " Barton-Davis recalled. But that attitude quickly changed because, "I was getting disillusioned working in the CS&E department. I was interested in doing a lot more programming that what I was doing there. There were also some internal issues going on within the department that made it a less attractive place to work. Some time after that, I decided to get in touch with Jeff." After a telephone interview, Bezos and Barton-Davis met a couple of times face-to-face. "I distinctly remember meeting him on campus and sitting outside and shooting off about various wild ideas I had for ways that you could build an interface that would let you have the look of a very large bookstore. Jeff was not particularly forthcoming with a lot of the expansive details, although he was very clear that the big selling point was going to be that there were going to be a lot more books [available through Amazon.com] than you were going to get at a physical store."

Bezos struck Barton-Davis as "somebody who definitely had a vision of what he wanted to do. Even at that point, he clearly had enough understanding of the software side of it to understand what was going to be easy and what was going to be difficult. He had a clear idea of what he was getting into. He's also a very friendly person and a high energy kind of guy. I thought he would be interesting to work for."

But the final test before Barton-Davis could be hired as the second employee was how well he got along with the first employee, Shel Kaphan. So, in October 1994, Bezos asked Barton-Davis to meet Kaphan, who was house-hunting at the time in Seattle. Meeting on the University of Washington campus, the two chatted for a while. "Shel is a somewhat more reserved person than I am, but I think that we certainly clicked enough to know that there weren't going to be any huge personality conflicts," said Barton-Davis. Soon after that meeting, Barton-Davis joined the team. Bezos's selection of Kaphan and Barton-Davis—neither of whom had much experience writing the user-level business software or retail systems software that Bezos needed—showed how from the very founding of his company, Bezos believed in hiring the best, smartest people available, regardless of previous experience.

If Kaphan was a hardened veteran of start-ups and flops, Barton-Davis was not. Thinking back on his first visit to the fledgling Amazon.com operation, he sensed "things being very exploratory; there was nothing in the way of anything actually being set up to do anything. I think there was maybe one SPARCstation [computer server] in there at the time, a desk made out of a door, a bunch of books about business, some stuff from the American Booksellers Association floating around. I wasn't expecting very much, but it was a little bit of a shock. I was thinking, 'Boy, this really is Ground Zero.'" As a going-away present, his colleagues in the UW Computer Science department gave him a coffee mug with three dollar bills stuffed in it. "I don't know how cynical a gesture that was," he recalled. "To be honest, that was a fairly realistic assessment. There were a lot of Internet start-ups at that point and they were all going bust in a couple of months. It was a realistic assessment of the risks, but it might not have been a realistic assessment of either the technical aspect of it or the potential upside."

That September, Bezos made his first purchase online—a network router from the Internet Shopping Network.

GOING TO "BOOK" SCHOOL

Before he could revolutionize the book business, Bezos had to learn something about what it was like to actually *sell* a book. So, on September 22, 1994, he traveled down to the Benson Hotel in Portland, Oregon, where he took an introductory four-day course on bookselling sponsored by the American Booksellers Association, the trade group for the nation's independent booksellers. The ABA Prospective Booksellers School course covered topics such as "Developing a Business Plan," "Selecting Opening Inventory," "Ordering, Receiving, Returning," and "Inventory Management."

After lunch on the first day, Barbara Theroux, owner of Fact and Fiction Books in Missoula, Montana, who was the dean for the program, asked the 40 or so attendees to introduce themselves and tell the others about their aspirations for the book business. Predictably, most of the people in attendance said they wanted to open their own store. "When it was Jeff's turn," recalled Jennifer Risko, one of the attendees, who was then working for a Seattle book distributor, "here was this kind of cute, dorky guy who stood up and said, 'I'm going to start an Internet bookstore.' The room fell silent. I'm sure half the people were confused and the other half was thinking, 'Yeah, a computer geek. Whatever.' "

Over the course of the four-day session, the students and four instructors got to know each other through small group sessions, lunch, cocktail hour, and the sheer proximity of staying at the same hotel. One of the instructors, Richard Howorth, owner of Square Books in Oxford, Mississippi, and current president of the American Booksellers Association, said, "I remember Jeff very well. He struck me as being very bright and personable. Early on, when you're teaching at an ABA school, you tend to form an idea about the people. You think to yourself, 'This one's serious and this one's not; this one's going to make it and this one's not."

On the second day of the course, Howorth spoke to the students about the importance of customer service in the bookselling business.

The centerpiece of his presentation was this story:

> One day the manager of my store comes upstairs to my office and says, "Richard, there is a customer downstairs who is real upset and I can't deal with her. You're going to have to deal with her."
>
> In a perverse way, I like that because I feel I can always turn every situation around—even though I'm not always able to. But it's the only attitude to have.
>
> I go downstairs and see this woman who is steaming. I ask, "What may I do for you?"
>
> She tells me she parked her car outside, next to my store, which is two stories with a balcony along the side of the second floor. There are a bunch of potted plants on the balcony. She says, "Somebody has thrown dirt from the balcony onto my car and my car is now dirty. My husband just washed it this morning. My husband is a lawyer."
>
> I just look at her and say, "May I wash your car?"
>
> She says yes. And I say, "Let's go."
>
> We get into her car. She has a friend with her. She and her friend get in the front seat; I get in the backseat. I direct her to a service station, which has a car wash. We get there, and the service station is being rebuilt, so the car wash is out of order. She's getting more mad at me because this service station doesn't have a car wash. I can't think of another car wash in town. So, I say, let's go to my house. We drive to my house on the other side of town. I get out of the car, I go in my house, I get a bucket and detergent and a hose and I wash her car. It doesn't take very long.
>
> The funny thing about this is that it's a really crummy car. The paint is coming off of it. There's no way of telling that her husband washed the car. It was ridiculous. But I pretend like I'm washing a late model Cadillac.
>
> I get back in the car with her and we drive back to the store so she can let me off. By the time we get to the store, she's beginning to apologize to me and thank me. Then she comes back in the store later that afternoon, and buys a whole lot of books from me.

> The next day, somebody on my staff tells me that she had been having breakfast at the Holiday Inn that morning and there was a group of women sitting around a table. She overheard that woman telling this story about my washing her car.
>
> There is no such thing as going too far with customer service and in the book business, particularly, you will have to go this far.

Bezos would later recount the experience of hearing that story in a conversation he had with Avin Domnitz, the executive director of the ABA. After hearing Howorth's example of customer service above and beyond the call of duty, Bezos told Domnitz that he took to heart Richard Howorth's "customer service gestalt," and was determined to make customer service "the cornerstone of Amazon.com," by giving the customer a shopping experience that couldn't be equaled online. Bezos later went on to say that he wanted to make Amazon.com the most customer-centric company on the planet. The seeds of that idea were planted by Richard Howorth and the story of the dirty car.

The next time Howorth saw Bezos was a couple of years later at Booksellers Expo America, the trade show in Los Angeles. "When I ran into him in the aisle, I recognized him but I couldn't place him," Howorth recalled. "I had no idea who he was. Then I looked at his shirt and noticed the 'Amazon' logo on his shirt pocket. I said, 'It's you! You're the one!' That was the first time that I realized that *that* was Jeff Bezos, who had been in the class. He said, 'That's right,' and we both started laughing."

That might have been the last time that anyone in the bookselling business had a laugh about Amazon.com.

TAKEAWAYS

Jeff Bezos methodically went about figuring out what business to get into, where he was going to do it, and how he was going to convince others to buy into his vision. He also took advantage of his contacts to find his way into the separate communities of bookselling, programming, and, eventually as we will see, investments.

- Follow your dream.
- Be bold in your decisionmaking.
- Abandon your comfort zone.
- Hire the smartest people you can could find and compensate them accordingly.
- Learn the basics of the industry.
- Hire what you don't know.
- Map out a strategy, but be prepared to scrap it all if something more efficient comes along.

chapter four

garage in, garage out

What one man can invent another can discover.

—Sherlock Holmes

In November 1994, Jeff Bezos, Shel Kaphan, and Paul Barton-Davis set up shop in the converted garage on 28th Street N.E. in Bellevue, and began the task of creating Amazon.com.

It was a modest setting for a company that in just a couple of years would become the most famous Internet retailer in the world. The room, which was long enough to fit a car-and-a-half, was crammed with desktop computers, assorted file cabinets and bookshelves, and a large round table. To make more room, they removed the potbellied wood stove that had been in the center of the garage. Although little natural light sneaked through the windows, it was still a bright space, thanks to halogen lights, a white linoleum floor, and white drawing boards on the walls. The technological heart of the operation were two Sun Microsystems SPARCstation computers, which provided high-performance graphics, lots of processing power, and the ability to carry out several tasks at the same time.

The trio was keenly aware of the other companies that were already selling books on the Web. (In fact, according to the records of the owners of Computer Literacy, Bezos ordered the book *How to Be a Computer Consultant* from their clbooks.com website, probably as a test of their system.)

"We looked at a company like Books.com and we knew that we needed to make sure that we did at least as good a job as those guys," said Barton-Davis. "There wasn't this sense of 'My, God. We've invented this incredible thing that nobody else has seen before, and it'll just take over.' " Although they weren't overly cocky about their prospects, the three felt that the other companies selling books online were, in their opinion, not doing it very well and that "we can do it better," recalled Barton-Davis. And if the three Amazonians could produce results that matched their ambition, they would be on their way to "building something larger."

Although the technical programming work was performed by Bezos, Kaphan, and Barton-Davis, the fourth key figure in the converted garage was Mackenzie Bezos. "We wouldn't have been operating without Mackenzie. She was vitally important," said Barton-Davis. An official employee of the company, Mackenzie did a little bit of everything. She made phone calls, ordered and purchased materials, and generally filled in at whatever odd job needed to be done, including secretary and accountant—an unlikely set of responsibilities for an aspiring novelist. The accounting duties, which were meant to be part time, turned into a full-time job for a year and a half, until the summer of 1996, when the company finally hired someone with an accounting background. Mackenzie learned the intricacies of Peachtree PC Accounting Software, an off-the-shelf program that small businesses used for tracking revenue and expenses. In those early days, all the financial dealings at Amazon.com were done on a cash basis, just as an individual would handle a personal checking account. "We certainly got our paychecks at the right time and things seemed to happen in the right way," said Barton-Davis.

Gina Meyers, who relieved Mackenzie of those accounting duties in 1996, and worked closely with her in the same room, described her as "extremely bright and fast on her feet. She was very diligent and conscientious with a lot of common sense." Mackenzie's other role is to keep Jeff "grounded," added Meyers.

As 1994 ended and 1995 began, most of the time and energy was devoted to programming the company's infrastructure, including the look of the website, the development of an operating system interface, the design of a database that would store all the orders, customer information, etc., and the creation of an e-mail interface with customers.

After researching the software that was available on the market, Bezos decided that he and his programmers would have to devise their own. Because they were creating a new online retail model that (at least in the beginning) would require no inventory, they would not be able to use existing software, which had been designed to accommodate traditional mail-order models for tasks such as order processing, order tracking, and inventory management. The available logistics software package for standard mail-order companies typically had just two availability categories: in-stock and back-order, while Amazon.com had seven availability categories: (1) shipped within 24 hours; (2) 2 to 3 days; (3) 1 to 2 weeks; (4) 4 to 6 weeks; (5) not-yet-published, shipped when available; (6) out-of-stock; and (7) out-of-print, shipped within 1 to 3 months if it can be found. Bezos estimated that about 85 percent of all of Amazon.com's software development in the first couple of years was concentrated in these back-end logistics systems—which are invisible to the customer—that processed and accounted for millions of books.

"Jeff wanted us to have a business model that was going to work for us, not a business model that was built into some other software," said Barton-Davis, who believed that one of the reasons for Amazon.com's eventual success was "Jeff's insistence on everything being done right."

Open-source software—source code written by thousands of programmers from all over the world and made freely available to all of them—was essential to the creation of Amazon.com, as well as other successful websites such as Yahoo! The readily accessible software lowered "the barriers for entry," said Tim O'Reilly, president of O'Reilly & Associates, Inc., the publisher of computer books, and a major advocate for open-source software. By not keeping their code private, software companies don't require a paid staff to maintain and upgrade their programs; that job is done for them by the rest of the world's programming community, who delight in doing their own tweaking and modifying.

In the beginning, virtually the entire Amazon.com system was written in a popular open-source software program called "C," which is the most commonly used language on UNIX systems. "Shel and I were both C programmers at heart," said Barton-Davis. C was also used for writing the Amazon.com compiler program. (A *compiler* processes statements written in a particular programming language and converts them into the code used by a computer's processor.) The C software was supported by Perl, a computer language that is best loved for manipulating and editing the contents of text files. For example, the Amazon.com programmers used Perl to generate a large list of books that had to be special-ordered, then reconfigured that list into different formats, which would be printed out for the Amazon.com staffers responsible for fulfilling special orders. "The ease of using Perl for formatting text made sense, instead of trying to do it in C," said Barton-Davis.

O'Reilly called Perl "the duct tape of the Internet, and like duct tape, it is used in all kinds of unexpected ways. Like a movie set held together with duct tape, a website is often put up and torn down in a day, and needs lightweight tools and quick but effective solutions." When Amazon.com was being created in the winter of 1994, there were no ready-made applications for managing a lot of text. But versatile open-source tools (called freeware) such as Perl enabled upstart companies like Amazon.com (and Yahoo!) to perform "quick and dirty applications," said O'Reilly.

O'Reilly believed that there is a new paradigm that underlies sites like Yahoo! and Amazon because they change all the time. "You can't have a heavyweight process of producing something where you've got millions of pages, where a large percentage of them are changing every day. The (programming) tool set that Amazon used was really adapted to the new era."

Barton-Davis said that, "Open-source software provided the infrastructure for us to write programs, to develop them, and to debug them. It provided us with the tools to do what we were doing. Without them, we would have been using commercial software from, for example, Sun Microsystems or Digital Equipment, which, for the most part, didn't work as well. The [open-source software] tools we were using were sufficiently evolved."

Today, Amazon.com uses much more sophisticated programs for its increasing complex needs. For example, the company now uses Veritas software for storing data; Bottomline Technologies for electronic bill payments; and i2 Technologies for monitoring processes and streamlining inventories (particularly for dealing with a spike in orders after Oprah Winfrey recommends a book).

E-MAIL STORE

By the end of 1994, there were about 10 times as many e-mail users as Web users, according to the *Internet Report.* At that point, AOL, Prodigy, CompuServe, and the other online services didn't yet have Web access; and hypertext transfer protocol (HTTP)—the software standard for transporting multimedia information between Web servers and Web browsers—was relatively new. Consequently, there was little purely Web-based commercial activity. So in the first six months of working together, Bezos, Kaphan, and Barton-Davis wrestled with trying to find the balance between providing customers with an e-mail catalog and conducting business *strictly* on the Web. "Things were changing incredibly rapidly," said Barton-Davis. "It was clear that the Web store was going to be important. But in the meantime, we wanted to be able to reach as many people as we could, and the way to do that was via e-mail. At that point, Jeff thought that e-mail would probably be more important than the Web."

In those early months, Amazon.com hedged its bets by focusing on being both an e-mail store and a Web store. Under the e-mail system, when a customer e-mailed Amazon.com with a request for a particular book, the company would run a search for the book, and e-mail the results back to the customer, who would then send another e-mail to place the order. This process was similar to using a Web search engine, where the response was in e-mail time rather than real time. The language that was going to be used for e-mail was also the core language of the search engine on the Web.

"It's a pseudo-natural search language that lets you specify the books that you're looking for," said Barton-Davis. The customer would type in a request for a title (perhaps just a word or two), the first few letters of the author's name, and the approximate year the book was published, and that information would be converted into a message that the software program could understand. "We got to the point where you could send e-mail to a particular address and receive something back. Then you'd send something else and get other results. But it was becoming apparent that we needn't do any more on [the e-mail application] because by the time we opened our doors to the public, the Web will already be so big. So, we dropped it. But it didn't matter, because nearly everything that had gone into [the e-mail application] ended up being used on the website as well, which we always knew would be the case."

GATHERING DATA

One of the reasons why selling books on the Internet was a feasible idea was the ready availability of an extensive database of books. Initially, Amazon.com's database came from *Books in Print*, the book industry's definitive reference source, which is published by R. R. Bowker of New Jersey. Bowker, which is the official registry agency in the United States for International Standard Book Numbers (ISBN), distributed a CD-ROM (periodically updated) to bookstores, libraries, and other book repositories; its 1994–95 version listed 1.5 million titles. Transferring that entire list of titles from the Bowker CD-ROM to the Amazon.com database was a tedious and time-consuming process because only 600 titles could be retrieved at a time. Kaphan compared the process to emptying a swimming pool using a drinking straw. The transfer of Bowker's weekly update of changes, deletions, and corrections took almost an entire day.

Another potential source was the Library of Congress, which contains all the books ever printed in the United States. "I was particularly interested in the Library of Congress route because they assign a hierarchical classification for subject," said Barton-Davis. "Most books typically have a three-level hierarchy. Something like 'History-United States-Labor Disputes.' But dealing with the Library of Congress was a very frustrating process because the people I spoke to failed to comprehend what we were asking them for. The subject classification of books is a fairly finite set of words. If you pick out a word that the Library of Congress doesn't use, then you're out of luck. When I would type in what I thought was an obvious word and it came up with no books, I'd have to think of synonyms. We ended up doing virtually nothing with the Library of Congress materials."

Amazon.com also gathered up source material from the two major book distributors, Ingram and Baker & Taylor, which broke down the books into categories.

Bezos and company soon realized that the problem with using all these sources was that they would often provide conflicting information on the availability of the same title. The Amazonians ultimately figured out that the best way to deal with that dilemma was simply to order a book from a distributor—whether or not the distributor indicated the book was in stock—and then wait for the results. After comparing what they were told they could order—versus what was actually delivered—"We could then say, 'this company's information is reliable X percent of the time,' " said Barton-Davis. "For example, if a publisher said a book was 'out of stock,' that was not very reliable. If they said it's 'out of print,' then it was always out of print. Some of the suppliers would use a code like 'publisher out of stock,' which we later found out is a hedged way of saying that it's out of print. But you didn't really know."

Once the Amazon.com site was launched, customers began asking for an explanation of the status designation of a book. So the company refined the wording with the philosophy that it was better not to overpromise and underdeliver. In those early days, if a book was stocked by Amazon.com, it would be designated as available to be "shipped within twenty-four hours"; a book available at a nearby distributor was designated as "shipped in two to three days"; and books that had to be ordered directly from the publisher were listed as "shipped in four to six weeks or maybe never." Thanks to that extra cushion of time, Amazon.com would look like a hero if the customer received the book sooner than expected—and a villain to small publishers who thought the "four to six weeks but maybe never" designation hurt their business.

Another problem was devising a system for updating the list of books as new books were published and older books went out of print. As the company grew, Amazon.com programmers were faced with dealing with hundreds of megabytes of database files and a plethora of questions: How do you drop books that have gone out of print? Can you delete data from the middle of the file? If so, do you insert a flag that marks the data as deleted? What happens when Amazon.com makes its own corrections to the database? If that data is continually being pulled off the CD-ROM, how do you keep a copy of the changes?

Kaphan and Barton-Davis built their own database with an existing public domain software library from the University of California at Berkeley, called DBM (data-based manipulation), which is used for managing files. To soup up the system and make it extremely fast, Kaphan modified the DBM system to use the UNIX system called mmap, which capitalized on the intelligence of Amazon.com's operating system to store more information in its memory. "And as long as the operating system was doing the right thing for our purposes, it would manage it for us cleanly and in a way that made use of all of the physical memory that we had," said Barton-Davis. "That became very important. In those days, we were willing to have 25 or so megabytes holding information from the bibliographic database. We had the 1,000 most-requested books held—and managed efficiently—in memory. We were beginning to get everything in place that you needed for the visible part of the site."

PROGRAMMING THE SUPPORT SYSTEM

At the same time, Kaphan and Barton-Davis needed to figure out how to program Amazon's "back office" and warehouse requirements. After much consideration, they selected Oracle Corporation's relational data-based system because, they felt, it was reliable and gave the company room to expand. "We were aware that there were going to be a lot more requirements on that [system] as the company grew. We were going to need to have reports and other information for the people who used the databases. There was very little point in believing that we should reinvent that ourselves," said Barton-Davis. He felt that "the one bad thing about Oracle—and other relational data-based systems—is that they like to think that they are the whole system. That's rarely the case. You have to struggle with them being too much of a force on your computer. So, we put a [software] layer on top of what Oracle gave us."

Barton-Davis said neither he nor Kaphan were particularly knowledgeable about relational databases. "We made some good guesses and a lot of poor ones," he conceded. "The company now has people working for them who know relational databases very well."

By the time Amazon.com was launched in 1995, it was maintaining at least a two-gigabyte database that contained more than a million book titles. Each online customer was given a unique ID when he or she entered the site. As the customer worked through the site, everything he or she did was tracked so that Amazon.com's Web managers could analyze the individual's browsing and buying patterns.

At the developmental stage, Kaphan and Barton-Davis had to figure out the most basic procedure: how to actually process an order from a customer. In order to be able to deal with all contingencies in the operation, they asked themselves a series of "What if?" questions: What was actually going to happen to an order? What if a customer didn't want to provide his credit card on the Net and preferred giving it by phone? What happens when the customer telephones the company? What does the company do with that information? They addressed all these possibilities with a series of text-based tools that provided prompts for Amazon.com customer service representatives. These tools helped to assure a corporate consistency at each step of the ordering process.

Of course, today, Amazon.com employs some of the most sophisticated programming in the world in order to run the myriad aspects of its business. But the basis of the operation can be traced back to the efforts of Kaphan and Barton-Davis, who built a system that was able to grow, reasonably smoothly, because they were writing code that had an eye on the future.

"We were trying to come up with ways of doing what we needed at that time, but we were also trying to do it in a way that was paying attention to the idea that this was going to grow, and that the demands would get larger," said Barton-Davis.

The dynamics among Bezos, Kaphan, and Barton-Davis produced some interesting results. "Like myself, Shel [previously] hadn't done any visible kinds of business-level, user-level programs very much," said Barton-Davis. "He enjoyed working on something that people would actually see—a Web interface that you could actually click on, rather than some sort of strange internal component of a larger system."

With his own considerable programming experience, Bezos knew exactly how difficult or easy it would be when he asked Kaphan and Barton-Davis to come up with a particular programming goal. After they came up with whatever he was looking for, Bezos would take a look at it, and "make excellent suggestions. It was a really good synergy," said Barton-Davis. "When Jeff asked Shel and me, 'Can we do this?' it was clear that he had already spent a little while in the back of his mind thinking about what might be involved. And he was willing to listen to us in terms of what we should really do about it. He understood the issues involved."

CC MOTEL

In these early days of Internet commerce, many customers were wary about giving out their credit card numbers. (In the minds of most consumers, it was somehow safer to give their credit card number to a traditional mail-order catalog than it was to an online company.) Around the time that Amazon.com was getting started, a hacker had broken into an Internet service provider and stolen thousands of credit card numbers—but never did anything with them. Despite this well-publicized black mark on the industry, the Amazonians were convinced that the chances were slight that a hacker would bother to take the time to grab individual numbers. The more legitimate worry was someone breaking into an unsecured system and stealing many numbers at once.

For the Amazon.com model to work, it was important for Amazon.com to be out in front on the issue of credit card security. Barton-Davis came up with a secure credit card system that was dubbed "CC Motel," which was a play on the name of a commercial pest-extermination product called Roach Motel. "At Amazon.com's CC Motel, credit card numbers check in, but they don't check out," was the company slogan. The CC Motel system consisted of two separate computers, which would communicate across a serial port connection using their own protocol. Immediately after a book was shipped to a customer and the customer's credit card was charged, the transaction information was transferred onto a floppy disk. Then an Amazon.com employee removed the floppy disk from the first computer and *literally* walked it over to the second computer, which was connected via modem to the credit card processing center. This process was known affectionately as "sneakernet."

In the very early days of the company, the computer that was connected to the credit card processing center was the same machine that was used for ordering books—because that was the only machine with a modem.

"That became an interesting [timing] problem as we began to get more volume," recalled Barton-Davis. "We ordered books in the morning, and we had to get that process finished in time so we would be able to start running the credit card numbers."

As far as the people at Amazon.com were concerned, this system was as secure as you could get because the only way someone could steal a stored credit card number would be to have physical access to the floppy disk and the computer. There was no place in the computing protocol where a potential thief could ask for a credit card number. Even if someone actually managed to figure out what the protocol was, the server didn't even understand the idea of being asked for a credit card. The only way someone could get the credit card number of an Amazon.com customer was to actually be in the Amazon.com office and have an understanding of the "sneakernet" security system.

"One of the reasons I designed it that way was so we could specifically claim that it's secure because it's *off* the Internet," said Barton-Davis. "I almost wanted to make the claim that even if you broke into the rest of our system, you *still* wouldn't be able to get the credit card numbers. Once we received and stored your credit card number on CC Motel, there was no way to get it back out other than to walk it into the office where that machine is. In retrospect, it's not totally clear that you need something that secure. And, in fact, the system they have now definitely works differently. There are no floppies going around."

Barton-Davis recalled that he used to have nightmares about the system because, "We didn't take seriously the responsibility of keeping that data in a good state." Although, *theoretically*, the machine was backed up every night, sometimes people would forget. "We kept asking, 'What happens when there are too many credit cards to fit on a floppy?' It was not taken that seriously. Since then, I've thought, what if we lost them all?' "

Back in those days, no one at Amazon.com was conversant in how exactly credit card transactions work. "We had some fundamental misconceptions about how credit cards were processed," recalled Nicholas Lovejoy, an early employee. "We set up our own terminology that wasn't quite reflective of how things really worked. It made sense to us but it didn't correspond exactly with the way the bank thought of it. So whenever we talked to the bank, we thought, 'My God, those guys are idiots. They don't know what they're talking about.' They were thinking the same of us, but really, we were the idiots, or oddballs, because we were using our own terminology that we had made up to represent all this stuff."

Mistakes were made, of course, particularly when a misreading of the documentation from the credit card company led to Amazon.com employees' misunderstanding of how credit card companies processed information. On more than one occasion, Amazon.com lost an original file with a couple of hundred credit card transactions. The only way of retrieving the information was to go back to CC Motel, print out a copy of the file with all the credit card numbers, call the credit card company, sit with them, and go through the list of numbers to make sure that each transaction had actually been processed. This tedious process could take an hour to deal with a relatively few credit card numbers. (Of course, that was back in the old days when the company was dealing with a relative handful of orders.)

Sometimes, someone would mistakenly overwrite the file of transactions that had been sent to the credit card company. To recuperate that information, Amazon.com would ask the credit card company to fax back the list of transactions, but that list contained only the last four digits of the credit card number, so someone would have to take the time to match those numbers with a list of transactions. The programmers fixed that problem by archiving every transaction.

When Amazon.com began selling to the public in July 1995, half of their customers phoned in their credit card number. The company initially had expected most credit cards to be taken over the telephone and very few on the Web, but that was never true, not even in the very early days. Some customers paid by check, while others chose to place their orders online. The latter group had to enter only the last five digits of their card number online, then call Amazon.com by phone with the remaining digits.

By this time, customers were using built-in encryption systems; the most popular was Netscape Navigator on the browser side and Netscape Secure Commerce Server on the server side, which made it very difficult for a hacker to gather private information. "That was not something that we could have done ourselves; that's something that had to be built into the browser that people were using," said Barton-Davis.

BECOMING USER-FRIENDLY

Back in those formative days, if a customer sent in a request to Amazon.com and then followed up with another request—even if it was a fraction of a second later—the company's computer had no notion that it had previously communicated with the customer's computer. So, for example, if a customer was searching for a new book by John Updike and then wanted to search for other books by John Updike, the web protocols had no way of knowing that this was a series of exchanges between a customer's computer and Amazon.com's server.

At the time, many Internet companies were working on various remedies to the problem through the use of Common Gateway Interface (CGI) scripts. CGI, which is attached to a hypertext link, enabled a Web server to communicate with another piece of software on the same machine. For example, a CGI program could take data from a Web server and convert the content into an e-mail message.

Amazon.com's CGI program created a 19-digit session identifier on the Uniform Resource Locator (URL) that was generated by a combination of random and specific information. (URL is a web address that all browsers recognize.) "As soon as you connected to the system for the first time, we figured out a new session key for you and then we would essentially edit the URLs of everything you would get back. Whenever you sent us another request, it would have that session key as part of the URL, so we could keep track of what people were asking for," explained Barton-Davis. "At that point, this was nothing terribly new. Various people had come up with some tricks to do this. Much of the same functions could be performed by some perl libraries, which was the dominant language for Common Gateway Interface."

After the order was taken, Amazon.com needed to establish a transaction history for the customer, and came up with the metaphor "Shopping Basket," said Barton-Davis. "There were three terms floating around. We didn't like any of them. Shopping Basket was the least offensive." For people acquainted with the Amazon.com website, the shopping basket has become a familiar icon.

As the Amazon.com engineers were trying to put out a product, much of the technology for the Internet was developing. With browser standards changing every six months, the company made sure that it continued to perform well with text-only browsers (since the site was mostly text). "That continues to be a feature on Amazon's site that people have commented on—that you can actually still go into the site using Lynx, which is a text-only browser, and the whole site still makes sense," said Barton-Davis. "On some sites, if you don't have graphics, you can't use their website. None of the eventual changes meant that anything that we had done previously was now broken; it just meant that there were better ways of doing it. But the old ways still worked satisfactorily. And that has continued to be true right through to the present day."

Because most home-users of the Web were running on slow 9,600 bits per second or 14.4 kilobits per second modems, it was important to make sure that pages could be downloaded in just a few seconds. With people already calling the Internet, the "World Wide Wait," Amazon.com, from the beginning, concentrated on the *text* of the site, with graphics definitely taking a backseat.

"We were talking about what the download time—in seconds—was for an image of a particular size," said Barton-Davis. "We really wanted to stay very small and compact, and also to try to reuse graphics. For the text part, it was not that much of an issue. Although 9,600 and 14.4 are a little slow, if you are just using text pages, it's pretty acceptable in some respects, even today. But with the graphics, it clearly was not. That meant an emphasis on trying to reuse graphics a lot. With most of the browsers at that point, if they just downloaded a particular graphic from the previous page, and it was reused, they didn't have to download it again. So, you would attempt to come up with motifs on the pages that would be used over and over again. For example, we talked about replacing the horizontal bars going across certain pages with pictures of animals that lived in the Amazon rain forest. Even by the time I left, there were remarkably few graphics. We never really got into a relationship with any good graphics house."

Tim O'Reilly, the book publisher, praised Amazon.com for building an easy-to-use interface that focused early on functionality. "A lot of people were spending a lot of time and energy making sites that were hard to use because they had all kinds of fancy graphics," said O'Reilly. "Amazon.com was so stripped down. They realized that what they were building was not a brochure; they were building an application."

MONEY TIME

During these first six months of operation, Jeff Bezos was personally funding the company out of his own pocket. In July 1994, as founder, president, chief executive officer, and chairman of the board, he purchased 10,200,000 shares of common stock for an aggregate price of $10,000, and also made a $15,000 interest-free loan to the company, followed up with another $29,000 loan in November, according to public records. During this period, he personally guaranteed the obligations of the company under a merchant account with Seafirst Bank of Seattle.

But he couldn't keep going back to his own well. In February 1995, he sold 582,528 shares of common stock to his father, Miguel A. Bezos, at a price per share of $0.1717. The infusion of $100,020 bought the company time and enabled it to make a move out of the garage into larger quarters.

These first six months produced an impressive infrastructure, but the company still had a long way to go. In fact, Amazon.com was about to enter its most critical period.

TAKEAWAYS

By the time he, Shel Kaphan, and Paul Barton-Davis set up shop in the converted garage, Bezos had already established the tenets of Amazon.com. Even with just three other employees (including his wife, Mackenzie), he was creating a nascent corporate culture, from the standpoints of both people and technology.

- Fully understand the available technology.
- Tailor that technology to your own needs.
- Create your own software if you can't buy it off the shelf.
- Take advantage of the availability of open-source software.
- Be adept at changing course when necessary, as Amazon.com did when it went from the strategy of selling books via e-mail to selling them on the World Wide Web.
- As you're strategizing, consider every "What if?" scenario, so you'll be able to make adjustments, when necessary.
- Constantly look to the future to figure out what's next.

chapter five

out to launch

Whether you believe you can do a thing or not, you are right.

—Henry Ford

I know why people move out of garages," Jeff Bezos has joked. "It is not that they run out of room, it is that they run out of electrical power."

By the time the ranks of Amazon.com employees had swelled to five people—with the temporary hiring of Nicholas Lovejoy, a high school math teacher in his early twenties—the lone circuit breaker in the converted garage wasn't up to the task of powering all of the hardware. So the quintet got creative. They ran long orange extension cords that curled Medusa-like into the garage from all the other rooms in the house, which were on separate circuit breakers. But even that power was not enough. By siphoning the entire house's power into the garage, it got to the point where Mackenzie couldn't turn on a hair dryer and Jeff couldn't vacuum the living room without blowing a circuit breaker.

In addition to the power problems, it was so crowded in the work space that all appointments with non-Amazonians had to be held somewhere else. As it turned out, the most convenient place to meet was a little café just about a mile or so away from the house. In a delicious bit of bookselling irony, the café was located inside the Barnes & Noble superstore in Bellevue.

During the late spring of 1995, the company began beta-testing the website with the help of several hundred friends—some computer savvy, some not so—who were invited to put the system through its paces by browsing for books and making pretend purchases. "We were prepared to handle real ones, but if they wanted to just do a fake one, they could," said Barton-Davis. Bezos beseeched all the participants: "Don't tell anybody what we are doing."

Glenn Fleishman, an author of Web-related books, who participated in that beta test (and who later went to work for Amazon.com) noted, "Today, companies are forced to launch a site, no matter how many warts are on it. Amazon, even in Internet time, took months to work out the kinks with real people."

Although the beta-testing produced much useful feedback, "most of it was already on our list of stuff that we wanted to change or extend or do," said Barton-Davis. "When the test was over, Shel and I were extremely satisfied that the only bug reports we got were when there was a choice of at least two ways for us to do something, and somebody didn't like the one that we had chosen. By the time we launched the site, we knew that we'd already ironed out 98 percent of the glitches. I remember having this satisfied feeling for some number of weeks that we weren't getting any feedback that hadn't been covered during that beta test."

This period saw the introduction of a variety of Web browsers such as Lynx, NCSA's Mosaic, Netscape Navigator, and Microsoft Internet Explorer; each was vying to be the next standard. Because they had neither the manpower nor the desire to test each browser for themselves, the Amazon.com engineers elected to devise a platform that worked for all browsers. "We waited until we had the feedback from the beta test," said Barton-Davis. "If there was going to be a diversity of browsers, it was much easier testing them with 200 or 300 people than doing it ourselves."

After the bugs were worked out of the system, the company sent an e-mail to all the people who participated in the beta test and told them that Amazon.com was ready for them to make *real* orders, thank you, and to pass the word on to their friends.

With the beta-testing completed, the company moved out of the Bellevue garage and into a space on 2714 First Avenue South in an industrial section of Seattle, across the street from the headquarters of Starbucks Coffee, about a mile from the Kingdome stadium. Because it is south of the Dome, the neighborhood is known locally as SoDo. Amazon.com, which shared the building with a tile retailer called Color Tile, occupied 1,100 square feet of office space on the second floor and had the use of a 400-square-foot warehouse—about the size of a two-car garage—which was located down two flights of stairs, in the basement. "Fortunately, though the physical warehouse was in many ways a toy, the software we had built to manage our . . . inventory system was not," Bezos told a Harvard Business School study. "We had put a lot of work into the system in advance."

Nicholas Lovejoy, who joined the company in June 1995, recalled that on the first day he went to work at the Color Tile building, "there were five rooms and only four employees. One of the rooms was used to store cardboard boxes, so I collapsed cardboard boxes," said Lovejoy, a graduate of Reed College in Oregon. Lovejoy, who had worked with Jeff and Mackenzie at D. E. Shaw & Co., had left the corporate world to teach mathematics at a private school in Redmond, Washington, the Seattle suburb that's best known for being the headquarters of Microsoft Corp.

"A friend of mine was in town for the summer and I called Jeff to see if he wanted to employ her," said Lovejoy. "Jeff immediately said, 'Well, what about you? What are you doing for the summer?' " Lovejoy went to Bellevue to talk to Bezos. "I didn't really get interviewed. Jeff knew that I was hired at D. E. Shaw, so he figured I was material for Amazon. I was an instant 'in' for him. So I basically took a summer job with Amazon. Jeff initially wanted me to work 50 hours a week—the full time Amazon commitment. I wanted to work 20 hours a week. We finally agreed on 35. I was hired to be an editor and write little book-review blurbs, to do whatever [odd jobs were necessary], to hire someone by the end of the summer to replace me, and to train that person."

A couple of months later, when he decided to quit teaching and cast his lot with Amazon.com, Lovejoy was technically the sixth permanent employee because Tom Schoenhoff had joined the company while Lovejoy was a part-timer. Both men have a legitimate claim to being the Amazon.com employee number five.

Although it was a roomier improvement over the Bellevue garage, the First Avenue office space was a motley mishmash of an operation. As soon as the group moved in, they pushed out the ceiling tiles, punched holes in the walls above the ceiling tile level, and crammed through the network cables, including the T1 Internet connection line, which hung clumsily from the ceiling. A cheap metal shelf held the CC Motel and the Internet hub and router. The phone system was installed by an independent contractor.

Lauralee Smith, who worked briefly for Amazon.com as a special-orders clerk, recalled that when she showed up at the Color Tile building, she thought, "For a company that was as high tech and visionary as it was, the actual geographical location was a little bit uninspiring. It was a very shabby collection of offices that gave you the impression of being put together with duct tape."

The 400-square-foot basement warehouse space was nothing more than some shelves (which could hold a few hundred books), a couple of tables with packing supplies, a metered scale, and a Pitney Bowes mailing instrument. Perusing these less-than-impressive facilities, Kaphan cracked: "I don't know if this is hopelessly pathetic or incredibly optimistic."

Although Bezos took the "incredibly optimistic" position, he conceded, "We had very low expectations for starting off, and thought it would take a long, long time for consumer habit to adopt to buying online at all." He tried to talk Ingram and Baker & Taylor into letting his fledgling company order less than the minimum requirement of 10 books. "We asked if we could pay a twenty dollar fee or whatever to get *one* book. We didn't want to go buy the book at Barnes & Noble because we wanted to actually test and exercise our systems," said Bezos. The distributors held firm on the 10-book order.

Part of that reluctance might have been a total lack of understanding of what Bezos was trying to do. As John Ingram, chairman of Ingram Book Co., told the *Washington Post* in 1998, "Before 1995, I'm not sure I knew what the Internet was."

Amazon.com was able to find a loophole in Ingram's policy. "Turns out that with both the wholesalers . . . you just had to *order* 10 books," said Bezos. "If you ordered 10 books, but nine of them were books they didn't have in stock, they would ship you the one book. Both wholesalers carried an obscure book on lichens, but they didn't have it. So we tested all of our systems by ordering one [other] book and then nine copies of this lichen book."

Back in those formative days, a crucial ingredient in the Amazon.com retailing model was that the company would maintain little or no inventory because inventory costs money. (As we will see later, it wouldn't be long before Bezos abandoned that idea and turned his business model on its head.) In the early 1990s, in order to cut down on the costs of their inventory, many traditional bricks-and-mortar retailers worked with their suppliers to popularize a system called "just-in-time" delivery, i.e., the goods would arrive in the store just when the retailer needed them. "We came up with a phrase 'almost-in-time' delivery," said Barton-Davis. "In other words, we don't have the books you want, but we can get them real soon."

A cynic wouldn't have trouble making a convincing argument that Amazon.com didn't *carry* over a million titles (as the company initially claimed), but that Amazon.com could *get* the customer any one of those million titles—as could any other bookstore, real or virtual.

Before Amazon.com could afford to launch the website to the public, the company desperately needed a new infusion of cash. In July 1995, according to public records, the company (read: Bezos) sold 847,716 shares of common stock at $0.1717 to the Gise Family Trust, for which Jacklyn Gise Bezos was the trustee and beneficiary. The sale brought in $145,553. "We didn't invest in Amazon," said

Jackie, "we invested in Jeff." Also that month, Jeff personally guaranteed the obligations of the company under a bankcard merchant account with Wells Fargo Bank; in April 1995, he had personally guaranteed company credit cards.

Amazon.com's timing was perfect because the summer of 1995 was the ideal time to launch a new site. If they had launched a year earlier, there would barely have been enough personal computers connected to the Internet to keep the company afloat; a year later and the competition would have had an insurmountable lead. In the summer of 1995, with the Web's infrastructure in place, several major developments were transforming the Web from being a static online magazine or kiosk into a more compelling and user-friendly interactive medium. In April, Silicon Graphics released Web Space, which contained Virtual Reality Modeling Language (VRML), making it the first Web browser to be able to display three-dimensional scenes (HTML created only two-dimensional environments). An even more significant launch occurred the following month, when Sun Microsystems released Java, a secure programming language that made it possible for virtually any type of application or interactive content (such as animation) to be run in a Web page. By treating all operating systems the same, a Java mini-application (called an applet) could run on Windows, a Macintosh, or on a UNIX workstation. With the widening in 1995 of the transmission band to 128 kilobytes per second, both picture and audio could easily be transmitted over the Web. Also that summer, Netscape released the Navigator 2.0 browser, which was soon being used on almost 10 million computers. When Netscape, which had not made one penny of profit, had its initial public offering (IPO) on August 9, 1995, the stock soared more than 100 percent over its official opening price—ending the day with a market cap of $2.7 billion.

With the coming-out party of Netscape, the Internet had barged into the corporate American consciousness. Even more important for Amazon.com, Netscape's successful IPO showed the investment world that an Internet stock could—should—be valuated not on past performance, but on a vague but compelling promise of a radically different online future, where all the rules have been broken. Whoever could weave the best story would be the winner, and no one told a story better, or more engagingly, than Jeff Bezos and Amazon.com, whose strategy of GET BIG FAST would make them the biggest beneficiaries of this brand of New Think.

On July 16, 1995, the Amazon.com website was launched. When a user logged on, he saw on the upper left-hand corner of the computer screen the first Amazon.com logo—an aqua blue letter "A" in the form of a pyramid with the top squared off. From the bottom up through the middle of the letter was a representation of a flowing river that was wide at the bottom and increasingly narrow as it reached the top. When you looked at the figure one way it looked like it formed an "A." When you looked at it another way, it looked like a flowing river. Written under the "A" was the tagline "Earth's Biggest Bookstore."

The opening page was essentially a list of informational text with textual navigation bars at the top and bottom of the page. The top of the page said: "Welcome to Amazon.com Books! Search one million titles. Enjoy consistently low prices."

The only artwork was the logo and the cover of a highlighted book, which was part of a changing daily feature called "Spotlight." In those early days, the only books that were eligible to appear in "Spotlight" were those that came with a lot of content, such as a synopsis, reviews, author information, etc. Those books were always discounted at least 20 to 30 percent—compared to the 10 percent off for all the other books. Not surprisingly, those books sold well and "Spotlight" became a big favorite among customers. In the ensuing months, the company hired experienced book editors to take responsibility for the Spotlight and other areas. The first full-time Spotlight editor, Jonathan Kochmer, "really put a lot of love into it," recalled Lovejoy. "Each Spotlight would have a theme and each day it would have a new twist to it. And if the books that Jonathan wanted to spotlight didn't have reviews, he would quickly write some. So [Spotlight] changed from being just a collection of the books we had reviews on, which were randomly selected, to more of an editorial piece."

Bezos, Kaphan, and Barton-Davis were proponents of concise web pages, and often used a term that has since become very popular in e-commerce: "frictionless shopping," i.e., keep the whole shopping process as simple and fast as possible. The customer should be able to come in, find what she wants, buy it, and be done in just a couple of minutes.

Amazon exploited the advanced searching capabilities of the Web by enabling users to execute searches by author, title, subject, publication date, and keyword throughout the entire catalog, and then to be able to narrow the searches even further. In addition to a basic search engine, Amazon.com provided two additional services for its users, Editors and Eyes. With Editors, Amazon.com's in-house editors provided customers with book recommendations—based on the customer's previous purchases—that the editors had read from preview book galleys or advance reviews. Eyes alerted users to the availability of books by their favorite authors or about subjects that they expressed an interest in. For example, users of the service could be automatically notified when the new John Grisham book was available in paperback, or if a new customer service book was on the market.

"What hangs it all together is that the search language defined inside the whole system lets you move queries inside the system in some standard form," said Barton-Davis. "So, when you have just completed a search for something, the system knows what the query was. When a customer tells you, 'I'd like to be told about books like this in the future,' the system takes that query and stuffs it away somewhere. Then that evening and all subsequent evenings, it takes that query and runs it against the database [of books], as if you had just typed it in yourself."

Bezos was issuing the dare of interactivity to bricks-and-mortar bookstores. "We're not going to replace the bookstore," he said in a 1995 interview. "One of the things that's interesting about books as a product is that people go to bookstores in part because they want books, and in part because they want a nice place to go. It's a challenge for all interactive bookstores to make their site as engaging as possible."

Very soon, the company received its very first paying customer. "It is very exciting when you get your first customer who is not a relative," cracked Bezos. When the order came in, "All the staff were saying: 'Do you know this person? I don't know this person. Hey, how about you? Do you know this person?' "

Barton-Davis thought it would be a great idea to have a gauge of how much activity the site was generating. "It's one thing to have a look at the sales record at the end of every day or every week," he said. "It would be much more visceral for us to hear something telling us that there was a sale right now. If today it's only a minute to the next one, and next week it's only 10 seconds to the next one, it would be, it seemed, a good psychological thing."

To that end, he tweaked the Web server code so that every time the company made a sale, a command sent a message to all of the computer screens in the company, which would cause a nice loud BEEP! and an on-screen message flashed the amount of the sale and the number of books sold. Whenever they heard the BEEP, the Amazonians would let go with a rousing cheer.

For a while.

In those first few days, when it was just half a dozen sales a day, the beep was a happy novelty. But as orders started coming in more frequently, the novelty quickly wore off. "It was amazing how much of a low frequency [of sales] was needed in order for it to become *incredibly* annoying," said Barton-Davis. "I thought it would be fun up to about a 10-second interval. But it turned out that if there was one every five or 10 minutes, it would tend to disrupt what was in the window [of the computer screen] you were working in. Or it would happen in a window that you couldn't see, but you'd hear it, and it was indistinguishable from all the other beeps. You'd ask yourself: "What happened? Did I do something wrong?' "

Three days after launching, Amazon.com received an e-mail from someone at Yahoo!, another brand-new Internet company. The guys at Yahoo! loved the Amazon.com website and asked if they could include it on the Yahoo! "What's Cool" list, which, at that time, was the most trafficked Web page on the Internet. "He said we were going to get a lot of traffic, and if this wasn't the right time to send all these people [to the website], we can do it in a month or whenever you want," Bezos recalled. "Today, to get Yahoo! to do something like that, you'd have to pay them tens of millions of dollars. Then, it was just an e-mail exchange. So, we sat around, seven or nine of us, eating Chinese food, discussing whether or not we were ready for what Shel Kaphan said, 'might be like taking a sip through a fire hose.' We talked about it for five minutes and said, 'Yeah, let's do it.' "

Kaphan was prescient, the deluge of orders *was* like taking a sip through a fire hose. The first week Amazon.com was in business, the company took in $12,438 worth of orders but was able to ship only $846.00 worth of books. The annoying sales beep was deprogrammed after one week and was replaced with an on-screen script, which could be run at any time if someone wanted to check to see what the sales had been in the last hour or five minutes. The following week the company took in $14,792 and was able to ship $7,302 worth of books.

At first, this wasn't enough volume to justify ordering more than once a day from the book wholesalers. But as that began to change, Amazon.com reached a point where if the company didn't start running the ordering program by about 10:30 in the morning, they wouldn't have enough time to put in the order for the day—because they had to use the *same machine* for checking credit card numbers and other things.

Although the number of orders was relatively small, it was huge compared to what the expectations had been. "Our business plan does not even begin to resemble what has actually happened," said Bezos. "I think one thing we missed was that the Internet was exclusively made up of early adopters at that time. So all the people online, even though it was a relatively small number compared with today, were those who liked to try new things."

As the leading online retailer of books, Amazon.com quickly became one of the most widely known, used, and cited commerce sites on the Web, offering what the company called "an authoritative selection" of more than a million titles at competitive prices. (Although the company always listed 1.5 million titles on its site, it professed to carry only 1.1 million. This was done, said a former insider, so that the company could later claim that it added another 400,000 titles.) During the first month online, Amazon.com shipped orders to 45 countries and all 50 states. By October, the company recorded its first 100-order day. The first 100-order hour came less than a year later. (100-order minutes eventually became common.) Customers were finding obscure books they'd been looking for for years and when the book would arrive, they would tell their friends.

And then things got even busier when Netscape put the Amazon.com website on its popular "What's New" page.

"I think it's important not to underestimate the amount of good luck involved," said Nicholas Lovejoy. "Amazon starts with an A. In 1995, a tremendous number of the lists of neat websites were alphabetical, and Amazon was at the top of the list. That was hugely important, in my opinion."

Of the 1.1 million titles that Amazon.com "carried," the 300,000 books in stock at Ingram and Baker & Taylor were all discounted 10 percent, and the top 20 or so paperback and hardcover titles were discounted 30 percent. A special group of books selected by the staff was discounted up to 40 percent. Of course a per-book shipping charge of $3.95 cut into the discounts on small orders, but for someone buying several books at a time, Amazon's prices were competitive with the deep discounts that were a normal way of life at Borders, Barnes & Noble, and other national chains, plus Amazon.com charged state sales tax only to customers in Washington state. On the other hand, it could take Amazon a week to deliver a book that wasn't a bestseller, and even longer for obscure titles.

Those early orders produced some humorous curiosities. In August, one customer ordered a dozen books whose only common thread was that the word "Marsha" appeared in every title. The customer's name was not Marsha. In September, in a cross-shipping mistake, a handsomely color-photographed atlas of skin diseases was sent to the wrong customer. The customer ultimately returned the tome, but admitted in an e-mail, "I've been staring at it in horrified fascination for days." (Four years later, the same customer had placed almost 100 orders.)

Every week employees would collect a list of the 20 oddest titles on order, and Bezos would award a prize for the most entertaining one. Some examples: "Training Goldfish Using Dolphin Training Techniques," "How to Start Your Own Country," and "Life Without Friends."

The programmers, Kaphan and Barton-Davis, were pleased that even though sales were growing exponentially, the system was still running fine, and they were easily able to identify areas that needed to be tweaked. "That's because we were paying attention to the engineering of the system, and trying to do it in a way that it would grow," said Barton-Davis. "We made a lot of mistakes. Subsequently, the [programmers and engineers] the company brought in corrected those mistakes because they knew a lot more about certain programs—Oracle for example—than we did, or they were able to spend a lot more time than we had focusing on a particular issue. I would like to believe that the design decisions that we took early on really paved the way for the company to grow so dramatically."

In those first few weeks, the company wasn't prepared for major sales volume. No one had been hired to do any packing. "We were trying to figure out how we were going to get enough bandwidth to actually hire more people to do this," Bezos recalled. "We were literally working until midnight every night shipping out 100, 200, 300 packages a day. So everybody pitched in." To make matters worse, there were no packing tables, so everybody had to get down on the concrete floor on their hands and knees to pack and wrap the books with CoreSeal, a corrugated self-adhesive cardboard product that sticks to itself but not to the book. "It was backbreaking work," said Bezos. "Our knees would be raw."

It quickly reached the point that Bezos said to Nicholas Lovejoy, "We've got to do something about this. We've got to get knee pads." Lovejoy "looked at me like I was a Martian," said Bezos. "But I was serious. That's the solution that I came up with." Then Lovejoy said, "What about packing tables?" "I thought that was the most brilliant idea I had ever heard in my life," Bezos recalled with a laugh. "It truly dramatically improved things."

Back then, with just a handful of employees, everybody did a little bit of everything, whether it was packing books or answering customer e-mail. All of the e-mail came through Amazon.com's one e-mail address, was logged into the system, and somebody would answer it—often it was answered by Bezos himself. "People were working long and hard, but we also would have two-hour lunches," said Lovejoy. They would all sit around a big table that Kaphan had brought with him from California (it didn't fit into his Seattle house) "and talk about all kinds of things in an almost philosophical way. We'd hypothesize about different aspects of the business: the website, privacy issues."

Lauralee Smith remembered the informality of it all. Rather than buying or leasing a photocopier and having it on the premises, all the duplicating was done at the PrintMart shop, which was several blocks away. "I didn't have a car, so several times a week, I would march across the railroad tracks to the copy shop with huge armloads of materials, wait for the order and then carry all the copied material back across the railroad tracks," recalled Smith. "It was the kind of operation where if you needed office supplies, you bought your own and you gave them a bill at the end of the month and they tacked it on to your check. It was a very different way of doing business."

To generate content on the website, company workers reviewed 10 new books a week in each of a dozen or so traditional retail book categories—fiction, business, etc. Initially, all the content covering the individual books on the site came from the CD-ROMs supplied by the book distributors and publishers, and were combined into one catalog. But there wasn't much information beyond bibliographic data, such as book title, author, and publication date. For additional information, Lovejoy frequently went to the Elliott Bay Book Company, the legendary bookstore, which was in the Pioneer Square neighborhood, about a mile down First Avenue from the new Amazon.com headquarters. At Elliott Bay, he would peruse the books and take notes from the dust jacket copy.

To add graphical elements, Lovejoy scanned book covers with a newly purchased Hewlett-Packard scanner, and wrote some software to manipulate the graphics. For some decorative art for the page, he vertically stacked some books together—with one book leaning against the stack—and scanned their bindings. "It was basic graphics, which I'm sure any graphics artist would have cringed at, but it added spice to a site that, apart from the logo, had been entirely text," he said.

At one point, someone came up with an idea of featuring particular books as part of special promotions with a publisher. "The publisher would sell the book to us at a deeper discount and we would advertise it in many places on the website and do an in-depth spread," said Lovejoy. To test the idea, he randomly selected a coffee-table book entitled *A Hundred Years of Gibson Guitars*, and spent a couple of weeks writing five Web pages for the book, including an interview with the author. "I tried to scan in the whole first paragraph with text recognition software, but in '95, that didn't work very well. So I pretty much typed in the first chapter; just huge amounts of data on this one book. I thought that there were some obvious reasons why people would want to buy the book. It was handsome and had lots of great pictures, and we featured it all over the place. Six months later, we sold our first copy. Clearly, this was not a hit."

THE AMAZON EXPERIENCE

Beyond giving customers the ability to conduct searches for a particular book or author, the freedom to browse from among the book selections that the company highlighted, and the opportunity to buy the latest bestsellers, the Amazon.com site promoted the idea of creating a *community* of customers. The company fostered this clubby feeling by encouraging readers to write and submit book reviews (which Amazon.com would post on the website). This "audience participation" gave readers the feeling that they were making a contribution to the thoroughness of the website's information. Authors of the books were not left out of the equation; they were invited to participate by answering a series of online interview questions. As was previously mentioned, customers could also register for personalized services such as Eyes and Editors, take part in promotions, and check the status of their order.

Ordering was a snap; a customer merely clicked a button to add books to his virtual shopping basket. If he changed his mind, he could easily remove a book from his shopping basket prior to making the final purchase, just as he could in a bricks-and-mortar store. When he was finished shopping, the customer just had to click on the "buy" button, provide his credit card number, and select from a menu of delivery services, including overnight and various international shipping options. Gift wrapping was a featured option. This ordering process is commonplace today, but in the summer of 1995, it was revolutionary in its simplicity.

Unlike many other Web retailers, Amazon.com had a system where orders were recorded, registered, and processed at one time, in real time. The customer was immediately apprised of the status of the order, how long it would take to ship the book, the amount of shipping costs, and how much sales tax (only for Washington state residents) had to be paid. The company instantly sent an e-mail message that confirmed all the previously mentioned details; a follow-up e-mail alerted the customer that the order was shipped. By using his Amazon.com password, a customer could use the Amazon.com website to follow the status of his package through the various delivery services, such as UPS and Airborne. This system minimized delays and miscommunication, and helped to promote Amazon.com's reputation for attentive customer service.

"The execution on the site was really, really good, and the site was light and airy and straightforward," said Craig Danuloff, the founder of iCat, an e-commerce software company "Part of that was to keep it simple. Their suitability-to-task was so rare. It did what it was supposed to do. By far, the greatest failing of commercial websites has been oversimplicity. In other words, they don't satisfy the need of the user; if you want to buy something, you don't know what to do."

In those early days, Amazon.com was able to earn a lot of positive points with the general Web audience, which "was simultaneously the most forgiving and the most unforgiving," said Danuloff. "They didn't care if something was slow or broken because they knew [the technical state of the Web at that time]. But if it was systemically bad and you weren't doing something about it, then they would go into chat forums and hatchet you."

From day one, Bezos knew that Amazon.com had to establish customer loyalty. Initially, the return policy was that customers could send back a book within 15 days, but that eventually was expanded to 30 days. In fact, Bezos was so insistent on the maxim that the "customer is always right," that it sometimes frustrated Kaphan and Barton-Davis.

For example, soon after launching the site, the company received an order from a customer who lived overseas. The customer sent Amazon.com a money order that was for the wrong amount. "Then he cancelled part of the order, so that we now owed *him* money," recalled Barton-Davis. "But then he decided to order some more books. He wanted to merge that order into the one he had already put in, and he wanted to pay for it with the remainder of the money order and a *new* money order.

"Jeff's response to this was that the customer gets it *his* way. There were no exceptions to that. The only exception was when someone wanted something that just couldn't be done because it was a physical impossibility. Otherwise, we made the software fit what the customers were telling us."

When the first customer returns began coming in, the company had no mechanism for processing and archiving them. "We sent requests to Shel, who would go directly into the database and update them," said Lovejoy. "From an accounting perspective, it was a nightmare. Shel helped to define how to handle the software development to accommodate the accounting and the physical requirements to run a warehouse, such as how to handle the returns from customers, how to handle returns to distributors, how to handle when a book gets damaged or stolen. What happens when a book disappears? What happens when it reappears?"

Although all these contingencies were nothing new to book retailing, they were brand new to the neophytes running Amazon.com. Each and every one of those original employees—none of whom had any experience in books, or in the warehousing or distribution of any kind of tangible product—had to figure it out on his or her own. "It was such a raw place that people were just expected to figure it out and get it right," said Lovejoy. "People can do that—given the right combination of motivation and resources, plus the willingness to work hard, to try things, to make mistakes, and to admit having made a mistake. We developed a can-do attitude. And we had a lot of skills. Jeff knew a lot about business and Mackenzie was incredibly attentive to detail and accounting."

As the company was quickly growing, Lovejoy was put in charge of recruiting. One of the first people he hired was a fellow classmate from

Reed College named Laurel Canan, who had been working as a carpenter for a Seattle construction company called Saltaire Craftsman. "Laurel's contribution shouldn't be overlooked by any means," said Barton-Davis. "One of the first things he did was to build some excellent packing tables. He completely framed in the warehouse so we had a real space to work in. Right from the start, he was a very enthusiastic person, despite the fact that he was just packing books, and clearly intellectually capable of doing a lot more than that."

According to Barton-Davis, Canan demanded to be allowed to buy stock in the company. "That was quite a leap of faith. Jeff tried hard to persuade him from doing it, but he did buy stock. He was committed to being there and doing everything he could to make it work." Canan went on to run the warehouse for a long time. Although he had no background in running a warehouse, neither did anyone else at Amazon.com.

With Canan taking over the day-to-day operations in the warehouse, Lovejoy concentrated even more recruiting, eventually bringing in two other Reed College friends, Fred Eiden and Knute Sears. "Although [recruiting] was my primary duty, it was always a team effort. Jeff made the last call in terms of whether we hired someone," said Lovejoy.

Bezos built himself a desk out of a 1¾-inch-thick solid core particleboard exterior door that measured 63 inches by 34 inches. The 80-pound door, made of birch veneer covered with polyurethane, was attached to four 30-inch-high 4 × 4 legs made out of fir. "Jeff built the first two of those, and I built the next four," said Lovejoy. "I had to make some structural improvements to Jeff's. Jeff's didn't have the triangulation quite right, so they were initially pretty wobbly." (Saltaire, the company that Laurel Canan used to work for, eventually got the assignment to build all the door desks for Amazon.com; to date, they've built several thousand of them.)

Bezos's original door desk ultimately became a symbol of Amazon.com's commitment to keeping costs down (in order to give customers the best possible price). It was cited in virtually every long interview with Bezos (and was featured in a photo shoot in *Vanity Fair*), and helped fuel the positive, quirky early press the company received.

In April 1999, when Amazon.com launched its auction site, that first desk was put up for bid as part of a charity auction for the World Wildlife Fund's habitat and wildlife preservation efforts for the benefit of the Amazon River Basin. The online bidding was intense. Among those vying for the door desk were John Doerr (no pun intended), the Kleiner Perkins venture capitalist and Amazon.com director, and Bezos's friend Nick Hanauer. The winning bid brought in $30,100. Who was the winner? Jeff's mother, Jacklyn Bezos.

In those formative years, Bezos repeatedly reminded employees that Amazon.com's customers didn't care what the offices or the desks look like; he continually reinforced the virtue of frugality. All the furniture—with the exception of the door desks—was purchased from garage sales or auctions, or wherever they could find it.

"At one point, Jeff wanted us to put little stickers on the furniture to show who bought it and how much money we saved on it. But we never followed through on that," recalled Gina Meyers, who was the company's first comptroller. "He just continually reinforced [the idea] that we weren't going to spend money where we didn't need to, where it didn't ultimately benefit the customer. Sometimes, that meant spending a little bit more to reinforce the idea that we weren't wasting money. Jeff would say, if [a piece of furniture] looks cheap—even though it's a little bit more expensive—we should buy it, because it reinforces our culture of being cheap and not wasting money."

"We have a strong focus on trying to spend money on things that matter to customers and not spend money on us," said Bezos. "Our wealth vanishes the instant we stop doing a good job for our customers, and that's real. That has happened to companies in the past. . . . What our furniture looks like does not matter one whit to our customers. Instead, we spend money on things that matter to customers."

TAKEAWAYS

Preparation was evident at every step of the way as Amazon.com approached its launch. Bezos might have been making it all up as he went along, but at the core of all this activity was a belief in finding good people and helping them make the right decisions.

- Beta-test the website in order to work out the kinks.
- Keep overhead low. Customers don't care what your office looks like; they only care about getting great service.
- Keep your website simple.
- Create a wonderful customer experience.
- Create a community of customers.
- Spend your money on systems; not on things that the customer will never see.
- If necessary to stay afloat, be willing to spend some of your own money.
- Hire people who are smart enough and flexible enough to come up with solutions.
- Find ways to make your customer feel loyal to you, i.e., the customer is always right.

chapter six

get big fast

Money is a terrible master but an excellent servant.

—P. T. Barnum

Although Amazon.com was steadily bringing in modest, but promising, sales—$12,438 the first week and $14,792 the second week, but a drop to $9,548 the third week—the company was quickly running out of cash. According to papers filed with the Securities and Exchange Commission, from July 5, 1994, when it was founded, to the end of 1994, Amazon.com lost $52,000; the eventual loss for 1995 was going to be $303,000.

Jeff was "dead broke" in that summer of 1995, according to Eric Dillon, who was then a stock broker for Smith Barney in Seattle. "He was out of his personal funds, he was out of his family's ability [to fund the company], and he was [going to be] out of money in 45 days." With the doors about to be closed, "it was a huge crisis; a critical stage for the company."

Despite that grim situation, "I don't know if Jeff ever worried about financing because he was so focused on the business plan," marveled Dillon. "He was just so sold on where he was going that he just naturally assumed that it would take care of itself." Seeing how committed Bezos was "was powerful to me."

To illustrate that confidence, Bezos was fully prepared to wait for the rest of the world to come around to his idea. He was ready and willing to lose money for *five years* before turning a profit, and if he did make any profits, they would be immediately plowed back into the company to improve the web site. "There's a whole set of habits that need to be learned for people who want to shop in this way," he said. "The landscape of people who do new things and expect them to be profitable quickly is littered with corpses."

Despite his cool confidence, he did need money. He told his friend Nick Hanauer—who had wanted to invest ever since Bezos came up with the idea—that, yes, he did need to raise money, and that he was trying to decide whether to get it directly from venture capitalists (most likely from Silicon Valley) or from a round of financing from local Seattleites. Hanauer, a Seattle native with a wide circle of personal and business relationships in town, argued for the local route, and ultimately convinced Bezos, who in his 12 months in Seattle had come to know relatively few locals in a position to invest.

Concentrating the raising of funds in Seattle was not going to be easy because, at that time, the investment "angel" community in the city was infinitesimal compared to Silicon Valley. With few exceptions, the Seattle area's legion of Microsoft millionaires had not yet fully unleashed their investment power on cash-starved local start-ups.

"Today, if you want to raise a million or five million dollars for a good idea, with good management, I could do that for you in 10 phone calls," said Hanauer. "But back then it was hard. That was because no one had done an Amazon.com. Today, Amazon.com is the example people use to prove that you can make hundreds of millions of dollars on a small angel investment. It's the metaphor for angel investing. But we didn't have that in 1995. So getting people to write checks for $20,000 or $40,000 or $60,000 or $100,000 was hard, hard, hard."

Hanauer began setting up pitch meetings for Jeff with potential investors that Hanauer knew personally and with wealthy people who had been recommended by Hanauer's friends. The first phone call Hanauer made was to Eric Dillon, a tall, blond stockbroker in his mid-thirties, who had participated in other venture capital deals. Dillon's immediate reply was that he was not interested, but agreed to meet with Bezos as a courtesy to the persistent Hanauer. Dillon fully expected his involvement with Bezos and Amazon.com would go no further than that one meeting.

Before that meeting, Hanauer was concerned about Bezos's performance because, in Hanauer's estimation, his friend was not particularly proficient at the fine art of asking people for money. "He didn't know how to present himself very well," Hanauer recalled. "Jeff has always been a compelling guy. But how compelling he was as a person was not as obvious to most people as it was to me. I knew as soon as I met Jeff Bezos that he was going to be a rock star. But if you had asked most of the people who had met him in Seattle in 1995 whether he was going to be a rock star, I'd have been the only one." In Hanauer's opinion, Bezos was not projecting "how smart he was, how accomplished he was, and how focused he was."

After the first meeting with Dillon, Hanauer told Bezos that there were several things wrong with his presentation. Chief among them was that Bezos didn't talk about his own credentials and track record. "He was either not confident enough or too self-conscious or just didn't understand how to sell people well enough to bring that to the fore," said Hanauer. "Jeff was the *only* thing we had to sell. Nobody knew what the Internet was and being in the book business on the Internet in 1995 just didn't sound like that big of an idea. It was sort of an amusing idea at the time. But people don't want to invest in amusing ideas."

Dillon concurred that he wasn't particularly impressed with Bezos's presentation, which he described as "totally scattered. It went, 'Hi, we have an online bookstore and I think we're going to do well.'" But whatever Bezos lacked in his presentation did not ultimately matter to Dillon, whose recollection of some of the other details of that first meeting differs from Hanauer's. "Jeff got me," said Dillon, who went into that meeting thinking there was no chance he would ever get involved with Amazon.com. "I was fascinated with Jeff Bezos from the get-go. He had a burning passion and a raw intelligence that I had rarely witnessed. Additionally, he had just come from D. E. Shaw. One of the businesses that I had started was an investment pool that invested exclusively in hedge funds. So, we had that in common. He was one of the few people who understood the type of investing that I was doing, so we talked about that. Being involved with Wall Street as long as I had, I was able to understand his career at Bankers Trust and the other places he had worked."

The most convincing factor to Dillon was that Bezos had given up a seven-figure-a-year job at D. E. Shaw to take a flyer on the Internet. "The fact that he had left that kind of [situation] overwhelmed me," said Dillon. "It gave me a very, very powerful urge to get involved with this guy."

As part of his presentation, Bezos told Hanauer, Dillon, and other potential investors that he had calculated Amazon.com's market worth at $6 million. At their second meeting, Dillon told Bezos that he thought the $6 million figure was arbitrary and without any basis. He asked how Jeff had plucked that number out of the air. "Jeff's answer to me was, 'Eric, I actually tried to be very *thoughtful* about how I arrived at the valuation,' " Dillon recalled.

Valuations for a new company are calculated by comparing it with existing companies with a track record in the same industry. Since this was the summer of 1995, there were few pure-Internet-play retail companies like Amazon.com with any kind of performance history, so there really were no comparables. But Bezos did have some information on how much other Internet companies were trying to raise in the private equity market. "Jeff had a good handle on what was going on," said Dillon. "We went back and forth. At the end of the conversation, the valuation was reduced from $6 million to $5 million, and that's where that initial funding was done. Jeff said, 'You're a hard bargainer. You need to be on the advisory board of this company.' "

Although, on its face, that $1 million difference in the initial valuation might not sound like much, it was colossal because it increased the value of the shares of the original investors by a whopping 18 percent.

Over the course of the growth of the company, including the many times the stock has been split, the reduction of the valuation from $6 million to $5 million eventually added tens of millions of dollars to the pockets of those original investors. The ultimate enormity of that financial decision "was probably the biggest valuation negotiating that has ever been done at Amazon.com," according to Dillon.

Meanwhile, Bezos was also talking to other potential investors in Seattle. An attorney working with one local investment group contacted Tom Alberg, one of Seattle's leading business and political powerbrokers, and told him about Jeff Bezos and his idea about selling books on the Internet. A graduate of Harvard University and Columbia University Law School, Alberg had been most recently involved in the cellular phone business, first as president (and a director) of LIN Broadcasting Corporation, and later as executive vice president of McCaw Cellular Communications, Inc. (Both companies are now part of AT&T Corp.) The low-key, fifty-ish Alberg, and the attorney who initially called him, attended an introductory meeting with Bezos, who laid out his business plan, which consisted of some 20 pages, with a few financial projections. One statistic that jumped out was that Amazon.com could produce the equivalent of 70 turns a year on its inventory, compared to the industry average of 2.7 turns a year for traditional bookstores.

Alberg was interested. "I was intrigued with the Internet," he said. "I was an early user of Netscape. I was trying to figure out how to do things online back in the late eighties when GE had a horrible online system."

The other lawyer in the meeting, who represented the other venture capital group, "did a very good, classical due-diligence," said Alberg. "He called everybody in the publishing business, he checked all over town. He checked around the country. He concluded that Amazon didn't stand a chance because [he thought] when Barnes & Noble launched their site, they would crush Amazon. Barnes & Noble got big discounts from the publishers. Amazon could never compete with them. They'd be wiped out."

That lawyer declined to invest. Alberg understood why. "Books didn't seem quite like the right market. I think one of the big stumbling blocks for potential investors was that we all liked to go to bookstores. I heard that from people a hundred times: 'I just love to go to bookstores. Why would I buy over the Internet?' "

Bezos had the answer to that question. He believed that Amazon.com could succeed because it was a singular business that could not exist anywhere but the Internet. He provided this rationale to researchers from the Harvard Business School, which conducted a 1997 study on the formation of the company:

> Books was one of the few—maybe the only—category where computers have already been very helpful in selling the product. For a long time, bookstores have had information desks, where you walk up and somebody uses a computer to help you find what you're looking for. Computers were already helpful in selling books. You could see how with a large number of products, the sorting and searching could help. But that wasn't the main thing. The main thing was that you could build a bookstore on the Web that simply couldn't exist any other way. The Web is an infant technology. If you want to be successful in the short-to-medium term, you can only do things that offer incredibly strong value propositions to customers relative to the value of doing things in more traditional ways. That basically means that, right now, you should only do online what you cannot do any other way.

What Amazon.com could do online was implement a business model based upon managing a fast-turning inventory from a centralized, low-overhead operation. The model was spectacularly capital-efficient. On day zero, an ordered book would enter Amazon.com inventory. Eighteen days later (on average) a customer would buy it. Two days after that, the credit card company would transfer the money into the bank account of Amazon.com, which would have *53* days to pay the supplier. That meant that Amazon.com would have a negative operating cycle of 33 days. By comparison, in a physical bookstore, the customer purchases a book, on average, 161 days after the book is in stock. The store gets its money on day 163, and it has to pay its supplier on day 84, giving it a positive operating cycle of 79 days. By comparison, Amazon.com's negative operating cycle of 33 days, would give it a huge cash flow advantage. Because the company didn't order most books until after it sold them, it could potentially turn over its relatively small stock (primarily bestsellers at that time) 150 times a year, compared with an inventory turnover of less than four times for traditional stores. Amazon.com receives its money very quickly by credit card, so for about a month, it earns a "float" of interest-free money. That money, which adds up to tens of millions of dollars a year, helps pay a significant amount of Amazon.com's overhead.

Amazon.com was a business that was going to be built on the altar of *scale*, with a core belief that as it increased the number of customers, costs would not increase. It seemed to make sense. Unlike a brick-and-mortar store, a website was inexpensive to build. The external infrastructure already existed in the form of customers' personal computers and connections to the Internet, enabling the company to reach a worldwide audience from one central location. With many of its costs already fixed (with the exception of order-fulfillment and customer service), the company could generate cash through sales that would help offset cash used for operating expenses. As a result, if Bezos was right, Amazon.com would have more cash to invest in systems and services, such as branding, comarketing, enhanced product features, and customer service. (Of course, these variable costs would later turn out to be enormously expensive.) And as microchips got cheaper and faster, and bandwidth widened, even greater scale and efficiency could be achieved. Finally, Bezos knew that by being able to keep track of the purchasing patterns (and other pertinent data) of online consumers, he could provide a unique level of personalized service as well as better anticipate customer demand for products.

Confident that the greater the growth, the greater the opportunities to make the system more efficient, Bezos believed that Amazon.com had to grow as quickly as possible before the competition realized what was happening.

Despite this proverbial rosy scenario, at the time, Bezos was uncertain as to how quickly consumers would adapt to making their purchases online and deal with what he called "this primitive, infant technology." He told an audience that "the hardest part with doing something totally new for consumers is that they don't adapt to the new habit—no matter how convenient it is. Even if they have Web access on their desk, they don't think about swiveling to their desk and ordering a book. They do what they've always done, which is stop on the way home and buy a book." Bezos spelled out in his initial business plan that he expected it was going to take several years of patiently training customers before they would be completely comfortable buying books online.

But, much to his happy surprise, that's not what happened. "The thing that we had overlooked was that at that time, everybody on the Internet . . . was what demographers call 'early adopters.' These were the first people to use computers, to use cell phones. They are the first people to do *everything*. These guys were very facile in learning new habits. They adopted this very quickly." This development was supported by a 1996 survey prepared by the American Booksellers Association, which revealed that 28 percent of all book buyers—nearly double the national average of 17 percent—were likely to use online technology. Half of book buyers under the age of 50 said they were likely to order books online. Clearly the market was there, and it was ready and waiting for a clever entrepreneur to grab the business.

Although he wasn't about to make any firm commitments, Alberg was impressed with Bezos, who kept in touch with Alberg by sending him Amazon.com's weekly sales figures, and telling him when orders would come in from a new state or new country. "In retrospect, it's easy to say it was clear how smart, dedicated, and analytical he was," said Alberg. "He seemed to have the thing well thought through. You know when people have successful CEO characteristics only after they've been in it for a while. On Day One, people thought Bill Gates was very smart, but they didn't know he was going to be so good at being a CEO. The same with Jeff. Jeff was good with numbers, but probably the strength of the presentation was not in the financial analysis, because it wasn't the most sophisticated [plan]. However, his analysis of the marketplace was good because he had an answer to a lot of the questions. On the other hand, the projections that were in the original financial statements were unbelievably modest compared to what happened—and they showed a profit. Quickly."

Bezos's 1995 proposal included two scenarios: moderate growth and rapid growth. His moderate growth plan projected a profit of $49,504 by the end of the fiscal year ending September 30, 1997, on sales of $11,522,584; the fast-growth scenario was for a profit of $142,605 on sales of $17,735,703 in the same time period. The fast-growth projection didn't show the company topping $100 million in sales until September 30, 2000. Amazon.com's eventual success would soon make those numbers laughable.

But, privately, Bezos confided his optimism to his employees. "I remember him telling me that he was going to build a billion-dollar company by the year 2000," said Nicholas Lovejoy. "I thought it was ridiculous, but at the same time, I loved his energy. He really meant it."

Although he didn't mention it to potential investors, Bezos always knew that Amazon.com was eventually going to be much more than books. "Books were always a prelude to other things," said Lovejoy. "At that time, I was doing quite a bit of kayaking. [Jeff] would say, 'In the future, when you come to Amazon.com, I don't want you just to be able to search for *kayak* and find all the books on kayaking. You should also be able to read articles on kayaking and buy subscriptions to kayaking magazines. You should be able to buy a kayaking trip to anywhere in the world you want to go kayaking, and you should be able to have a kayak delivered to your house. You should be able to discuss kayaking with other kayakers. There should be everything to do with kayaking, and the same is true for anything.' That amazing vision was there then, very clear, unambiguous. No doubt about it; books were just a starting point."

Mary Meeker, the famed Internet analyst for Morgan Stanley Dean Witter, hit the nail on the head when she discussed Amazon.com's future direction with the *Wall Street Journal* in December 1999: "Maybe a decade from now we'll be looking at books and concluding that it was a Trojan horse that built the rest of the company."

His optimism aside, Bezos still needed money. "I need you to write a check," a frustrated Bezos told Hanauer. "I need somebody to make a move. No one will make a move. It takes one." Hanauer agreed to write a check in exchange for stock options. Soon after, another 20 people also wrote checks, including Tom Alberg. Most of the amounts were for $30,000, according to one of those pioneering investors. By the end of 1995, Bezos was finally able to secure $981,000 in funding. "If he had to raise $5 million," said Alberg, "he could never have done it."

Bezos's behind-closed-doors confidence about the success of Amazon.com was contradicted in a speech he gave in 1998 that described his travails in raising money. Acknowledging the long odds facing start-up companies, he told an audience at Lake Forest College, "I suspected that we would fail. I told all of our early investors that they would lose their money for sure. I think this is a good technique when you're taking money from friends and family because you still want to be able to go to Thanksgiving dinner."

Because Bezos was the only Amazon.com employee with any previous corporate management experience, in December 1995 he asked Alberg, Hanauer, and Dillon to form a board of ex-officio advisors to the company.

By that point, the Amazon.com website was getting 2,200 visits a day, which was a significant number in 1995 (it would grow to

80,000 a day by the spring of 1997). As the company began 1996, "stuff is rolling out the door, orders are going up, and we're beginning to start to understand what has to happen next. We need to move to a bigger space," said Paul Barton-Davis. Before they could move, the landlord in the Color Tile building let Amazon.com temporarily expand its space from 1,100 square feet to 2,000 square feet.

Although that was still a tiny space for their needs, "it was organized in a great way; a very fun way; different from the way our distribution center is organized today," said Bezos. In those early days, the way the system worked was that orders were accumulated directly in the warehouse and place in bins that were labeled with the individual customer's name. One could walk through the warehouse and look at the grouping of books that comprised a customer's order. Seeing the combination of books that people were buying, "was very interesting," said Bezos. "One day, I saw a three-book order that included *101 Ways to Make Love to Your Husband*, *101 Ways to Make Love to Your Wife,* and *Hawaii Vacation Planning Guide*. I looked at this order and said, 'I think we know what's going on here.' "

In early March 1996, Amazon.com moved for the second time in five months; this time just a couple of blocks north to 2250 First Avenue South, to a two-level 17,000-square-foot building with a large open area for warehouse space. "Jeff said we would be in this building for only six months; 10 at the most," Barton-Davis recalled. "Shel and I were wondering what he was talking about. We walked into that space and thought, 'You've got to be kidding. There's no way we are filling this in six months.' No one was tremendously thrilled with that property, but it was the best we could find. It did have big space, some offices and room for expansion. It looked like there was plenty of room to grow for ages. But in reality, it was not very long before that space was totally filled. Five months was the right answer."

By early 1996, Amazon.com was on course for an annual revenue run rate of about $5 million. "We started to see the evidence of how quickly the business was growing without us stirring the pot any," said Dillon.

ENTER THE VENTURE CAPITALISTS

In early 1996, Ramanan Raghavendran, who was then a senior associate at General Atlantic Partners, a large private equity investment firm based in Greenwich, Connecticut, was surfing the Web and came upon the Amazon.com site, which was still an essentially unknown entity to anyone who wasn't a member of the digerati. "I just picked up the phone and cold-called Jeff Bezos," said Raghavendran, who was the first representative of a venture capital fund to contact Bezos. Raghavendran was the person most responsible for pursuing Internet-related investments at General Atlantic, a firm that specialized in funding software companies. "I had a phenomenal conversation with Jeff. We got along like a house on fire because I completely bought into his vision."

Raghavendran then went about the process of trying to convince his firm that Amazon.com was a good investment. "That was a little bit of a challenge because General Atlantic is a late-stage investor, and Amazon.com was a very early-stage company," said Raghavendran.

"We were amazed that someone would have an interest," said Dillon. "Right away, Jeff asked, 'What does this mean? What are we *really* worth?' "

Raghavendran and some colleagues from General Atlantic flew to Seattle to meet with Bezos, Alberg, and Dillon. "We continued to fall in love with the business and with Jeff in particular," Raghavendran recalled. A short time later, Raghavendran called Bezos from Hong Kong, and outlined the terms of a deal between Amazon.com and General Atlantic. To the best of Dillon's recollection, General Atlantic offered to invest $1 million at a market capitalization for Amazon.com of $10 million. Raghavendran, who is now a general partner at Insight

Capital Partners, declined to confirm these exact numbers, but did acknowledge that "the investment size was larger [than what Dillon recalled], but the valuation range is not far from what we had thought."

The General Atlantic offer was a watershed for Amazon.com. "We thought it would be fabulous if we could get $20 million or $30 million," said Alberg. The Amazonians quickly came to the realization that "if they're willing to give us money, it makes sense to get a *bunch* of money and build this business as fast as we can," said Dillon. "When I first got involved [in the company], Jeff was focused on the fact that we could make profits right away." But, when they started getting phone calls from venture capital companies, the Amazon.com principals reached what Dillon described as "a crossover point" when "we stopped talking about profits and we started talking about dominating the market" and creating a multibillion-dollar business. "We started to realize that this thing was much bigger than we ever thought it could be; and that we *were* the market leader and we were going to do whatever it takes to retain our position as the market leader. That's when we all said, 'We're going for it! We're going to build a franchise and we're going to do it right.' We changed our whole focus to one that was driven by momentum. We had the momentum and we had to keep the momentum. We needed to bring in money. We needed to be the first one to do national advertising."

Amazon.com's new approach was very much in the spirit of entrepreneurship in the formative years of the Internet. Marc Andreessen, the cofounder of Netscape, put it succinctly: "One of the fundamental lessons is that market share now equals revenue later, and if you don't have market share now, you are not going to have revenue later. Another fundamental lesson is that whoever gets the volume does win in the end. Just plain wins."

Robert Reid, the author of the 1997 book *Architects of the Web*, expanded upon that notion:

> This growth profile has fostered a mind-warping mentality and behavior for Internet companies; tossing aside just about every experience-honed

> tenet of business to build business in a methodical fashion, Internet businesses have adopted a grow-at-any-cost, without-any-revenue, claim-as-much-market-real-estate-before-anyone-moves-in approach to business. This mentality has come to be known as "Get Big Fast."
>
> Behind it lie two strategic points: The first is that Internet opportunities—whether in software or in banking—are new and unclaimed, and hence available for the taking.
>
> Secondly, these opportunities will ultimately deliver big rewards to whoever gets claim to them.
>
> Hence, Internet company after Internet company is wisely going for it, spending lots of bucks far, far in advance of revenues to both develop offerings and claim market real estate in order to claim stakes in the Internet gold rush that will—hopefully—reward them with unprecedented returns. This is the hypergrowth, hyperspeed, hyperbucks world of the Internet.

"Get Big Fast" was quickly becoming the mantra at Amazon.com. When the company put on its first employee picnic in 1996, Bezos handed out T-shirts to everyone in attendance. Emblazoned on each shirt were the words "Get Big Fast."

The momentum began picking up on May 16, 1996, when Amazon.com and Jeff Bezos were the lead story on the front page of the *Wall Street Journal* with the headline "How Wall Street Whiz Found a Niche Selling Books on the Internet." The article raved that the website "has become an underground sensation for thousands of book-lovers around the world, who spend hours perusing its vast electronic library, reading other customers' amusing online reviews—and ordering piles of books." The overwhelming positive story talked about how Amazon.com had customers in 66 countries, including Bosnia, where orders were placed by more than two dozen homesick American soldiers stationed in that war-torn country. Army Lt. Clyde Cochrane III e-mailed Amazon.com from Bosnia: "This will help make this deployment a little more tolerable."

The genesis for that pivotal *Journal* story can be traced to a March

1996 meeting of the American Association of Publishers. The *Journal* reporter asked Alberto Vitale, then chairman of Random House, Inc., what was new and exciting in the business. "I told him, 'If you want to explore something different and truly cutting edge, go to Seattle and explore Amazon,' " said Vitale. "He later did the article. And that launched Amazon."

And how. The *Journal* article created an incredible spike in traffic that nearly overwhelmed the site and the company. "The size of the business basically doubled that day," recalled Nicholas Lovejoy. "That was a permanent shift. The business kept growing the next day and the next day and the day after that."

Bezos would later characterize that *Journal* story as both a blessing and a curse. Because Amazon.com was not yet spending money on advertising, and was relying strictly on word-of-mouth and public relations, the article was a blessing because it generated a lot of exposure and awareness for the company and produced many new customers. "If we treated them right, those people became evangelists for us," said Bezos. Jane Radke Slade, an Amazon.com customer-service specialist, agreed: "If we hadn't been on the cover of the *Wall Street Journal* and most people hadn't seen us as a solvent company, they wouldn't be handing us their credit cards."

On the other hand, the article alerted Amazon.com's competition to the fact that the company existed.

In the meantime, Bezos and company deferred a decision on the General Atlantic offer. Thanks to feedback from their Wall Street contacts, the Amazonians were getting positive indications of what was going on in the private VC funding arena. "We figured out pretty quickly that we should be thinking north of $50 million for what we should raise in our next round," said Dillon.

At the same time, they also explored opportunities for strategic partnerships with companies such as the cable television giant TCI and CUC International Inc., a discount shopping club that sold goods by catalog and phone and had recently gone online. None of those talks led to any deals. (CUC later changed its name to Cendant, and eventually purchased Books.com.)

The venture capital company that Bezos and the others most dearly wanted was Kleiner Perkins Caufield & Byers, the leading VC firm in Silicon Valley, which had funded companies such as Netscape, Intuit, Sun Microsystems, Compaq, Marimba, @Home, and Macromedia. Kleiner's most illustrious partner was the lanky, bespectacled L. John Doerr, who has been dubbed "the avatar of the Web" and is considered by many as the person who recognized the potential of the Internet before virtually everyone else. One of the chief tenets of Doerr's investment strategy was to create what he has described as a *keiretsu*—the Japanese term for a network of general trading firms with interlocking directorships and joint investments that are connected by a central bank.

Doerr's digital version of *keiretsu* was a mutually beneficial network among Kleiner Perkins companies. For example, Intuit's Quicken software incorporated the Netscape Navigator; and Netscape and Macromedia were early adopters of Sun Microsystem's Java software. The principals in these companies meet periodically to build and cement relationships and to assist each other in their respective businesses. "*Keiretsu* are rooted in the principle that it is really hard to get an important company going and that the fastest and surest way to build an important new company is to work with partners," said Doerr.

"I left four phone messages for John Doerr directly," Eric Dillon recalled. "I've been in sales all my life. I know how to sell. I left him the most sales-y oriented messages you've ever heard. He never returned any of my phone calls."

Amazon.com was not without connections to Kleiner Perkins. Leslie Koch, who had at the time had been hired as vice president of marketing for Amazon.com, knew Doerr from when Koch had worked at Microsoft. Tom Alberg served on the board of Visio Corp., the Seattle-based maker of graphics software, with Douglas

McKenzie, a Kleiner partner. Finally, not long after the first meeting with General Atlantic, Bezos got a phone call from Kleiner. "I was in Jeff's office when the call came," said Dillon "Basically, Jeff told them, 'We have a great deal with somebody else. If you want to be in on this deal, you need to pony up and you need to be here tomorrow.' " Bezos, Dillon, Hanauer, et al. were feeling cocky "because we had the money" from General Atlantic. Suddenly Amazon.com was the most popular girl at the dance.

The company was being deluged by calls from venture capitalists who wanted to get involved. "We joked that we were going to have to change our voice-mail system to say, 'If you're a customer, press one. If you're a VC, press two,' " said Bezos, who invited Doerr up to Seattle for a meeting and to tour the Amazon.com operation. The two apparently clicked on a personal basis, but Doerr told Bezos that he thought Bezos's valuation of the company was inflated. No deal was immediately forthcoming.

In the meantime, Bezos, Dillon, and Leslie Koch had a meeting with General Atlantic at the VC's midtown Manhattan office. "I remember sitting with Jeff in the GA offices the night before the meeting, going through the financial model that he was going to present," said Ramanan Raghavendran. "As you can imagine, it was an outrageous model. He portrayed Amazon.com growing to $800 million in revenues in no time at all. I said, 'Jeff, this may well be true, but for a group of rational investors, you want to tone down your projections.' He said, 'I think this is what we're going to do.' In hindsight, he overperformed against those projections."

Dillon called this meeting "the final dance" with General Atlantic. "Jeff was having me be the fall guy in this thing. I was happy to do it. It was my skill set." After an hour and a half of discussion, it came down to agreeing upon the valuation of the company. "We decided before the meeting that we would take money from [General Atlantic] only if they would give us a $100 million valuation. I didn't say a thing for that whole hour and a half time. All of a sudden, every eye turns to me.

"I said, 'We still feel that we should do more due diligence and figure out what our best path is in taking money. We're only willing to sign a deal with you guys today if you're willing to give us a valuation of $100 million.' Everybody at the table looked as though we had dropped a huge dose of cyanide down their throats. They really wanted this deal. They understood Jeff and they understood this business. But it was too far out of the realm of possibility—ever. We came up with the figure of $100 million because it was just a staggering, outrageous stop-us-in-our-tracks number. Outside of that, we were still going to do our due-diligence" in researching other VC companies. "Afterwards, Jeff and I went out to dinner and we just laughed all night long about their reactions. In the annals of Amazon, it was just a really fun day."

Kleiner was not yet out of the picture. "We had to compete like crazy for the right to invest in Amazon," said Doerr. "Jeff approached us the same way Intuit's Scott Cook did. Jeff said, 'I'm not going to publish 30 business plans along Sand Hill Road (Silicon Valley's most prestigious stretch of VC real estate). No one will pay attention. Instead, I'll work through my network of friends to find the good firms and best fit for Amazon.' "

General Atlantic came back with a valuation of $50 million. "Jeff said, 'We already have an offer of $50 million. How about $70 million or $80 million?' " Alberg recalled. "The theory was 'Let's just test this market.' Then Doerr said, 'We could go to 40 or 50, but we bring a lot to the table and we should get credit for that.' Then [General Atlantic] proposed a $60 million to $70 million evaluation," but it was based on a contingency to what a future initial public offering could bring. "They had this offer on the table. We had a term sheet proposal from them; the whole works."

Finally the lure of Kleiner Perkins tipped the scales. "Ultimately, we lost out for two reasons," said Raghavendran. "One, Kleiner brings a phenomenal footprint in the Internet space, and that's pretty compelling, and two, we were just not comfortable at the valuations where the deal ended up getting done. In relation to where the market cap of Amazon.com is now, it was insignificant. But that's 20/20 hindsight. I would have done the transaction at a much higher valuation. The reality is that GA was constrained by its own investment discipline, which I commend, because you win some and you lose some."

Bezos and company decided to go with Kleiner, which was the trophy VC fund. But before agreeing to the deal, Bezos had one final detail to be settled: Who on Kleiner would join the Amazon.com board? Bezos asked Alberg who he should ask for. "I said we should try to get John Doerr," Alberg recalled. But Bezos said that Doerr indicated he wasn't interested in joining any more boards. "But I said we should get Doerr." So Bezos said to Kleiner Perkins that Amazon.com would agree to the deal *only* if Doerr joined the board.

Doerr initially declined. Bezos was playing "a little bit of brinkmanship," said Dillon. "Jeff was absolutely willing to walk away." At the end of the day, however, Doerr agreed to become a director. Amazon.com accepted the Kleiner offer of $8 million in cash based on a $60 million valuation, or a little over 13 percent ownership of the company, which bought Kleiner 3,401,376 common shares at $2.35 a share.

"An $8 million financing is nothing compared to what people are doing today even in the Internet space," said Alberg. "It was a remarkably small amount." By holding the Kleiner investment to 13 percent, Bezos limited the dilution of the stock and maintained the share value for the original stockholders. "It's similar to the story of Microsoft," added Alberg. "They almost never raised money [from outside investors]. That's why Bill Gates owns such a large percentage of the company. That's why Jeff owns such a big percentage [initially, 42 percent personally, with another 10 percent owned by his family]. Amazon has never raised very much in the way of equity. Jeff has sold very little stock. He wasn't taking a lot of cards off the table."

Alberg also compared Bezos with Alberg's old boss, Craig McCaw, who after selling McCaw Cellular to AT&T for $11.5 billion in 1994, got right back into the telecom business with companies such as Nextlink Communications and Nextel Communications. "People keep thinking Craig's supposed to sell, but he doesn't do it. He's a true entrepreneur. It isn't just the money; it's the idea of believing in something and getting fulfillment by doing it in a big way and having a big impact. Craig has a vision of how to spread wireless phones throughout the world. In Jeff's case, it's the power of the Internet in the e-commerce world, with ali its many implications."

Bezos said that he selected Kleiner Perkins because "Kleiner and John are the gravitational center of a huge piece of the Internet world. Being with them is like being on prime real estate," meaning that Kleiner was so well connected in terms of strategic alliances *(keiretsu)* and recruiting outstanding managers. In one of his first moves after investing in Amazon.com, Doerr convinced Scott Cook, the chairman of Intuit, to join him on the board. "Scott's a very compelling and thoughtful guy and Jeff desperately wanted him for the board," said Dillon. "He begged him."

Doerr was less successful when he asked Michael Dell, the founder and chairman of Dell Computer to join the Amazon.com board. According to people who were privy to the details of the telephone conversation, Doerr told Dell that "Jeff Bezos was the Michael Dell of the Internet." To which Dell replied: "John, I thought *I* was the Michael Dell of the Internet."

With the infusion of Kleiner capital in the spring of 1996, Amazon.com was thinking big. "We were going to grow a franchise, and we were going to create an enduring huge company that was going to be a market leader," said Dillon. From then on, "everything that we were going to do had to support that. Now, we were able to think about spending a million dollars on an advertising program or signing up to be on Yahoo. There was no stopping the company at this point. We were going to do anything and everything to dominate our market. We never worried about money again. The sky was the limit."

TAKEAWAYS

Like any other successful entrepreneur, Jeff Bezos did whatever needed to be done, and told people what they wanted to hear. There was nothing unethical or immoral about what he did, but it was informative that he would tell early potential investors that the company would reach sales of $100 million by the year 2000, and that he told employees he expected that figure to be $1 billion by 2000. He would tell some people that he expected to turn a profit in two years; he told others that the company would not turn a profit for at least five years.

- Be willing to lose money if you believe in the project.
- Find ways to improve on the business model that exists in the physical world. For example, Amazon.com's cash flow is far superior to that of a bricks-and-mortar bookstore, and once it reaches scale, it is also more efficient.
- The personal charisma of the entrepreneur is sometimes more important than the idea.
- If you can't afford advertising, employ a clever public relations campaign to keep your brand name out in front of the public.
- Keep open the lines of communication with potential investors. (Bezos would send them weekly sales figures.)
- Tell investors one thing, employees something different.
- Get big fast.

chapter seven

raise the bar

Take my assets—but leave me my organization
and in five years I'll have it all back.

—Alfred P. Sloan

With the venture capital money secured, Bezos began the task of getting big fast by going on a hiring binge of middle managers, executives, and warehouse workers. By the middle of the summer of 1996, the building at 2250 First Avenue South was crowded with people and equipment. Soon the ground floor parking garage was converted into office space, a move that later prompted Bezos to quip: "We're the only start-up company I know that started in a garage and then moved to another garage."

Gina Meyers, employee Number 40, recalled: "All of the office space was taken up. Nicholas Lovejoy, Mackenzie, me, and one or two temps were in the kitchen area. We just started lining the door desks up. It was very crowded, noisy, and hot."

In the midst of this chaos, meetings were held with bankers, who were often seen parked in the center of a room while hordes of frenetic people worked around them and various dogs—including Jeff and Mackenzie's golden retriever, Kamala, and a corgy named Rufus, who belonged to the newly hired Eric and Sue Benson—were running out and about. (Kamala was named after a metamorph in an episode of *Star Trek: The Next Generation*, entitled "The Perfect Mate.") Although the bankers were unaccustomed to such feverish informality, they were willing to put up with it because they had already read that pivotal *Wall Street Journal* story on Amazon.com.

Meyers was hired from Data I/O Corporation, a Redmond data-processing company, to be corporate comptroller and to relieve Mackenzie Bezos of the accounting responsibilities. Other than the programmers, she was one of the few people working at Amazon.com who actually had education and training in her field. Hiring an experienced numbers person was an essential preliminary step toward taking the company public; Amazon.com needed to move from a seat-of-the-pants, cash-based checkbook operation to a business run according to general accounting principles.

Setting about to build a corporate culture from the ground up, Bezos focused on hiring the absolute best people he could find, thanks in part to the insistence of John Doerr. A self-described "glorified recruiter," Doerr said that, "In the world today, there's plenty of technology, plenty of entrepreneurs, plenty of money, plenty of venture capital. What's in short supply is great teams. Your biggest challenge will be building a great team."

Paul Barton-Davis recalled an early example of Bezos's unwavering insistence on hiring the best. As Amazon.com drew closer to its launch, "it was becoming clear to Shel (Kaphan) and me that we needed more people," said Barton-Davis. "We were pushing Jeff to hire people and we interviewed at least a half-dozen candidates. The discussions weren't acrimonious, but there was a genuine philosophical difference between the two of us and Jeff over whether we should hire any of the people that we saw. Our attitude was that we need a body in here, and if they're reasonably good and can probably do the work, then let's hire them. Jeff's attitude was if they aren't on the A list, then we aren't interested."

Interestingly, back in those early days, Barton-Davis and Kaphan feared that the company was not going to be able to attract the kind of people that Bezos wanted to hire "because we didn't have the sorts of challenges that they would be interested in," said Barton-Davis.

That problem rarely happened. From the very beginning, Bezos said, he looked for "intense, hard-working, smart people," who were secure enough to "hire other great people. When I interview somebody, I spend about a third of the interview asking them questions designed to ascertain whether or not they can hire great people. It's sort of the meta-interview." He told the *Wall Street Journal* that managers who lack the confidence to hire stellar performers "have to understand that if they don't hire them, they'll be working for them down the road." For Bezos, it was an article of faith that Amazon.com would continually raise the bar for hiring talent and that, "Five years from now, employees hired today should be saying, 'I'm glad I got hired when I did, because I wouldn't get hired now.' " He also wanted to attract people who had a talent or quality—unrelated to the job—such as music or athletics, which would add a dimension to their value because, "When you are working very hard and very long hours, you want to be around people who are interesting and fun to be with."

Eric Dillon referred four of his good friends to Amazon but none were hired. "It was brutal," he recalled. "Jeff demanded that you exhibited a track record of success in everything you did. And he demanded that you be smart. He operated on the theory that the best athlete is the smartest athlete. He cared a lot less about relevant experience—because there wasn't any relevant experience—and a lot more about people who demonstrated a track record of being super smart."

David Risher, who became a senior vice president of Amazon.com in early 1997, and who was a classmate at Princeton with Bezos, told the *Wall Street Journal* that instead of quizzing applicants on their previous job experience, he talks about values, personal interests, and approaches to work problems, such as "How would you design a car for a deaf person?" According to Risher, "the best candidates say they'd plug their ears and drive around in their cars to experience what it feels like to be a deaf driver. They put themselves right into the customer's mind and body, to find out what they need."

Essential to be hired on at Amazon.com is a desire go give oneself over to the company's intense us-against-them, we're-changing-the-world corporate culture. "I'm looking for people who want to care," said executive editor Rick Ayre. "I'm looking for people who want things to do that matter, a group of people who want a life with meaning, who want a career with meaning, and we offer that to people because it's a company that provides everyone with a voice and a responsibility for their actions."

In those early days, the interviewing and hiring process was so exhaustive, that managers—who already had plenty to do and were putting in 60- to 80-hour weeks—were required to spend many additional hours interviewing, researching, and evaluating job applicants. Department managers had to interview each applicant and then write up a report that covered what was discussed during the interview, their impressions of the applicant, and any other relevant thoughts or comments. Each candidate had to supply three telephone references. Those references were also interviewed for a half-hour or so by the human resources people, who then wrote up a transcript of *those* interviews as well. "Those telephone references were intense," recalled Maire Masco, a customer-service manager.

Then each of the four or five people who interviewed the candidate was given as many as 100 pages of information on each candidate. A former Amazon.com manager recalled a hiring meeting for a programmer in which the largest conference room was filled with people involved with the hiring process. (For a programmer position, upwards of a dozen people could be involved.) These pages included the transcriptions of all the interviews with the references, the individual's résumé, and three writing samples (programmers showed code they had written). Masco considered the writing samples "a clever tool," because they showed how well the candidates communicated in written form. The writings also offered an insight into the applicant's personality and shined a light on other talents and interests that might not necessarily come out in a standard interview or application. Some candidates for customer-service positions submitted poetry or a short story; others a business plan. One woman handed in an erotic novella. "If somebody was interesting but maybe a little rough around the edges, as long as they could communicate clearly, we would take them on," said Masco.

The group involved in hiring would sit around and read these stacks of papers, according to Masco, who estimated that at one point, she was spending 80 percent of her time either interviewing people or taking part in those follow-up meetings. "Then the discussion would begin. It would start out with initial impressions: thumbs up or thumbs down. Then you would go around the room: 'Is this an appropriate candidate for this position? Not for this position? Perhaps for another position?' It was a fascinating process. I admired it. But it was exhausting." Although the first 40 people in customer service were hired in that fashion, the company was bringing in so many customer-service representatives that they eventually had to farm out some of the hiring process to a local employment agency.

In the early days, up until early 1997, Bezos interviewed every salaried employee and had the final say on whether a person should be hired. That was one way to preserve the culture. "Jeff would find things wrong or right with people that no one else spotted," said Glenn Fleishman, who was hired in September 1996 as catalog manager. But Fleishman recalled one episode when Bezos did miss something.

Fleishman and other managers were discussing the hiring of a person for a low-level position that did not require Bezos's direct involvement. During the discussion, Bezos called the office from a plane and spontaneously jumped into the review process. He agreed with the consensus that the candidate should be hired. "After Jeff gets off the phone, I'm looking through the résumé and I see that the candidate had gotten some years wrong, and there were some typos," said Fleishman. "This person was being hired for an area where attention to detail was involved. We thought the person was superior enough to be hired. But we all agreed that we would never tell Jeff because if we did, the person wouldn't have been hired." That person still works at Amazon.com.

Above all, Bezos wanted to hire *smart* people. When he joined

Amazon.com in September 1996, Fleishman felt, "it was like going to the world's best college. I was surrounded by smart people." All applicants were asked for their SAT scores and college grade point average and if the scores weren't high enough, they might not be hired. As a result, Bezos snared a lot of the smart people he was after. Many were Ivy League graduates, and two—Dana Brown, who was put in charge of ordering, and Ryan Sawyer, the vice president for strategic growth—were fellow Rhodes Scholars at Oxford.

"We went to Harvard, MIT, and Columbia and recruited the smartest people we could get our hands on," said Brown, who came to Amazon.com with a B.A. in political science and Russian and a masters degree in Russian and Eastern European political science from Rutgers University. Back in those formative days of 1996, "we got a few people, but we had a hard time selling people into coming to work for us because of the low salary—$35,000 a year for people with a B.A. We were small fry. Nobody knew who we were. We didn't have people lining up out the door to interview with us. If we could get 10 people, we were lucky. The recruiting officers were somewhat skeptical."

Scott Lipsky, who joined the company in July 1996 as vice president of business expansion, after an executive stint at Barnes & Noble, said, "The recruiting effort at Amazon was enormous, just to support the growth, which was organic."

Early on, Bezos established relationships with the University of Washington Computer Science & Engineering Department. He often addressed students in their classrooms, and used the UW as source of strong technical help.

CREATING A CULTURE

It was Bezos's task to mold a corporate culture from people who had come to the company from a variety of different corporate backgrounds. "Competitors can never copy a culture," he said. He often told employees he wanted a place that was "intense and friendly. . . .

In fact, if you ever had to give up 'friendly' in order to have 'intense,' we would do that. So if we needed to be 'intense' and 'combative,' we would do that before we'd be 'not intense.' "

Microsoft, the company that defined the Seattle business culture in the 1990s, was a model for the nascent Amazon.com culture. "I think they recruit better than any other company that I know of," said Bezos. Lauding Bill Gates for being "a smart guy," Bezos added that, "what impresses me is the hundred people underneath him who are incredibly smart executives in their own right."

But Bezos was looking to create a more benign atmosphere than the Microsoft model. "We often talked about how we wanted to have the same sort of demanding nature as Microsoft, without being so internally competitive," recalled Nicholas Lovejoy.

That recollection was echoed by Gina Meyers: "Jeff would say, 'You can be like Microsoft but you don't have to be as combative as Microsoft to be a congenial place to work.' That was the intent at the beginning."

Although Bezos may have talked about shaping his company into a merciful Microsoft (a contradiction in terms?), in reality, in the quest to get big fast, the seemingly mild-mannered Bezos is a fierce, take-no-prisoners competitor, who has been unafraid to battle for Amazon.com's interests in the marketplace and the courts.

Bezos also cited FedEx as a model "because it grew up out of nowhere and changed the dynamics of an industry. That was something everyone could relate to. He said FedEx didn't let things get so out of control where they couldn't deliver their packages. He wanted us to continue to push forward and never be satisfied with where you are."

Bezos also admired the vision and innovation of Walt Disney. (He's visited Disney World at least a half-dozen times.) "The thing that always amazed me was how powerful his vision was," said Bezos. "He knew exactly what he wanted to build and teamed up with a bunch of really smart people and built it. Everyone thought it wouldn't work, and he had to persuade the banks to lend him $400 million. But he did it."

Bezos believed that an entrepreneur starts his company with an idea of what he wants the culture to be, and then the early employees carry the torch of what that culture represents. He estimated that the eventual corporate culture ends up being "a blend of 30 percent of what you set out for it to be, 30 percent who your early employees happen to be, and 40 percent random chance. The bad thing about the random chance part is that once it's set, you've got it. There's really no way to change a corporate culture."

From the beginning, Bezos was, not surprisingly, "the soul of the company," said Scott Lipsky. "He's a leader who can inspire people with his success, his intelligence, his brilliance, his ideas—and the fact that he had these great ideas before many other people did."

While agreeing with Lipsky's characterization of Bezos, Gina Meyers, who had come from the more staid and conservative Data I/O, found working at Amazon.com "a little bit of a culture shock. It was so chaotic and everything was changing so fast."

Maire Masco, who came from Aldus Corp. (a part of Adobe Systems, Inc.), recalled coming in for her first interview and being "immediately enthralled by the speed and quickness" of the operation. "People were dashing back and forth. There was a huge sense of camaraderie. A reporter and a camera crew were following Jeff around. Construction people were bringing in desks and computers. It was total mayhem. I thought, 'This is great. I want to work here.' "

With so many new managers, Amazon.com—just as Bezos had predicted—outgrew the 2250 First Avenue space in seven months. In August 1996, management moved a couple of miles north to the Columbia Building on Second Avenue. Only a block east of the Pike Place Market and a few blocks north of downtown's tony retail corridor and in the shadow of the sleek high-rise office buildings, this was one of the last seedy blocks in the area. The Columbia Building was around the corner from Wigland, the Holy Ghost Revivals mission, assorted T-shirts-for-tourists storefronts and across the street from the Seattle-King County Needle Exchange (and I don't mean the Space

Needle). It was a neighborhood where winos would relieve themselves in the alleys. The offices within the Columbia Building were only a small step up from what was happening on the street. The carpet was worn and stained with coffee. The walls cried out for a paint job.

The expanded warehouse stayed on First Avenue South until November, when it moved to a larger facility on Dawson Street in South Seattle. In all the company had been in five different locations in three years. "That's either poor planning or unusual growth, whichever way you want to think about it. I think every company should move every four months," Bezos quipped.

The warehouse quickly developed a subculture of its own, separate and apart from management. It was filled up by an army of Gen-X Seattleites—musicians, poets, geeks, students—in between gigs, who proudly displayed tattoos, multiple body piercings, and hair colors not previously found in nature. No wonder then-customer-service director Jane Radke Slade told the *Wall Street Journal* that she instructed temporary employment agencies (everyone hired for the warehouse started as a temp): "Send us your freaks."

Those first couple of dozen warehouse employees "were a bunch of funky rock musicians and starving artists trying to make ends meet," recalled E. Heath Merriwether, one of that original group. Looking out across the warehouse floor, "There was a purple head over there, and a blue head over there, and a green head over there. It was a very young crowd." It was that young energy that was able to keep up with the growth rate at Amazon. The original crew "really did bond. We were the core. We *were* Amazon."

Bezos would reinforce to the warehouse workers how important they were by reiterating that the only elements that customers knew about Amazon.com was the website and the book they received in the mail. Without the warehouse, he told them, there's no company. Bezos backed up his words with actions. He and many of the other managers regularly helped to sort and pack shipments.

"I remember the first time I heard someone in the warehouse call him 'Mr. Bezos,' " recalled Merriwether. "I said, 'That's *Jeff*.' He was one of the gang. He never put himself up on a pedestal. As Amazon grew, and it became more corporate, other people put him on this pedestal. But Jeff never put himself there."

One day in July 1996, Bezos walked into the warehouse and Merriwether and several others spontaneously began firing rubber bands at him. Without skipping a beat, Bezos picked some rubber bands off the floor and immediately shot back. Some of the new hires were "horrified that I was shooting rubber bands at the chairman of the company," said Merriwether. "They were even more horrified that the chairman shot back."

The following day, Al Gore visited the Amazon.com offices and briefly worked the customer-service phones for a photo opportunity. Seeing Bezos on television schmoozing with the vice president of the United States the day after the rubber band battle was "surreal; a *Twilight Zone* episode," said Merriwether. "I will say this about Jeff Bezos: I would want him on my side in a rubber band war."

On November 3, 1996, Amazon.com moved its distribution operations to a 93,000-square foot facility on Dawson Street in South Seattle. "It was so big, it was like being out in the country—you couldn't see your neighbor. The break room was about the size of the old warehouse," recalled Merriwether. "We figured we'd never fill this space. We figured we would last there for years. Three months later we were elbow-to-elbow."

The evening of November 3, the company threw a moving-in party at the new warehouse with a couple of kegs of beer and catered food from a Mexican restaurant. As part of an impromptu christening, warehouse manager Laurel Canan pulled out a copy of *The Dilbert Principle*. The Scott Adams bestseller was the first title that Amazon.com began shipping in mass quantities, so the warehouse was loaded up to the rafters with *Dilbert*. "Laurel took his beer and poured it over the book, ripped it apart, and threw it across the warehouse floor," said Merriwether. "We all stomped on it, because we all hated that book and most of us do to this day." That copy was deleted from the database. "We certainly didn't want to take a copy of a book that a customer was waiting on."

The organization of the distribution center "was an ongoing process," said Merriwether. As the company grew, it continually added new systems or improved existing ones, so "You had to adapt very quickly. Once we moved to the new distribution center on Dawson, it became more necessary for new employees to be even more flexible, because you learned something one week and it would change the next week."

Two months after moving into the Dawson Street warehouse, Amazon.com finally hired someone with previous logistics experience (before then, they were just making it up as they went along). Oswaldo-Fernando Duenas was a 47-year-old Mexican-American who had worked for Federal Express for 20 years. Duenas rose from being truck driver when FedEx was a fast-growth start-up to become a senior vice president. He helped build FedEx's first regional hubs and oversaw the transition from a system centered at a single hub in Memphis. He had also served as vice president of the Latin American division of International Service System, Inc., Latin America's largest integrated service company, where he oversaw sales, marketing, operations, and customer relations for the division and managed several thousand employees. As Amazon.com's vice president of operations, Duenas brought order and organization to the warehousing and distribution facilities. "At that point, we had a lot of people who had never worked anyplace before," said Gina Meyers. "They were figuring things out and doing a pretty good job. But it helped to have someone who knew how things were done so we didn't have to reinvent the wheel for everything. We immediately started looking at automation."

The office people had just split off from the warehouse, and there was beginning to be a breakdown in communication, according to several former employees. Duenas took it upon himself to bridge that gap. "Fernando could talk to anyone," said Nils Nordal, who worked briefly in customer service. "He could talk to an 18-year-old pothead in the warehouse, and he could talk to Jeff Bezos. He was the company adult. That was a pivotal role for him to play at that point in the company development."

The hiring of Duenas was part of a process of building up a senior management team that Wall Street would approve of. (At this point, Amazon.com was prettying itself up before its eventual initial public offering.) For most of 1996, the ever-growing company had little managerial bandwidth, and Bezos depended on Dillon, Alberg, and Hanauer to "pitch in wherever we could," said Dillon. "We tried to keep Jeff focused as much as we could on business." From the fall of 1996 to the spring of 1997, in addition to Duenas, the company hired a parade of executives, including:

- Rick R. Ayre, vice president and executive editor. Ayre was formerly executive editor for technology at *PC Magazine* and had launched *PC Magazine* on the World Wide Web. He also ran *PC Magazine*'s online services, including their online web site and PC MagNet, which was part of ZD Net on CompuServe.

- Mark Breier, vice president of marketing. He had spent two and and half years in a similar position with Cinnabon World Famous Cinnamon Rolls, and had worked in product management with Dreyer's Grand Ice Cream, Kraft Foods, and Parker Brothers. (Breier later became president and CEO of Beyond.com, the online software retailer. He left Beyond.com in January 2000.)

- Mary E. Engstrom (later Morouse), vice president of publisher affairs, had been vice president of marketing at Symantec Corporation, the developer of information management and productivity enhancement software. She had previously worked in several management positions at Microsoft Corporation.

- John D. "David" Risher, vice president of product development, who had spent the previous six years in a variety of marketing and project management positions at Microsoft Corporation, including team manager for Microsoft Access and founder and product unit manager for MS Investor, Microsoft's website for personal investment.

- Joel R. Spiegel, vice president of engineering, was another ex-Microsoftie, who was Windows 95 multimedia development manager, Windows multimedia group manager, and product unit manager of Information Retrieval. Spiegel, who had also worked at Apple Computer Inc., Hewlett-Packard, and VisiCorp., was able to hire many good programmers fast.

- Scott E. Lipsky, vice president of business expansion, came to Amazon.com from Barnes & Noble, where he had been chief information officer of B&N's superstore division and chief technology officer of B&N's college division. Lipsky had extensive experience in retail software development and systems integration.

Lipsky took a 50 percent salary cut to work for Amazon because, "When I met with Bezos and Shel Kaphan, it was just so utterly apparent that this was going to work," said Lipsky. He was sold on "the combination of the energy level, the intelligence, the out-of-the-box thinking" about book retail, where Lipsky had spent much of his professional career. Lipsky did, of course, get some generous stock options, but, he ripostes: "Who the hell knows what is going to happen with stock options? There were no guarantees."

Although those new executives were definitely essential to bringing Amazon.com into the next phase of its development, "There were a lot of tensions," said Dana Brown. "They were given new high-level, well-paid positions. They were relying on our knowledge of the company to accomplish their goals. A lot of us took that very hard. I couldn't even make my student loan payments with the salary I was making. I felt offended in a way. It's tough making ends meet. I'm working 18 hours a day. I don't have time to read any of the books I'm supposed to be ordering."

During that time, the company added another director—Patricia Q. Stonesifer, an independent management consultant whose clients include DreamWorks SKG. She had been senior vice president of the Interactive Media Division of Microsoft Corporation. (A close friend of Bill Gates, she heads the Bill and Melinda Gates Foundation.)

Another key addition was Maryann Mohit, who became the company's site producer. Although not a vice president, Mohit has had more influence over the design of the website and the integration of its features than anyone other than Bezos, according to a former company insider.

Probably the most crucial hire was a chief financial officer who could help take the company public. By the middle of 1996, Bezos had set his sites on Joy Covey, who was then 33 years old, and had accomplishments that Bezos could admire. The daughter of a doctor, Covey grew up in San Mateo, California. Although she dropped out of high school at age 16, she went on to earn an equivalency degree from California State University at Fresno in 1982, and a B.S. in business administration, summa cum laude. After earning the second-highest score in the country on the accounting exam, she became a certified public accountant at 19. Following graduation, Covey worked for four years at Arthur Young and Co. (now Ernst and Young LLP) as a certified public accountant. (Her first assignment was counting beans at Denny's restaurants.) Covey went on to earn joint degrees in business and law, graduating with honors from both Harvard Business School and Harvard Law School in 1990. After an eight-month stint as an associate with Wasserstein Perella & Co., the New York mergers-and-acquisitions advisory company, in April 1991, Covey became chief financial officer of DigiDesign, Inc., a random access digital audio systems and software company and helped take the company public in 1993. Two years later, DigiDesign merged with Avid Technology, a Boston-based developer of digital media systems. After serving in a transitional role at Avid in Boston as vice president of business development, Covey left the company in February 1996 with a desire to hook up with a Silicon Valley start-up.

"I had interviewed with nearly 40 high-tech companies (including Excite Inc. and Marimba Inc.)," Covey told a Harvard Business School study. "I was very particular, though I was not focused on a specific role. I wanted to help build something significant, I wanted to work with very high-quality teammates, I wanted to build a business with a strong, virtuous-cycle business model, and I wanted it to be on the [San Francisco Bay Area] Peninsula," in order to pursue her other passion: windsurfing.

In August 1996, an executive recruiter asked Covey to meet with Bezos. She declined the invitation. But the headhunter was persistent, and Covey agreed—as a favor—to a lunch with Bezos. Despite acknowledging that her curiosity was piqued by the involvement of John Doerr, Covey spent the first 10 minutes of the meeting reiterating that she had no interest in moving to Seattle. "She said there was no way she was leaving the Bay Area and wanted me to understand that it was a waste of time to try to get her to," Bezos later told the *Wall Street Journal*. "But after that, we had an incredible lunch, since the pressure was off to impress each other."

After the meeting, "I couldn't sleep," Covey related in the Harvard Business School case study. "I could not stop thinking about Amazon. It was clearly a 'category formation' time and I wanted to be part of the team." The next day, Covey called Bezos and asked him if she could commute between Seattle and her home in San Francisco, and Bezos went along with it. Covey was hired in December 1996 as chief financial officer and vice president of finance and administration. (In March 1997, she became secretary and treasurer.) For the next eight months, Covey spent her weekdays in Seattle and her weekends in San Francisco, before moving full time to Seattle in the spring of 1997, just in time to run the initial public offering.

When Covey joined at the end of 1996, Amazon.com had 150 employees and $16 million in sales. She immediately established stringent financial controls, and eventually installed a million-dollar Oracle accounting system.

Gina Meyers, who had been brought in to do the basic accounting, was part of the group who interviewed four or five of the candidates for the CFO job. (Bezos interviewed many more people than that.)

Meyers recalled being impressed by Covey's energy level and smarts. "At the CFO level, you get a lot of people who are risk-averse," said Meyers. "The other candidates felt that Amazon.com should slow down because the company was growing too fast. Joy had the attitude, 'We're going to do this tomorrow,' and do it. Joy could think out of the box and quickly grasp the important points. It was a different business model than most people were used to."

Nicholas Lovejoy stated flatly: "Nobody is a quick as Joy. On her second day at Amazon, she cornered me and Shel and spent three hours with us to have us overview the entire system. And she's not a systems person. She asked great questions. She understood every bit of it. She can cope with incredible volumes of information in incredibly short order." On the downside, said Lovejoy, when it comes to "human interactions skills," Covey is "a bulldozer. She just crushes people."

Covey brought fiscal discipline to Amazon. For the first time, managers had to work within budgets. Prior to Covey's arrival, "I never had a department budget or was aware in any way of the finances of the company," said Dana Brown. "We sort of went ahead and did things. It was very loosely organized. There weren't many limits on what we could do or plans for the future. It was just as it came up at the time. Joy Covey imposed more of a broader view on us and forced us to do budgets and plan and project growth."

In March 1997, Shel Kaphan, the first employee hired and the architect of the basic Amazon.com system, was named vice president and chief technology officer. Nicholas Lovejoy, who worked closely with Kaphan, affectionately described him as "crotchety," but quickly added: "I love him. He was an incredible grounding influence on Jeff." When it came to Bezos's marketing ideas, Kaphan "was a reminder to Jeff that you can't pull the wool over the customers' eyes." He was constantly hammering away: "They're gonna hate that! That's marketing bullshit!"

Gina Meyers called Kaphan, "the nuts and bolts behind the whole system" and the reason why it was so well thought out, reliable, and flexible. "Yeah, we had a little down time every once in a while when something crashed, but when I look back on it, it was just incredible what he and one or two other people created."

For his efforts, Kaphan has been greatly rewarded. In the November 19, 1999, issue of *Forbes ASAP*, Kaphan was picked as the Internet's thirty-eighth wealthiest millionaire, with a net worth (on paper) of $808.9 million.

In fact, there was remarkably little down time on the system. The site went down in June of 1997, when a routine maintenance check turned up a computer problem, and twice in 1998, and three times in November 1999, when a raft of new products were added to the mix. In January of 1998, the site went down at about 11 a.m., and was out of service for several hours. In September of 1998, it was shut down for 10 hours because a problem that occurred during routine maintenance. The company gave out $5 gift certificates to customers who visited the site and couldn't order. The Amazon.com system tended not to break down in those early days because of Kaphan's insistence that things got done in the right way. Some called his attitude "technical pessimism."

"I remember a very small detail very early on," recalled Paul Barton-Davis. When the company moved into the Color Tile building, "We suddenly had a vast explosion of network cabling, since we now had three or four rooms with wires going through them. Shel was very insistent that all these wires got labeled at both ends. That was the kind of thing that I would tend just to shrug off. In fact, when we did end up having problems with one or another machine, it became very easy to go in and unplug the wires and not spend hours figuring which one is which. That technical pessimism that he's got has been a real upside to the company in that he tends to want to make sure that things get done in the right way."

BUILDING THE BRAND

"It's very important, when planning a business, to look at what is the brand promise that you're going to make to customers," said Bezos. "And the brand promise that you make has to actually coincide very,

very closely with the things that you can deliver. That's an important, but sometimes overlooked, component."

With its new injection of cash, Amazon.com could finally afford to advertise; up until that point, the company relied on positive word-of-mouth and free website placement. In the spring of 1996, the company hired the Portland, Oregon office of USWeb/CKS, a Silicon Valley–based advertising agency, to put together its first creative campaign. "We took the point of view that here were these 11 people in Seattle that want to take down Barnes & Noble and Borders," said Bernie Schroeder, who worked on the Amazon.com account with creative director Mahesh Murth. "But we couldn't do it in a way that made us look like a tiny little David against Goliath. So how do you appear to be a Goliath without having a reputation as a Goliath? And how do you back up Amazon.com's claim of being 'Earth's Biggest Bookstore'? The only way you can really run with a proven brand is to demonstrate something that a typical consumer can understand."

If Amazon.com—a company that most people had never heard of—made such a claim, how could the company back it up? After working on the project for about a week, Mahesh Murth walked into Schroeder's office and said, "163 books on marriage. 798 books on divorce." It was a clever, eloquent illustration of the vastness of the Amazon.com selection. Plus, it opened up all sorts of intriguing combinations for a sustained campaign.

"We immediately dove into their database and we looked at every section that they had and every title that they carried," said Schroeder. "We had categories upon categories of books."

The urbane and amusing campaign included headlines such as "16 books on male pattern baldness; 128 on hats;" "859 books on cooking; 1,985 on dieting;" and "460 books for Marxists, including 33 on Groucho." Online banner ads invited browsers to "Click here to enter" the Amazon.com site. USWeb/CKS also placed satellite storefronts on about 600 websites, which enabled browsers on a recipe or cooking site to hyperlink to Amazon.com's cookbook selection.

The bulk of the media buy was spent in major mainstream publications, such as the *Wall Street Journal,* the *New York Times Book Review,* and *USA Today,* in order to reach literate, educated adults; only a small percentage, said Schroeder, was spent online. Soon Amazon.com began making strategic advertising alliances with general-interest media such as National Public Radio, *Commentary, Salon,* the *New Yorker, Atlantic Monthly,* and *Wired* to establish in the mind of the consumer that Amazon.com offered the most comprehensive selection of books on the World Wide Web.

BARNES & NOBLE COMES CALLING

With all the attention Amazon.com was attracting, it was inevitable that Barnes & Noble would sit up and take notice. Bezos enjoyed playfully tweaking both B&N and Borders. In 1996, he said that he understood—but did not share—the two retailing giants' disinclination to make a commitment to selling books online. "I think it's rational for those guys at this point. They're big enough to break into the market," he said, "after it's been validated."

At that time, Leonard Riggio, the chairman and chief executive officer of Barnes & Noble, who had built the company into a 466-store chain, told Bezos he was interested in buying part or all of Amazon.com, according to Tom Alberg. "Len Riggio is smart and shrewd; a classic New York street fighter," said Alberg. Riggio and his brother Stephen, who is B&N's vice chairman and chief operating officer, "started calling Jeff. They said they wanted to do something. They didn't know exactly what they wanted to do. They said, 'You're doing a fantastic job, but, of course, we're going to kill you when we launch. But we'd still like to talk to you about doing something.' "

In the late fall of 1996, the Riggio brothers came to Seattle, where they had dinner with Bezos and Alberg at Dahlia Lounge, a popular Seattle restaurant where a dinner scene from the movie *Sleepless in Seattle* was filmed.

Alberg recalled that the Riggios were very complimentary about what Bezos had accomplished, but they also reiterated the claim, "We're going to kill you," when they launch their own website. The brothers expressed interest in putting together a joint venture. One suggestion was a website—separate and apart from the Amazon.com website—that would use the Amazon.com system and would carry both the Barnes & Noble and Amazon.com brands. To Bezos and Alberg, there were many thorny issues. What would the site be called? Would the companies eventually combine the two sites? Would the agreement be exclusive or nonexclusive? How would the brands be handled? What about other products, such as music? What would be the role of the B&N stores? "Len's style is, 'Let's do a joint deal. You own half the site; we own half the site. Split the profits. You guys name a price. I want to invest. I want to own 20 percent of you. I don't care what the price is,' " said Alberg. "I don't know whether that would be the case when it got down to negotiation. But he's very engaging. They were really determined. I don't think they offered to buy us 100 percent; it was more about joining forces."

Nothing ever came of the Barnes & Noble approach, but the story was leaked to the press. The January 28, 1997, edition of the *Wall Street Journal* cited "one senior book retailing executive" who said that B&N had "made overtures as recently as last week to acquire Amazon.com." That claim was denied by Len Riggio, who added: "I can't say whether or not we would be interested if it were offered." He also said that that B&N is "projecting to be the No. 1 bookseller on the Internet," and Stephen Riggio said, "We have to be a player. . . . Online bookselling is going to be a very big thing."

He wasn't kidding.

TAKEAWAYS

From the very beginning, Jeff Bezos insisted on hiring the brightest, smartest, most versatile, and entrepreneurial people he could find—people who were going to buy into his vision of the future and would be willing to work their tail off in order to achieve it.

Bezos's attitude was if a candidate was not on the A list, then Amazon.com wasn't interested.

- Hire the right, motivated people and don't be willing to settle.
- Constantly raise the bar for the qualifications of a job applicant.
- Sharpen communication skills to motivate employees.
- Find people committed to the corporate culture.
- Corporate culture is a blend of 30 percent of what you set out for it to be, 30 percent who your early employees happen to be, and 40 percent random chance.
- The leader is the soul of the corporation.
- Be playful. Bezos was noted for his horseplay with employees at every level.
- Hire the right executives to take you to the next level.
- Include managers in the hiring process.
- Begin early on to establish your brand.

chapter eight

"anal-retentive" about customer service

Businesses planned for service are apt to succeed;
businesses planned for profit are apt to fail.
—Nicholas Murray Butler

Jeff Bezos has often said that he wants to make Amazon.com "the most customer-centric" company in history. Even before he launched the website in July 1995, he made customer service the top priority for the company because he knew that positive word-of-mouth buzz would have a greater impact on consumer perception than any kind of paid advertising. (Anyway, in 1995, he couldn't afford to spend money on advertising.) This is something that Nordstrom, Inc. has always understood. Nordstrom has never run an ad or sent out a press release boasting about its customer service. The company's reputation for superior service is 100 percent through the unsolicited accolades of satisfied customers. "It was seeing how successful word-of-mouth was in that first year that really led us on this path of being obsessively, compulsively, anal-retentively focused on customer service," said Bezos.

Word-of-mouth is even more powerful online than it is in the bricks-and-mortar world because, as Bezos has said many times, in the real world, if you make a customer unhappy he'll tell five friends; if you disappoint a customer on the Internet, he'll tell 5,000 friends—or maybe 50,000—friends. Bezos understood that there are always going to be people who will "flame" a company on cyberspace bulletin boards and news groups, and that he couldn't possibly hire enough people to monitor those sites and respond to the flames. But what he *could* do is build incredible customer loyalty so that when the company does screw up, there will be enough satisfied customers to come to its defense. Happy customers will become evangelists for a company they like and will use the Internet as a megaphone to spread the word and help bring in new customers.

For example, in early 1997, Microsoft's online magazine *Slate* conducted an ordering test to see who could deliver a hot bestseller faster—Amazon.com or a local Seattle bookstore; the store won. But loyal Amazon.com customers besieged *Slate* with flame mail and defended Amazon.com against the criticism. The Amazon.com PR department had intended to reply to *Slate*, but discovered they didn't have to, because the customers did it for them.

No naif when it comes to the longevity of customer allegiance, Bezos has said, "When people ask me if our customers are loyal. I say, 'Absolutely, right up to the second that somebody else offers them a better service.' " That's why Amazon.com's "mantra" has been "that we were going to obsess over our customers and not our competitors. We watch our competitors, learn from them, see the things that they were doing good for customers and copy those things as much as we can. But we were never going to obsess over them." He considered that the primary reason "behind our growth and our ability to cope with that growth is our focus on customer experience. We've been completely obsessive" about customer service. "I tell folks inside Amazon.com to be anal-retentive about this. But not orally fixated. I think," he said with a smile, "that would be going too far."

With today's consumers armed with extensive product and price information, and the freedom to move from one website to another with a mere click, the balance of power in online commerce has shifted from the merchant to the consumer. "The Internet is this big, huge hurricane," said Bezos. "The only constant in that storm is the customers." Therefore, he believed, merchants must refocus the emphasis in their operations. "So, if the optimal business decision in the old world was to spend 30 percent of your time, energy, focus, and dollars on building great customer experience, and 70 percent of your time, energy, focus, and dollars on shouting about it, today that's inverted. Today, the optimal thing to do is to spend 70 percent of your time, energy, focus, and dollars on building great customer experience and 30 percent shouting about it.

Through anecdotal evidence, focus groups, and quantitative research, Amazon.com found that the three things that mattered most to customers were *selection, convenience,* and *price.*

Bezos understood that the customer-service experience is an end-to-end proposition, taking in every aspect of the interaction between buyer and seller—the amount of time it takes to download the home page, the ease of use of the website (from searching for the product to placing the order), all the way through to the delivery of the right product to the customer's door, and everything in between. Like many companies who have committed to a customer-service culture, Amazon.com was going to make sure that the customer experience was a positive one—regardless of immediate costs.

The raison d'être for Amazon.com (or any other online company) is offering something on the Internet that can't be done in any other way. From the beginning, Bezos's philosophy was that a successful online retailer must add enough "value" to convince potential customers to change their buying habits and try a new way of shopping. The value proposition "that you have to build for customers is incredibly large," he said, because "the Web is a pain to use today," with slow modem speeds, slow downloading websites, telephone line disconnections, and browser crashes. "So, if you are going to get people to use a website in today's environment, you have to offer them overwhelming compensation for this primitive, infant technology."

The whole customer service equation boils down to nothing more complicated than the Golden Rule. "Jeff doesn't want to have his time wasted," said former employee Gina Meyers. "That's how he expects to be treated and that's how he expects customers to be treated. The whole vision is: 'How do you want to be treated as a customer?' "

Bezos knew that in real life, people don't go to bookstores *just* because they need a book; they go because it's an enjoyable way to spend a couple of hours on a rainy Sunday afternoon. "We will never make Amazon.com fun and engaging in the same way as the great physical bookstores are," Bezos admitted. "You'll never be able to hear the bindings creak and smell the books and have tasty lattes and soft sofas at Amazon.com. But we can do completely different things that will blow people away and make the experience an engaging and fun one."

WEBSITE EXPERIENCE

For the online user, the experience starts, of course, at the website. That's also the place where the customer will be turned on or turned off—so turned off she may never visit your site again. In the early days of the Web, many established retailers limited their efforts to nothing more than a glorified kiosk that provided basic information such as products, phone number, location, directions, etc. The *Wall Street Journal* in June of 1996 called the Internet "mostly a game of bait-and-switch," where users were attracted to the web page, and then told to contact the company by phone or fax "to get the real goodies." The *Journal* added that the Web "was little more than an electronic yard sale" and that online retailing "is just barely in the shopping-center phase."

Even when companies realized that they could actually sell products online, most of them viewed the experience from the standpoint of *selling merchandise* as opposed to *completing a transaction with a customer.* Scott Lipsky, a former Amazon.com vice president, believed that most of these online companies "were thinking traditional retail from the get-go—as opposed to thinking, 'What is going to make someone buy online?' The thing that's going to make them buy online is to make it easy, fast, and economical. . . . If you're thinking about what it's like to walk into a store and view your merchandise, you're starting off on the wrong foot."

In the mid-1990s, many companies thought that the way to drive traffic to their site was to put up the fanciest, prettiest, coolest stuff they could find, without considering that most people were dialing in at the tortoise speeds of 9,600 bits per second baud and 14.4 kilobits per second and did not want to wait for all this cool stuff to download. Amazon.com, on the other hand, knew that the key to the user experience was the convenience of ordering a book online versus having to drive over to a store and buy it. "I abide by the theory that says in the late twentieth century, the scarcest resource is time," said Bezos. "If you can save people money and time, they'll like that."

Bezos understood that the Amazon.com website in the customer's perception was not the layout of pixels on the screen's home page, but what the experience is like. The Amazon.com website was initially a bit clunky and crowded, but it did change every day in order to encourage people to come back. For the first two years, the site retained its simple format so that it could always be fast and functional. (Two years after the launch, increased bandwidth helped make the site more graphical and appealing as well as easier to navigate.)

Back in the summer of 1996, when customers logged on to Amazon.com, the Web page, made up mainly of text, downloaded quickly, and users would be greeted with the words: "Welcome to Amazon.com Books! Search one million titles. Enjoy consistently low prices." For example, "The Spotlight" on August 8 proclaimed: "Losing weight, getting fit, brain surgery and Southeast Asia; forbidden books and tropical oils; melatonin and TCP/IP; Internet investments, business traveling; all discounted 30%!" (There was generous use of exclamation marks!) The two featured covers were *Rogue Trader* ("crashing global banks") by Nick Leeson and *Let's Go Asia*. The company offered daily excerpts of "spotlighted" books online.

Visitors could use the efficient search engine to hunt for a specific book, topic, or author, or browse through a database, which, back then, consisted of 1.5 million titles in 23 subject categories. Three book editors read book reviews, perused customer orders, and reviewed current events to determine what books would be featured. With these editors, the company conveyed to users that they were getting the same kind of literary feedback they would find in a small independent bookstore. "If you spend a lot of time on the site, I hope you get a sense of the quirky, independent, literate voice, and that behind it all you're interacting with people, and that it's people who care about these things, not people who are trying to sell you these things. My mantra has always been 'the perfect context for a purchase decision,'" said Executive Editor Rick Ayre.

"People don't buy books just because they need a book," Bezos observed. "There is a lot of serendipity to it, and we're trying to capture that." Part of that serendipity was the "displays" on the front page of the site that featured new releases, specials, and suggestions for gifts. Customers who knew exactly what book they wanted needed only to use the search engine to move on to a particular section: business, computers, gardening, etc. where they saw recommendations by experts on the subject. Many of the books included capsule descriptions, blurbs from publishers, as well as reviews from Amazon.com editors and taste arbiters such as the *New York Times Book Review* or Oprah Winfrey's book club. There was also "self-administered interviews" with the authors, who were free to discuss their own books or respond to readers' comments. Some of the best-known authors, including Bill Gates *(The Road Ahead)* participated in question-and-answer interviews conducted by Amazon.com editors.

Customers were invited to "Click and 'Write Your Own Review of this Book.'" One reason for doing that was to create a sense of "community"; a more pressing reason was that the Amazon.com website had all this white space to fill so it needed a way to generate more content. By having customers write their own reviews—positive or negative—Amazon.com was able to spark some intellectual dialogue as well as add (free to Amazon.com) content to pages that would otherwise be virtually blank. (The company awarded cash prizes for the best customer book reviews.)

David Siegel, author of *Futurize Your Enterprise: Business Strategy in the Age of the E-Customer*, and a pioneer in Web design, described the Internet in 1995 as "full-blown counter-culture. It was a toy, it was fun, it was physics. It was universities, it was students. It was young. It was vibrant. It was breaking rules. It was about going against the grain. It really wasn't about selling. Amazon really catered to that by letting people put up reviews of books."

Amazon.com's corporate philosophy on customer reviews was "Attack ideas, not people," said Glenn Fleishman, the catalog manager, who helped monitor the customer reviews and who coined that phrase. Reviews that were negative or slanderous about something other than the book were removed. "We didn't want to prove objective facts and we filtered out dirty words, but I was never asked to remove things for content," said Fleishman.

Maire Masco, who was a customer-service manager, recalled a firestorm over an in-house review of Robert Heinlein's *Starship Troopers.* The Amazon.com reviewer charged that the book was misogynistic and supported the practice of beating children. The reviewer "didn't take it from a science fiction point of view, but a sociological point of view," said Masco. "Oh, my God! It was like the doors of hell opened! We were inundated with e-mails and counter-postings. I stopped counting after we posted 300 reviews by readers who condemned that review."

When publishers and authors asked Bezos why Amazon.com would publish negative reviews, he defended the practice by claiming that Amazon.com was "taking a different approach, of trying to sell all books. We want to make every book available—the good, the bad, and the ugly. When you're doing that, you actually have an obligation—if you're going to make the shopping environment one that's actually conducive to shopping—to let truth loose. That's what we try to do with the customer reviews."

But these "civilian" reviews are sometimes the source of mischief. In June 1999, the *Los Angeles Times* reported that the Amazon.com website posted a negative review of a book about Internet business planning by Lynn Manning Ross. The review written under the heading "Stupid Book . . . Don't Waste Your Time!" was signed by "Jeff Bezos," who listed his e-mail address as Jeff@amazon.com. Ross complained for a week before Amazon.com got around to deleting the review. It took that long to correct the problem because the system wasn't flexible enough at that time to move fast.

This anonymity is the part of the reviews that a lot of authors and publishers dislike because it makes it too easy to sabotage and slander other people's work in a very visible and public way. "Now that we have this community and a methodology for contributing to that community, the real question becomes: How do you prevent the misinformation," asked David Rogelberg of the Studio B Literary Agency in Fishers, Indiana. Rogelberg represents many writers of computer- and Internet-related books. "Now that it's become such an important information app in business decision-making, how do you prevent people from skewing it for their own benefit? That's going to be *the* question because if I had 12 people on staff and said, 'All I want you to do is go to Amazon and write up good reviews for our clients,' it would help their book sales, royalty rates, advances, book opportunities, etc. It would be a very inexpensive way for me to cheat the system. It's something that I would never do, but I'm not sure everybody's that honest. There are already people who are having their books reviewed [on Amazon.com], and the books are not yet published. How did that happen?"

Authors are invited to review their own works. A team of people scans those author reviews (which must include the author's e-mail address) and verifies the information with the publisher. Occasionally bogus reviews slip through. One time, "God" reviewed the Bible, and "Emily Brontë" critiqued one of her own works and moaned, "I just can't believe that Jane Austen got two miniseries and a full-length motion picture in one year."

Amazon.com's primary competitors also offered their own features and content. The Internet Book Shop, based in England, which referred to itself as the "Largest Online Bookshop in the World" offered 780,000 books, some at discounts. Cleveland-based Book Stacks Unlimited (books.com), offered more than 425,000 titles on a searchable database, and provided more than 190,000 book annotations and reviews, a daily Internet radio show covering literary news, and online book discussion groups. The very sophisticated site also offered free book bonuses (after a certain amount in purchases) and a "café" chat room for readers and guest authors. A service called Lyric provided real-time audio files of authors either reading from their works or being interviewed. Book Stacks published a magazine called *Cook's Nook* that contained information about cooking and cooking books. The site also offered excerpts, tables of contents, and story summaries on featured books. Bezos knew that in order to compete, he had to at least match—if not surpass—those features.

SELECTION

On the first day she went to work for Amazon.com in the summer of 1996, Dana Brown walked into a small room in the back of the warehouse at 2250 First Avenue. She saw two 486 PCs and one employee, and was told: "This is our ordering department, and you're in charge of it."

Jumping on a quick learning curve, she took the department from ordering 100 books a day in July to 5,000 books a day in December. She helped establish relations with the distributors in order to get better deals and more efficient deliveries. "There were a lot of mistakes and problems with the shipments, and we had no written agreements," said Brown. "We needed someone to manage the quality of their shipments." Adding to the problem was that Amazon.com had no return department. Many returned books were stacked up on shelves with no rhyme or reason. The company frequently lost track of which books went back to which vendors, and, "at the end of the day, you almost had to write a lot of them off."

Customer service "was central to what I was trying to accomplish," said Brown. "We were trying to reduce the amount of time between the customer placing the order and the customer receiving the order. That was our emphasis. That's how the productivity was measured." That summer, the company began in earnest developing relationships with the major book distributors—Ingram and Baker & Taylor—as well as book publishers, both large and small, in order to improve service.

In the beginning, the shipping time was four days for books that distributors had in stock, but Amazon.com was trying to cut it down to 24 hours. (Bezos knew that customers would be reluctant to order if they had no idea how long it was going to take to get the book.) "There was a lot that could be streamlined. Even the amount of walking that the warehouse people did. The basic physical layout of the warehouse could improve the speed and efficiency of the operation," said Brown. At that time, all books were hand-packed and the company had no barcode scanners, so every book's ISBN was keyed into the system. Most of the day's shipments were shipped in a minivan by a courier service. There weren't enough shipments for the post office to pick them up.

Despite the primitive conditions, the company was still stressing "that the product had to be perfect when it got to the customer and it had to be sent when it was supposed to," said E. Heath Merriwether, who began working in the warehouse in the summer of 1996. "They took as much care with a $4.99 paperback book as they did shipping the entire set of the World Book Encyclopedia." To ensure the efficacy of the packing, "Amazon overpacked everything. The trick was to take the [packaged] books and toss them across the floor, as a demonstration of how well Amazon packed. So you would take a book, pack it up, sling it across the floor, and unpack it. The book would be undamaged."

Scott Lipsky, the vice president of business development, and Glenn Fleishman, the catalog manager, also worked on developing the relationships with publishers, both large and small. They figured that one way to sell more books was to get more information on book titles from publishers. Fleishman helped smaller publishers get their information in the catalog from a number of sources, including distributors. “The home page aside, everything at almost every online bookstore seems to be the same thing,” said Fleishman. “The main determining difference might be discount or the amount of information you have,” such as a table of contents, excerpts, and other marketing information. “I told publishers that the more information they gave me on their titles, the more effectively they could compete with a bigger publisher. (That’s more likely to happen in nonfiction.) The attitude that I wanted to convey was that we are going to help sell more of your books. The way we’re going to do that is by giving you equal placement. Amazon gives books the same level of placement, whether you’re HarperCollins or a self-published author that sells one copy of one title once a month.”

INDEPENDENT PUBLISHERS

In February 1998, Amazon.com invited small, independent publishers—who had traditionally been shut out of many traditional distribution channels—to participate, for free, in its Publisher’s Advantage program, which would give that publisher a placement on the website equal to any major publisher. Amazon.com would stock five copies of a book on consignment and reorder them as they were sold. This program cut down the wait for customers trying to order hard-to-find books because books by participating publishers would be upgraded on the Amazon.com site to “usually ships in 24 hours,” instead of the usual four-to-six-week delivery classification for titles that had to be special-ordered. Amazon.com also scans the book cover for free, includes the title’s detail page, and adds descriptions, excerpts, tables of contents, and author and publisher comments.

In this way, the Internet provides infinite shelf space so that books that can’t get distribution in physical stores can still be merchandised to a worldwide audience. One author/publisher who has taken advantage of this program is Christina Crawford, the author of the 1978 bestseller, *Mommie Dearest*, about her mother, the famed screen actress Joan Crawford. Christina Crawford self-published the twentieth anniversary edition of the book through her own company, Seven Hills Press, and sells it almost exclusively through Amazon.com. "It's very democratic and egalitarian in the best sense," said Crawford. "Amazon.com will take a single title [from a publisher]. That alone created the underground phenomenon [among self-published authors] of Amazon.com because it suddenly filled a need that nobody talked about. It makes possible worldwide distribution with the click of a mouse and a credit card. Amazon.com orders from me by the carton. I simply send it to one of their warehouses as they designate with a purchase order number on the box. I pay the freight." Since Amazon.com orders a book from Crawford when they receive an order, "there are almost no returns. And unlike publishers that pay an author every six months, Amazon.com pays me every 30 days."

ALTERING THE BUSINESS MODEL

As orders across the board increased dramatically, it was becoming apparent that to supply the kind of total customer service Bezos had in mind, Amazon.com would need to warehouse and ship books in-house. The notion of an inventory-free online bookseller, which was the basis of the original model, was dead. Dana Brown selected what books should be inventoried in bulk so that they were available to be immediately shipped out the door. First it was limited to just the top 10 bestselling books but that quickly expanded to the top 25, and eventually the top 250. "We didn't have the room in the warehouse to store a lot," said Brown. Soon she was going from ordering 100 copies of a book to 10,000 copies, and "we were arguing over what on Earth do we do with 10,000 books in a warehouse that's not set up for them? Where do we put them? The answer: anywhere."

Soon, all the key personnel were working virtually around the clock—not an unusual occurrence for an Internet start-up. Books were ordered at 4:30 in the morning. Brown estimated she was putting in 15 to 18 hours a day, sometimes more. "I also had two pagers that went off all the time," she recalled. "Jeff was always there. I never saw him go home."

Gina Meyers described her two years at Amazon.com as "like being on a rocket ship and just holding on for dear life. It was fun, but after a while, it took its toll."

"I don't think anybody could predict all of the fires and complications" of moving the books quickly, said Laurel Canan, the warehouse manager. "We solve problems as we go." Or, as one former Amazonian said: "The attitude was, you can work long, hard, and well. At Amazon two out of three won't work."

In those early days, Amazon.com would not always get first dibs at the bestsellers from the publishers. "That was always a terribly sad thing when people would write that they saw the latest Tom Clancy book at Borders and they wanted to know why they hadn't received their copy from Amazon," said Maire Masco.

Customers weren't willing to wait more than two days to receive a popular bestseller they knew they could find on the shelf in any bookstore. So in November 1996, Amazon.com leased a 93,000-square-foot warehouse in Seattle from which it could pack and ship books to customers as soon as orders were placed. It stocked enough copies of the bestsellers so it could fulfill those orders quickly. Bezos convinced his two major distributors, Ingram Books and Baker & Taylor, to ship books to Amazon.com on demand so that he could keep down inventory and storage costs. Soon the company was inventorying 200,000 of the best-selling books in its Seattle facility, and later, in another warehouse in Wilmington, Delaware. They received the 200,000 to 400,000 top sellers from a network of about a dozen different wholesalers, and then the next 400,000 to 1.5 million directly from 20,000 different publishers. Ingram and Baker & Taylor ship almost every order the day it's received, with virtually every shipment delivered within 24 to 48 hours. But for that service, customers must pay the wholesale markup, which is a 10 percent to 20 percent over what they would pay if they bought the book directly from a publisher. Amazon.com had the additional costs of packaging and shipping books to customers.

Because discounting is an integral part of Bezos's idea of a "value proposition," Amazon.com slashed the retail prices on virtually all of these titles. He has often said it would be a huge mistake not to offer discounts. (But, of course, with shipping and handling, the buyer had to tack another $4.00 on to the price of the order.) Amazon.com could "afford" to discount because its overhead costs (including real estate and the number of employees) were about half those of a book superstore. In 1996–97, Bezos claimed that Amazon.com generated more than $300,000 a year in revenue per operating employee, compared to physical bookstores that generated about $95,000 a year in operating revenue per employee.

In that summer of 1996, "We were growing so fast and trying to put systems and processes in place as we went," said Gina Meyers. "You had to be ready to have the business multiply by 10 times in two months. You had to keep pushing all of your processes to the extreme. We wondered, 'What's going to break?' You had to know [that something was] going to break before you get there, so that you can have a solution in place before it breaks." Thanks to the infrastructure that Kaphan and Barton-Davis had put together, the company kept solving logistical problems and increasing orders with only an occasional glitch in the system. "There were times I would go home and think, 'Oh, my god, how did we do that?' It's mind-boggling the number of transactions that we were able to do on this system that was homegrown, overnight, by people who weren't distribution experts and weren't order experts. That's what's incredible," said Meyers.

With the orders increasing exponentially, the company added two high-powered Digital AlphaServer 2000 systems (then considered the best servers available) with 64-bit processors in a symmetric multiprocessing configuration with one gigabyte of RAM, where the 3 million book titles were stored. The Digital AlphaServers showed, "This is not a fly-by-night sort of thing," said Meyers. "We were gearing everything to be the best possible customer-service company and we were making sure everything was tuned to fast response times."

The foundation of the software was an Oracle database, which was thought to be the best and most robust system on the market. For the sheer number of its real-time transactions, Amazon has probably been the most intensive user of Oracle products among online retailers. Bezos said that that the bulk of the company's investment in software development was spent on back-office logistics, including the ordering process.

ORDERING PROCESS

"What's really at the core of 'owning the customer's total experience' is an appreciation of what makes a customer nervous," Patricia Seybold wrote in *Customers.com*. "You need to deal with the unarticulated gnawing sense of anxiety the customer experiences whenever he doesn't know exactly what's going on." The Amazon.com site goes "a long way toward reducing customers' unspoken fears."

Bezos and Amazon.com took a systematic approach to every step in the process of buying a book on its website. The company is considered the first Internet retailer to divide the buying procedure into a series of specific steps, to literally number each step, and to guide the customer through it. The whole idea was to make it easy and enjoyable for the customer and to allay any fear or trepidation about this brave new world of buying something on the World Wide Web.

The five steps are:

1. What is your e-mail address?

2. What method of payment do you intend to use (credit card, check, or money order)?

3. Is this your first order from Amazon.com Books? (If you are a returning customer, you type in your password here.)

4. Is this order a gift? (If not you can skip to step 5; if it is, Amazon.com offers a selection of gift wrapping, for which it charges $2.00 per order.)

5. Press this button to continue to the next page. You will still have a chance to cancel or change your order. (This step takes the customer to a page that summarizes his purchases. From that page, with another click, the purchase is completed.)

At the Amazon.com website, customers shop by selecting a book and adding it to their virtual shopping cart. At any time during the process, the customer can make changes—additions or deletions—to her order. If she decides to halt the transaction and exit the website, when she returns to the site, the shopping cart—with all the previously selected books—are there waiting for the next move. A customer who makes a purchase from Amazon.com has his profile on file, including pertinent information—name, e-mail address, shipping address, credit card number, etc. If that information has not changed, the user clicks the "purchase now" button and is done. Changes of shipping address can be added to the profile, and the next time the customer orders, he will be given a choice of the shipping addresses in his Amazon.com file. If the purchase is a gift, the customer can write a card and choose among a variety of gift wraps. The final step is to confirm what books have been ordered, the bill total, the shipping address, and the shipping option (UPS, U.S. Postal Service, etc.). As late as 1999, of the 10 most visited shopping sites on the Internet, Amazon.com was the only one that offered on its home page a link to its "shipping policies," where a chart explained shipping and handling fees. The shipping costs are also posted at the final step of the registration and purchasing process. In addition, Amazon.com's site enables customers to review their purchase history, track orders, and personally customize virtually every aspect of the ordering process.

As the site has become more sophisticated, the service has become more personalized. Returning customers are greeted by name ("Hello, Robert Spector!") and presented with several titles that Amazon.com recommended, based on previous purchases. "I want to transport online bookselling," said Bezos, "back to the days of the small bookseller, who got to know you very well and would say things like, 'I know you like John Irving, and guess what, here's this new author, I think he's a lot like John Irving.' "

The Recommendation Center contains a more detailed list of relevant titles. This personalization is part of Amazon's philosophy of "mass customization," which tailors the experience to the individual customer's tastes, buying habits, and browsing behavior. Through the use of advanced relational software, Amazon.com was the first online retailer to post a message that listed other book titles—either in the same subject area or by the same author—that were purchased by other readers who bought the book that you just selected. Using a feature called Bookmatcher, Amazon.com asks customers to rate 10 books, which gives the company more information on the preference of readers, which ultimately helps the company suggest other books that the customer might be interested in.

By the time Amazon.com branched out into other products, its recommendation system had grown even more sophisticated. Instant Recommendations, which is based on previous purchases, has a button called "mood matcher," which enables the user to click on categories such as "feeling depressed," "dancing," and "party." There are even subcategories. If you click "feeling depressed," you'll find "get dumped" and "won't stop raining." (Very popular in Seattle.) In May 1999, *Interactive Week* reported that Amazon.com was ranked number one for this recommendations system: "What's remarkable about this system is that it even recommends CDs and videos with surprising accuracy, even if you've only purchased books from Amazon in the past."

Several minutes after placing an order, Amazon.com sends the customer an e-mail to confirm the order. (Amazon.com is considered the first online company to do this.) After Amazon.com ships the order, the company sends another e-mail notification. If some products are not yet available, Amazon will tell what was shipped and what is still on order. Regular customers are often upgraded in shipping priority.

In late 1997, Amazon.com launched "1-Click Shopping"—a trademarked and patented process—which adds a value proposition to the Internet shopping experience by enabling repeat customers to order with literally one click of the mouse. To make ordering as easy as possible, the user can designate a credit card number, shipping address, and shipping method (standard, two-day, or overnight, for example) for all future 1-Click transactions. After making his purchase, he hits the 1-Click key and the purchase is done. 1-Click lets the user add or amend his profile and gives him the opportunity to review the record of every purchase he's ever made.

"When we did focus groups and tested this new feature before launching it, the biggest problem was that people didn't think they had really finished the order," said Bezos. "So we had to change the text surrounding this thing to not only say, 'Thank you for your order,' but in parentheses, it now says, 'Yes, it really was that easy.' " After a myriad of online merchants began copying 1-Click buying, Amazon.com petitioned the court to protect its intellectual property. The company filed suit in October 1999 against Barnesandnoble.com, accusing the Internet bookselling arm of Barnes & Noble of illegally copying Amazon.com's patented checkout system with B&N's Express Lane 1-click checkout. Although Amazon.com began using the 1-click technology in September 1997, it did not receive a patent for it until Sept. 28, 1999. Barnesandnoble.com had been using Express Lane since early 1998. In December, a federal district court judge in Seattle, Marsha J. Pechman, issued a preliminary injunction that barred Barnesandnoble.com from using Express Lane 1-click ordering while the patent-infringement suit was pending. B&N switched to a system called Express Checkout, but vowed to fight the ruling and in a press release said, "we do not intend to sit back and allow Amazon to stake a claim upon any technology that is widely used."

Soon after Judge Pechman's decision, a boycott of Amazon.com was called for by Richard Stallman, an early developer of the Linux operating system and the head of the Free Software Foundation. On the Linux Today website, Stallman wrote: "Amazon has sued to block the use of this simple idea, showing that they truly intend to monopolize it. This is an attack against the World Wide Web and against E-commerce in general. . . . If this were just a dispute between two companies, it would not be an important public issue. But the patent gives Amazon the power over anyone who runs a website in the U.S. (and any other countries that give them similar patents)—power to control all use of this technique. Although only one company is being sued today, the issue affects the whole Internet."

Bezos saw the value of customizing Amazon.com for customers by offering a variety of promotional services that would tailor the site to individual tastes and desires. A feature called "Editors" provides recommendations of books in nearly 50 genres and subjects by Amazon.com's departmental editors, who preview book galleys and read advance reviews. The "Eyes" feature offers advance notification of new books on a specified favorite subject or by a favorite author.

The idea for "Eyes" grew out of Amazon.com's original idea of selling books via e-mail rather than on the Web, according to Paul Barton-Davis, who said, "We thought it would be great if you got e-mail (notification on a book) as if you had done the search. That came pretty naturally out of the search language." Customers could order in advance books that were scheduled for publication but not yet available in bookstores. (Amazon.com sends the customer the book when it becomes available.) Customers can also subscribe to newsletters on a variety of topics and genres from independent editors and independent presses.

"Amazon.com Delivers" is another service that provides recommendations from Amazon.com editors. The company will e-mail recommendations, articles, and interviews all tailored to the individual's tastes, from electrical engineering to Eastern religion.

To allay customers' fears about invasion of their privacy, the company posted the "Amazon.com Bill of Rights":

1. No obligation: Eyes & Editors Personal Notification Services are provided free of charge, and you are under no obligation to buy anything.

2. Unsubscribing: You can unsubscribe or change your subscriptions at any time.

3. Privacy: We do not sell or rent information about our customers. If you would like to make sure we never sell or rent information about you to third parties, just send a blank e-mail message to never@amazon.com.

By 1998, Bezos had stopped calling Amazon.com's business "e-commerce," and began referring to it as "e-merchandising," because "commerce is the simple find-it-buy-it-ship-it action. E-merchandising is much more about customer behavior online," he told an audience at Lake Forest College. Bezos explained that while much is known about customer behavior in the bricks-and-mortar world, relatively little is known about customer behavior in the nascent online world, and that he views Amazon.com as "an experimental laboratory" to figure out this behavior. "At the same time, we can use advanced technology to not only understand our products on an individual product-by-product basis but to understand our customers on a customer-by-customer individualized basis."

Stating that Amazon.com's goal is to "enhance the discovery process," Bezos said that he believed that Amazon.com could use advanced technology to dramatically improve the odds that a customer could find a book "because we will not just let readers find books, we will let books find readers."

With its work on software development, Amazon.com is "very much a technology company," said Bezos. "In fact, I think of us, in many ways, as sort of a small Artificial Intelligence company." In recent years, to help people discover products online, Amazon.com began using simple but sophisticated techniques such as collaborative filtering, which looks for the individual customer's "affinity group"—other Amazon.com customers who presumably share your tastes and interests and who previously bought the same book(s) as you—and then searches for books that that group of customers has bought and that you haven't (at least not yet).

By 1998, Amazon.com was customizing the user's home page based on past activity and stated preferences. "You don't even notice this unless you sit right next to someone and see that their version of Amazon.com is slightly different from yours. This is something we've wanted to do forever," said Bezos. "We don't have to have the average store for the mythical average customer. The goal is to make the perfect store for everybody."

ASSOCIATES PROGRAM

In mid-1996, an Amazon.com customer asked the company for permission to link book recommendations on her website to Amazon.com. The company quickly agreed to it. With that innocent request, Amazon.com pioneered the concept of organizing a network of associates to help them sell books and, in the process, to build communities of interest. Soon, virtually any business or organization with a website on a particular topic was invited to join the program. On its site, the associate features books on its subject that it selects from the Amazon.com database, complete with reviews, recommendations, and commentaries. When a customer visiting an associate's website clicks to make a purchase of the book, the customer is hyperlinked (at no charge to the associate) to Amazon.com to actually make the purchase from Amazon.com. Amazon.com takes care of the order-taking, the logistics, the gift-wrapping, shipping, etc., and the associate earns 5 to 15 percent commission on the sale.

Associates could, of course, buy books directly from a distributor, and then make a 40 to 50 percent gross margin, like a bookstore, but then they would have to deal with inventory and fulfillment. Amazon.com showed associates that it would be better to make 15 percent net at the end of the day, with no other expenses, than to make 50 percent gross.

One reason for the program (which eventually was coordinated by Shawn Haynes) was to add credibility to Amazon.com by enabling the experts on the topic to make the recommendations. Because he owns a Labrador retriever, Bezos likes to use a website about Labrador retrievers as an example of the Associates program. If someone is an expert on Labrador retrievers, it's not logistically or financially feasible in the physical world for that expert to open up a bookstore that would sell only the best books on Labrador retrievers. But it's perfectly logical to sell those Labrador retriever books on a specialized website and provide the editorial context for those books.

"This is good for the customer because now they have an editorial authority sort of force-ranking Labrador retriever books," said Bezos. "It's good for us because it gives us new introductions to customers. And it's good for the Labrador retriever website because it gives them a new source of revenues and an ability to offer a new service to their customers."

In the first three months of the program, Amazon.com signed up more than 5,000 sites, ranging from Yahoo!, Netscape, and AT&T Business Network to Explore Madagascar!, the *Cigar Journal,* and Bezos's favorite, The Meteorite Market, which bills itself as "the Web's oldest and best place to buy meteorites." (By the end of 1999, the number of associates exceeded 350,000.)

Of course, Amazon.com's motivation for the Associates program is not entirely altruistic. The program enables the company to cleverly build affiliations with other websites, and minimize competition from specialty websites, who don't have to deal with inventory or fulfillment issues. Amazon gets the additional business, as well as the use of customers' names and addresses.

Although Amazon.com often talks about the "community" it has created with associates, one former company insider said, "I prefer not to call it a 'community'; it's 'new customer acquisition.' The idea is not for someone to keep going back to that other site and buy books through that channel every time. It's to get a new customer and keep him." If that customer never again goes through the original associate website to order books from Amazon.com, Amazon has essentially paid the associate a one-time finder's fee, and that's it—even if that customer buys another 100 books from Amazon.com. So Amazon.com has no shared costs for the future, and it still owns the customer. (Most unsophisticated associates neglected to negotiate a piece of the lifetime value of the customer. In addition, the associates know from their own records whether one of their customers linked to Amazon.com, but can't tell how much he spent.)

The creation of the Associates program was another good example of Bezos's thinking about how to do business on the Web. It was a classic "first mover" strategy that has since been emulated by hundreds of other Internet companies, such as C|Net, Lycos, Ask Jeeves, and Goto.com Inc., who pay cash to sites that send traffic to their sites. "It's a Tupperware party on steroids," said Forrester Research analyst Chris Charron. "The reason it's valuable is that affiliate networks take advantage of the diffuse nature of the Internet." According to Forrester Research, associate programs are the best way to drive traffic to a site. Of course, today, associate programs are more sophisticated, and canny associates now stipulate payment for the lifetime value of the referred customer.

CUSTOMER SERVICE

The backbone of Amazon.com's customer-service department, particularly in the early days, was a remarkable collection of bright, overeducated men and women who set the tone for the rest of the corporation. To be hired in customer service, the applicant had to have earned at least a bachelor's degree. "The smartest people at Amazon—with no training in a specific book-related field—were in customer service. They know the company better than anyone at the top level knows the company from the customer perspective," said Glenn Fleishman. "They brought in people at $10 or more an hour. The first ones coming in got exquisite stock options." (Those early customer service personnel, who stuck around for the initial public offering, are multimillionaires today.)

Richard Howard, who chronicled his brief, unhappy career as an Amazon.com customer-service representative in a blistering, oft-cited article in *Seattle Weekly*, wrote that, "I was stunned by the backgrounds and level of prior accomplishment boasted by members of my training class (a published book author, a former translator with the Moscow branch of the Soros Foundation . . .)."

"If you were a disaffected academic, the customer-service department was a great place to work," said Maire Masco, who joined the company in February 1997, when there were a few dozen people in Amazon.com's customer-service group. When she left a year later, there were over 200 people in the group. The people in this group "were very widely read. If somebody called up and wanted to know what the best edition of *The Iliad* is, chances are there was somebody in the group who had the answer. That was particularly so when it was a smaller group. There was a tremendous amount of sharing. People developed specialties such as children's books, contemporary literature, or science."

There were two levels of customer-service representatives: Tier One and Tier Two. (Since that time, a thid tier has been added.) Tier One was comprised of hourly employees who helped customers locate a book by running a search and sending the results to the customer. Tier Two representatives, who were salaried, "were supposed to be creative, responsible, and smart, and be able to search the entire database and understand the way the company ran," said Nils Nordal, a current college instructor who was once a Tier Two employee.

Not only did all customer service representatives have to learn the UNIX software code, they also had to grasp the entire scope of the Amazon.com operation—how books were ordered from publishers, how they were delivered into the warehouse, how they got from the truck at the warehouse to the shelf, how to match up the order to the books that were packed, and how to determine the best shipping method. "To do customer service at Amazon, you really had to know every single step in the company's operation in order to figure out where the process went wrong, so that it could be rectified, so that a book would end up on somebody's doorstep," said Nordal. "When a customer wrote in to ask the status of a book, you could reply, 'It's on its way. This is the reason why it wasn't immediately delivered. We apologize for the inconvenience.' "

Asked to define customer service at Amazon.com, Bezos said, it "means that if you order a book from us, we ship the book in the time frame that we say we'll ship the book. If it's two or three days, then we should ship the book within two to three days. . . . Likewise, if you send us an e-mail message asking about your order, we ought to respond to that e-mail message in a reasonable period of time. Good customer service is fulfilling the promises you make to your customers."

Reps went through a thorough three-week training program in a classroom before they came in contact with customers. "There was an additional period where they would be monitored and tutored, and have their work observed closely because it was so complicated, and it was so easy to accidentally delete an order or mess up somebody's password or whatever," said Masco. "Usually, with a call center, the whole idea is to bring people in to pay them nominal wages and to make it easy and quick for them so that your training time is quick."

Nordal said that customer service at Amazon essentially "boiled down to one of two things: (1) 'I'm looking for a book on something. I don't know how to use your website. Can you help me find it?' and (2) 'Where's my book?' So we would walk people through the ordering process: 'Now, you click on this and you click on that; now you type in your credit card, and then click complete.' This was essentially the mundane, repetitive queries via either e-mail or telephone.

Masco noted that, as the customer base evolved from early adopters to the mainstream, "customers would call up and say, 'Okay, I bought my computer, I want to buy books on Amazon. Where do I plug the mouse in?' They purchased a computer just to access Amazon. At that point, we became a helping hand to get onto this technology. If a customer asked for a book, we would not only tell them the book and show them where to find it, but also how they could have searched for it and found it themselves. So we were also teaching. That was another advantage to having so many disenfranchised academics. Many of them were teachers, so it was something that came quite naturally to many of them."

When someone sent a message to Amazon.com, it was lined up—in the order in which it arrived—in a holding tank called a "queue." There was an "order queue" and an "information queue." All new hires started in the "information queue," which consisted of helping to locate books, editions, or authors. As they became more skilled and more conversant with the protocols and the procedures, they advanced to the "orders queue," which dealt with lost or problem orders.

The logic behind this huge personalized customer-service process is driven by the notion that the online shopping experience is impersonal. A customer never sees an Amazon.com employee. The transaction is between the customer and the server that the website is posted on; the customer is interfacing with a search engine and computer-generated forms. There is no human contact that generates loyalty. So the one human point of contact that most people have with a company like Amazon.com is with the customer-service department. Therefore, the customer-service representative must perform above and beyond the call of duty. Amazon.com's attitude was if you're having a problem, we will be not only responsive, but we will respond in a manner that shows our commitment to you, the customer, and your shopping experience on Amazon.com. So customer-service people conducted searches for the books that customers were requesting by e-mail. They would pull up the search results, cut and paste them into an e-mail, and send them back with instructions:

"If you type in the following heading, you will get the book."

Nordal recalled, "You might get a query such as this: 'In 1944, when I was a little girl on a boat from Europe to the United States, fleeing the second World War, I read a book and the main character was named Mary and this is what happened.' That query would then get e-mailed around the department and it was amazing the number of times that people would write back and say, 'you are looking for such and such book.' The level of education and variety of experience of the people who worked there was such that they could identify esoteric books. A lot of the answers to those questions—once they left the realm of the search engine—actually were answered by the expertise of the people who worked there. If you had just hired a bunch of people lesser educated, they wouldn't have found the book. Somebody would write in, 'In the movie *The English Patient*, there is a book that the character is always holding under his arm. What book is that?' Two seconds later, someone would e-mail the answer."

As the company began growing exponentially, Bezos's insistence on virtually instantaneous e-mail responses to customers took its toll on already-overworked customer-service employees. "There was always a feeling that you could work harder. It was a Microsoft attitude," recalled Maire Masco. "I remember Jeff calling me up one day when we were a week-and-a-half behind in answering customer responses. We could keep up with the daily flow, but it was the backlog that was killing us. It was terrible because everybody was working so hard; I don't think anybody was working less than 10 hours a day and everybody was working 12 hours a day, seven days a week, and we had been doing it for three months.

"Jeff said, 'I want people to work harder.'

"I said, 'Jeff, there are only seven days in a week. I can't get people to work any harder. In fact, if I was really smart, I'd send everybody home and tell them to sleep for 24 hours. But I can't.'

"He was quiet for a while. Then he said, 'Okay, what do you think we ought to do?'

"Eventually, we ended up having a contest. At that point, the only motivation we could have was a financial one. Pizza wasn't doing it anymore. The idea was that we were going to take 48 hours in a weekend and empty the queues [of e-mail]. Everybody had to do a minimum of 10 hours that weekend—in addition to their regular shifts. And it was just e-mail. People turned it on. We paid people for the number of messages [they responded to]. Anyone who answered a thousand messages over a 48-hour weekend made $200. So we got caught up and we were good for a couple of months after that."

Although Amazon.com tried to confine customer contact to e-mail, Amazon.com reps did a lot of customer contact via telephone, particularly for matters such as changing passwords and taking credit card numbers for people who were wary of giving them out over the Internet. "We couldn't avoid those phone calls," said Masco. "But e-mail was more efficient for a lot of reasons. You could answer it 24 hours a day. If someone left a message, it could take you three or four attempts to catch that person. With e-mail you can give a timely response."

As Amazon.com developed its customer-service approach, it came up with a carefully crafted database of standard responses or "blurbs" that could be easily modified to personalize answers to customers' inquiries. Some inquiries would be rather esoteric. For example, regarding a series of science fiction books by the same author, customers would ask in what order the books should be read. "That was an example where you wouldn't necessarily know that blurb was there, until you got asked the question; it wasn't part of the regular training," said Masco.

"Probably the most important thing about the blurbs was the consistency," she added. Once, a customer ordered a book early in the day and called up later on in the day to order another book and wanted both books in the same order, but the company couldn't do it. Looking for a way to explain it to the customer, "We came up with a blurb that was very professional, but also a little lighthearted: 'This time we were too fast. Sorry we weren't able to merge your books.' That combination of personable responses and professionalism was one of the strengths of the blurbs. Even though people could add personal information at the end of a message by using one of the blurbs, we were always very consistent and we presented a common face to our customers. On occasion, you would develop personal relationships with customers who, for some reason or another you would have a lot of contact with. With those people, you might take more latitude."

From the beginning, Amazon.com employed customer feedback from e-mail to design the website and maintain a level of customer service. "One of the great things online is that the customers help you figure out what you're doing wrong and how to do things better," said Bezos. "E-mail is this great medium for receiving feedback because somehow e-mail turns off that little piece of everyone's brain that causes them to mostly be polite. . . . With e-mail, people have a certain amount of bravery, so they tell you the truth about your service."

Bezos has publicly cited some examples of how procedures changed from customer feedback. In Amazon.com's first year, it used a packaging method that made the package tougher to open. The company received an e-mail message from an 80-year-old woman, who wrote, "I love your service. I use it all the time. But I do have to wait for my son to come over to open the packages. You need a crowbar to get through your packaging material. Could you do something about this?"

In another instance, an unhappy customer wrote that he had spent hours and hours filling his shopping cart but he wasn't quite ready to purchase the books. There had been no activity on his account for 30 days, and the company had had a policy to clear out the shopping cart after that time period, and his cart was emptied. The customer wrote that he thought this was a stupid policy. "It probably was a stupid policy," said Bezos. "We've changed that. He also thought that at least we should have warned him. He was not polite, I assure you." Amazon.com technicians went back through their database and found the customer's shopping basket in raw data form and sent it to him.

Amazon.com created a culture of helping among its customer service staff. Maire Masco recalled a customer e-mailing the company that she had lost her favorite cookbook. The only description she had was that it had a red cover and was published by the Telephone Pioneers of the United States. "On a lark, I decided to find it," she said. "It became a matter of self-competition to help find books for people who had provided scanty information. Masco searched under "Telephone Pioneers" and "cookbook" and found it. Not only that, it was available from Amazon.com, even though it had been published by a nonprofit organization as a fundraising tool for their group: it had an ISBN number so it was in the catalog.

Masco felt that Amazon.com was making a difference for customers in rural areas that did not have bookstores, or who were ill or housebound. "People would e-mail us about how their world had widened through being able to order books through the Internet," said Masco.

Masco said that the customer-service department, "pounded into people that one of the things that made the Amazon customer-service department different than other customer-service departments was that we really empowered people to make decisions. So if a customer wrote in and said, 'I ordered this book three days ago. I asked for it overnight, and I still haven't gotten it.' There was no question at all that the shipping cost would be refunded. The individual customer-service representatives had it within their power to evaluate the severity of the situation and to make a judgment call."

Often, in the end, it's the small touches that leave the most lasting impression with a customer. Writing in *Customers.com*, Patricia Seybold added this personal note to her Amazon.com experience: "When I unpacked a box of books from Amazon.com last summer, I found a handwritten Post-it note on one of them. It said, 'We know you ordered the softcover version of this book, but it's out of stock, so we sent you the hardcover copy for the same price.' That little handwritten note cemented my love affair with Amazon.com."

That type of feeling is why Bezos has described Amazon.com as not a business about selling things, but rather a business about "helping people make purchase decisions. That is . . . a more customer-centric way of looking at the world. Along the way, we're going to confuse a lot of pundits" who try to describe what the company does. "The closest thing that I can come to is that we're not trying to be a book company or trying to be a music company—we're trying to be a customer company."

TAKEAWAYS

From virtually the very beginning of Amazon.com, customer service was at the forefront of Jeff Bezos's strategy. Taking a page out of the playbook of top customer-service companies, he understood that positive word-of-mouth comments from customers would count for more than any self-serving ads boasting of great customer service. (Anyway, in those early days, he didn't have the money for an advertising campaign.) He also understood that customer service takes in every aspect of the online experience—from the thoroughness and friendliness of the website to the timely arrival of the purchase.

- Commit 100 percent to customer service.
- Emphasize selection, convenience, and price.
- Save your customers time and money.
- Invest the majority of your capital into creating the best possible customer experience.
- Create the perfect context for a purchase decision.
- Add a value proposition to the Web experience.
- Enhance the interactivity of the Web experience.
- Promote a "community" by encouraging feedback from customers.
- You can work long, hard, and well. At Amazon.com, two out of three won't work.
- Make ordering as easy as possible.
- Create an Associates program for adding new customers by extending your community.
- Listen to your customer.
- Commit 100 percent to customer service.

chapter nine

toast of the town . . . or amazon.toast?

I buy books from Amazon.com because time is short and they have a big inventory and they're very reliable.

—Bill Gates,
in a May 30, 1996, interview in
PC Week's online edition

Thanks to customers like the Microsoft CEO, Amazon.com finished 1996, its first full year in business, with net sales of $15.7 million—an attention-getting *3,000* percent jump over 1995's $511,000. The other numbers were equally astounding: Compounded sales growth exceeded 100 percent every quarter, from the first to the fourth. Almost 180,000 customer accounts. Approximately 50,000 visits (not "hits") a day in December compared to 2,200 the year before. More than 40 percent of orders were from repeat customers.

On the other hand, Amazon.com was doing something that Bill Gates never did: hemorrhaging money—$5.8 million in 1996, compared to $303,000 in 1995. Some of that money was spent on recruiting people into the company as quickly as possible—Amazon.com ended 1996 with 151 employees, a 357.6 percent increase in one year. According to its filing with the Securities and Exchange Commission, sales and marketing expenses—online and print advertising, public relations and other promotional expenditures—increased from $200,000 in 1995 to $6.1 million in 1996; and product development expenses (mostly to improve the back-office system) increased from $171,000 in 1995 to $2.3 million in 1996. And why not? If he didn't spend money, how on Earth could Bezos get big fast?

Although Amazon.com's sales of almost $16 million were not even a blip compared to the domestic book-selling industry's $26 *billion*, the company's performance was a sign that commerce on the Web was becoming a trend that could not be ignored.

The timing was perfect.

First of all, there was a greater awareness of the Internet among businesses and consumers, who were benefiting from faster and better-performing personal computers (and modems) at home and work. The network infrastructure was getting better, and it was getting easier and cheaper to gain access to the Internet.

By the end of 1996, approximately 35 million people were using the Web, according to International Data Corporation, which estimated that the total value of goods and services purchased over the Web grew from $318 million in 1995 to $5.4 billion in 1996. More than half of regular Web users held a college degree or higher, and over 62 percent of the worldwide Internet users made at least $40,000 a year. Proof that Amazon.com was appealing to a particularly sophisticated and computer-savvy audience: the top-selling book on Amazon.com in 1996 was *Creating Killer Web Sites: The Art of Third-Generation Site Design* by David Siegel.

At the end of that year, Bezos appeared on *The News Hour*, the PBS television news program, to discuss the impact of the Internet, along with Esther Dyson, editor of the computer newsletter *Release 1.0,* and Clifford Stoll, the astronomer and author of *Silicon Snake Oil: Second Thoughts on the Information Superhighway.* While proclaiming it "a great year for business on the Internet," Bezos likened the state of the medium to the first 10 seconds after the Big Bang, where there is still "a huge amount to come." Conceding that there had been a tremendous amount of hype surrounding the Net, he argued that there was also a lot of substance. He said he was optimistic because the Internet is "ubiquitous," and that "whenever networks start to get ubiquity, that's when they really take off and the growth is always exponential."

With all that potential for growth, it was no wonder that new and increased competition was on its way. From the beginning, many potential investors were concerned about Amazon.com's ability to compete with bigger bricks-and-mortar booksellers. That became a greater concern in January 1997, when Barnes & Noble entered into an agreement to become the exclusive bookseller on America Online, where it would have access to AOL's more than 8 million subscribers. Like Amazon.com, B&N boasted a database of more than 1 million titles, speedy delivery of about half a million books and 30 percent discounts off the cover price of hardcover books—a steeper discount than it offered to customers who shopped in its stores. B&N also announced that it was going to launch its own website in early spring 1997 after hiring a staff of 50.

Around that same time, CUC International, a $2.3 billion consumer-services company, was developing a subscription-based online marketplace called NetMarket, which would sell a wide range of goods, including books, to subscribing members. Several major publishers and retailers had, or were planning to have, Internet sites. Random House Inc. had already been selling books online and in early 1997, Viacom Inc.'s Simon & Schuster unit launched something called "The Super Site." Borders Group Inc., the second biggest U.S. operator of book superstores, was preparing its own online bookstore. Borders had already been operating a tiny book site where customers could order books by sending an e-mail or a fax to a store in Ann Arbor, Michigan, where Borders is based. "We definitely think," said Marilyn D. Slankard, vice president of marketing for Borders, "it is time that Amazon.com had some competition."

Although Barnes & Noble was almost certain to be the next big retailer online, Borders was considered the bigger threat among people inside Amazon.com. "Nobody was worried about Barnes &

Noble launching because we figured they would do a bad job and it would take some time for them to get it right," said Glenn Fleishman. "The impression within Amazon was that Borders had a culture that was most similar to what Amazon's was. They would empower employees, have good people on the frontlines, and divert significant money and data processing resources to it."

Or as Bezos would later say: "Barnes & Noble isn't doing this because they wanted to. They're doing it because of us. That's just a fact."

In anticipation of Barnes & Noble's online launch, Bezos challenged Fleishman to come up with a new feature for Amazon.com's business. "Jeff didn't want a Barnes & Noble 'killer,' but he wanted something that would trump them," recalled Fleishman. Bezos asked Fleishman to create an out-of-print book division. Searching for out-of-print books was not, of course, a new industry, but it was ideal for the Internet. "Suddenly, I had more than 1 million out-of-print titles—or at least some skeleton information about them."

Rather than charge the customer for a search fee, Amazon.com instead marked up the price of the book, and promised customers it would keep looking for the book forever. Today, there are a myriad of Web sites that can search for out-of-print books, but Amazon.com's entry into that category in early 1997 was a signal that the company was going to keep moving ahead and adding new features.

THE INITIAL PUBLIC OFFERING

Amazon.com had to make expansion moves such as adding out-of-print books because Bezos had been spending the last half-year laying the groundwork for an initial public offering. In the summer of 1996, he began meeting informally with investment bankers so that he could learn their different styles and cultures.

But it was the hiring of Joy Covey in December 1996 that really accelerated the efforts. Covey, who said that she joined the company expecting to take it public "as soon as it was ready," spent her first couple of months on the job keeping investment bankers at arm's length while she developed the financial reporting infrastructure and systems required for a public company. By February 1997, with the business performing at a $60 million annually run rate, Covey believed Amazon.com was ready for discussions with the banks.

"While Jeff and I fully understood the benefits of going public, the decision to do so wasn't a no-brainer," said Covey. At the time, Amazon.com really didn't need to go public to raise capital. Although the company had a mere $7 million of cash available, its operating cycle didn't require a tremendous amount of capital. Plus, there was no shortage of investors who were clamoring to privately finance the company. But the lure of the kind of really big money that an IPO would bring in, money that would create a recognizable brand, among other things, was too tempting to pass up.

On the other hand, Bezos and Covey wanted to run a public company on their own terms. That meant, ". . . we were committed to not giving in to the short-term pressures which public companies often feel," said Covey. "We were committed to focusing on the long-term value of the business and on value to our customers, which we believed to be the best approach if we wanted to build an enduring global franchise." This controversial philosophy—sales growth and market share over profits and earnings—would be the Amazon.com mantra over the ensuing years.

In February 1997, Covey solicited proposals from eight leading investment banks that had historic strength in underwriting the public offerings of technology companies: Alex Brown, Deutsche Morgan Grenfell, Goldman Sachs, Hambrecht & Quist, Montgomery Securities, Morgan Stanley, Robertson Stephens, and Smith Barney. She told them, "This is not yet an official bakeoff [the competition to select the underwriter] but we want to meet you on February 26 and 27. Bring your team because we may move quickly when we actually decide to begin our IPO and may not conduct another full round of meetings." As was their wont, Bezos and Covey had no intention of sharing any internal financial numbers. They were, she said, "less concerned about valuation and more about banker quality, judgment, commitment, distribution, and analyst quality."

Covey, who was still living in the Bay Area, met with each of the investment banking teams (including their analysts and brokerage teams) in the Kleiner Perkins Caulfield & Byers offices on Sand Hill Road in Menlo Park, California. Bezos did not take part in the meetings, leaving the responsibility with Covey, because, Covey said, John Doerr had advised them that "the CFO should be the CEO of the going-public process."

She flew up to Seattle the following day and proposed to the board of directors that they choose Deutsche Morgan Grenfell (DMG) to lead the offering, with Hambrecht & Quist and Alex Brown as comanagers. "We decided that we liked DMG's approach," said Covey. "We were entrepreneurial and focused on long-term value and we wanted a bank that shared our approach. We also wanted a bank that had as much to win or lose if our IPO was a success as we did. DMG was a relatively new team and we were their first highly visible lead-managed IPO. We knew we would have their full attention."

Although the DMG team was newly assembled, it was made up of a highly publicized and highly regarded team of technology investment bankers led by managing director Frank Quattrone, who had just joined DMG after a 17-year-career at Morgan Stanley and was considered the John Doerr of technology investment bankers. Quattrone was founder and managing director of Morgan Stanley's Global Technology Investment Banking Group and had advised on over 100 IPOs, common stock and convertible offerings and merger & acquisitions for companies such as 3Com, Adobe, America Online, Apple, Cisco, H-P, and Netscape.

Another DMG star was Internet analyst Bill Gurley, who was picked as a member of the 1995 Institutional Investor all-star research team. In January 1997, Gurley, who writes a column called *Above the Crowd* (currently running in *Fortune* magazine), had vigorously defended

Amazon.com in his biweekly newsletter after *Slate*, Microsoft's online magazine, condemned the company in an article titled "Amazon.*con*." Gurley wrote: "Our fondness for Amazon should not surprise *Above the Crowd*'s long-term readers. After all, we've dedicated many issues of this newsletter to the inherent advantages of the direct PC-distribution channel, and the similarities among Amazon's advantage, and those of Dell and Gateway are strong."

From the beginning, Bezos and Covey saw the IPO "as just another step in our business development process," said Covey. "We saw an opportunity to access the public markets while helping to build our brand."

With supreme confidence in their business plan, they made it abundantly clear to potential investors that they were not going to be concerned about short-term profitability and traditional earnings expectations. Instead, they were going to focus on the long-term view, which meant continual and substantial investment in marketing and promotion, technology, operating infrastructure, and development of the Web site. "We hoped these investments would help us provide more value to customers and enable us to build scale faster," said Covey. "We believed that the right thing for our customers and for the long-term development of the business, and therefore, for our shareholders, was to extend our brand position and achieve sufficient sales volume to realize economies of scale."

Armed with that firm conviction, Bezos and Covey "decided to remain true to our long-term approach and hope that enough investors would agree with our strategic philosophy. We realized that in this evolving space, flexibility would also be very important and expectations drawn too narrowly would be a significant problem."

Although they were not going to share certain financial and competitive numbers, they did share with investment bankers how they approached making decisions and strategic moves. All the risks in the investment were presented in high relief in the prospectus. For example: "The Company believes that it will incur substantial operating losses for the foreseeable future, and that the rate at which such losses will be incurred will increase significantly from current levels."

Is there a clearer way of saying "We intend to lose lots of money for a long time"?

And lose money they did—$2.97 million in the first three months of 1997, for a grand total loss of $9.0 million since Bezos formed the company in mid-1994. But look at the sales numbers! Sales jumped to $16 million in the first quarter of 1997—more than the entire 1996 sales total—and had doubled every quarter for six consecutive quarters. The customer database was up to 340,000 names from over 100 countries. Average daily visits skyrocketed from 2,200 in December 1995 to 80,000 in March 1997 and repeat customers accounted for over 40 percent of orders.

Bezos and Covey had to argue for, and defend, those numbers when they hit the road for their investors road show, an experience Covey described as "brutal." The road show began in late April with a four-city European leg—Zurich, Geneva, Paris, and London—where the pair made nearly five presentations a day for three days to institutional investors. From London, they flew to San Francisco to attend Hambrecht & Quist's Technology Investor Conference, where they schmoozed with dozens of technology investors and analysts, and then onto the domestic leg—48 presentations in 20 U.S. cities in 16 days.

The pair were battered by skeptical investors who challenged the company's very viability as a (yet unproven) business model. What were some of complaints? They are familiar to anyone who follows the company: stiff competition, no profits, and a reluctance on the part of management to divulge strategic details.

Beyond Amazon.com itself, there was one other potentially thorny issue in early 1997: a sudden weakness in the IPO market for technology companies. This was a marked contrast to the previous 24 months, which saw several successful IPOs for Internet-related companies such as Netscape's in 1995 and Yahoo!'s in 1996. In the first half of 1996, a record 104 technology companies went public, raising about $8.6 billion. By comparison, in the first four months of 1997 a mere 40 technology companies went public, raising $1.2 billion, and the only three Internet companies in that group took in $52 million. New issues were hurt in March by the poor showing of public Internet companies, most of which were trading below their offering prices. Auto-By-Tel, the online car and truck shopping service, which was a highly visible Internet commerce company, had pulled its offering at the end of March, rather than accept a lower valuation.

As Covey flew home from London after her European tour was over, she opened up a copy of the *Financial Times* and was greeted with the headline: "Investors Skeptical on Internet Flotations," which included this comment from a U.S. analyst: "*Wired* fell out of bed, Auto-By-Tel didn't pop, and even with Amazon.com's top tier investment bankers, I think they'll have trouble selling the book."

Wrong. Bezos and Covey ignored the weak market by sticking to their investment plan and maintaining "the confidentiality of many metrics of our business despite inquiries by investors," said Covey. "They wanted to know details on customer mix, repeat buyer patterns, and successful marketing programs. We understand why investors are interested in these metrics—they are important underpinnings to our business model." Despite Amazon.com's reluctance to show a little more skin, Bezos and Covey were able to convince investors that Amazon.com would be a better investment if they kept that information proprietary for competitive and strategic reasons. Investors were understanding—and buying into—the company's long-term investment strategy. In fact, Frank Quattrone, Amazon.com's investment banker at lead underwriter Deutsche Morgan Grenfell, had told Bezos that he had never witnessed such a strongly attended road show presentation. (Quattrone later became head of the Credit Suisse First Boston technology group.)

Investors' positive reception to her candor was "really a relief to me," said Covey, who believed that her experience in helping to bring

DigiDesign public had "helped inform my perspective" on Amazon.com's IPO. "I had learned a key bit of advice from Roger McNamee [a well-known growth-company investor, who is a general partner at Integral Capital Partners]. Roger told me, 'You don't have to convince everyone of your story on day one—only enough to complete the IPO. Make the right choices for your long-term strategy.' "

Amazon.com was expected to offer 2.5 million shares of common stock at $12 to $14 each, but the road show had been going well and the offering was already oversubscribed. Eric Dillon recalled that Bezos was in New York discussing share prices with the people at DMG. After a long session, Bezos excused himself and went out to take a walk on the streets of Manhattan. While strolling down the street, he called Dillon on his cell phone. This is how Dillon remembered the conversation:

Bezos: "Eric, I know our offering is going very well. These guys want me to do this deal at $17. What should I do?"

Dillon: "Tell them that it's $20."

Bezos: "I can't go that high."

Dillon: "Tell them that it's 19."

Bezos: "Eric, I *knew* you were going to say this . . . I'm going to tell them 18 or nothing."

Eighteen dollars a share would be the initial offering price.

"That was a fun piece of the IPO," said Dillon. "I could picture Jeff, as giddy as he could be, walking around the streets of New York." And as he strolled down midtown Manhattan streets, Bezos didn't realize it, but he was about to get mugged—by Barnes & Noble.

On May 12, 1997, B&N unveiled plans for its own Internet site, Barnesandnoble.com, which, it claimed, was "designed as the preeminent Web destination for book lovers worldwide," and would feature partnerships with Microsoft Corp. and Hewlett-Packard Co., among others.

On that same day, three days before Amazon.com's IPO, and a couple of days before it launched its *own* website, B&N sued Amazon.com in federal court in Manhattan. B&N, which was about to bill itself as "The World's Largest Bookseller Online," charged that Amazon.com had falsely claimed in its ads and on its website to be "Earth's Biggest Bookstore," when, in fact, Amazon.com was not "a bookstore at all. . . . It is a book broker making use of the Internet exclusively to generate sales to the public." The suit challenged Amazon.com's claim that it "offers over one million titles, more than five times as many titles as you'll find in even the largest Barnes & Noble" was false because, "Amazon's warehouse in Seattle stocks only a few hundred titles. . . . Barnes & Noble stocks more books than Amazon and there is no book that Amazon can obtain which Barnes & Noble cannot."

The suit, which also sought unspecified damages, called for Amazon.com to immediately cease running its ads and issue new "corrective" ads. B&N further claimed that on January 28, 1997, it "demanded that Amazon cease and desist from making these false and misleading claims. To date Amazon has refused to do so." (Interestingly, in the light of Barnes & Noble's claim that Amazon.com was not a bookstore, Bezos said in 1999 that, "when we first started Amazon.com, we had very conscious discussions where we talked about the fact that we were not a bookstore, but we were a book service. I do think that is a better way to think about it. Thinking of yourself as a store is too limiting. Services can be anything.")

"I remember laughing about this stuff with Jeff," Nick Hanauer recalled. "We were like 'You're afraid of *us*?' " They were still laughing when, that May, Internet pundit George Colony, the CEO of Forrester Research, looked at the B&N competition and declared the company "Amazon.*toast*."

Colony's assessment aside, the company went public on May 15, 1997 with an opening price of $18 a share. Thirty-three-year-old Jeff Bezos, who held 9.88 million shares, was suddenly worth, on paper, $177.8 million. This was less than three years after coming to Seattle. And he sold only 10 percent of the company. He personally held 42 percent of the company; his family—father Miguel, mother Jacklyn, brother Mark S. Bezos, sister Christina Bezos Poore, and the Gise family trust—owned 10 percent, giving the Bezoses approximately 52 percent of the outstanding voting power of the company.

After five days of trading, the stock hit a high of $30, before tumbling below $18, when short-term investors began unloading it. On the fifth day of trading, 1.5 million shares—or half the traded shares—changed hands. By the end of 1997, Amazon.com stock soared 235 percent to $52 a share. It was the beginning of a roller-coaster ride for a stock that would be simultaneously lauded and reviled. (For more on reactions, see chapter 10.) Whatever the case, for Jeff Bezos, a guy who made an annual salary of $64,333, 1997 was less than half over, but it was already a pretty good year.

He wasn't the only one profiting from Amazon.com stock. Kleiner Perkins Canfield & Byers held an 11 percent stake in Amazon.com through a pair of its funds, and the preferred stock that Kleiner received in the previous year's venture capital transaction was converted to more than 3 million common shares in the IPO. Those shares were later distributed to the funds' limited partners, including Intel chairman Andrew Grove, Sun Microsystem's chief Scott McNealy, America Online's chief Stephen Case, Lotus Development founder Mitchell Kapor, @Home chief Thomas Jermoluk, cable TV magnates Ralph and Brian Roberts, and former publisher William R. Hearst III.

THE WAR HEATS UP

Amid the volumes of lawsuits, an online price war broke out. Barnesandoble.com began offering 30 percent off hardcovers and 20 percent off paperbacks. In June, Amazon.com extended the discount rate to at least 20 percent on softcover books, at least 30 percent on hardcover books, and 40 percent on selected books.

"We've always offered the biggest selection, and with these prices, Amazon.com offers the lowest everyday book prices anywhere in the world—online or off," proclaimed Bezos, who was now fully engaged in the PR war. He had decided early on that, "we weren't going to let [Barnes & Noble's] purchasing power get in the way. So we were going to fund any purchasing-power difference. We would have the same prices, no matter if our margins were lower. And we would adopt the strategy of 'get big fast,' so that we could eventually level the playing field in terms of purchasing power."

In his public utterances, Bezos was constantly drawing distinctions between Amazon.com's purely online business and the B&N and Borders hybrid of virtual and physical stores. "First of all, they [Barnes & Noble and Borders] are completely separate businesses," Bezos said at the time. "I wouldn't want to manage one physical bookstore because we don't know how to do that. I think that one of the huge advantages we're going to have is our ability to focus. We're going to be focused exclusively on selling books online, whereas Borders and Barnes & Noble are going to have to worry about two things: They're going to have to figure out how to sell books in the physical world [as if they hadn't figure that out already], which is a hard thing to do by itself, and they're going to have to figure out how to do a great job of selling books online." And, to add a little more insult, he said: "Frankly, I'm more concerned about two guys in a garage."

In August, Amazon.com showed it could play hardball, too. Filing a countersuit against Barnes & Noble in federal court in New York, Amazon.com claimed that B&N was engaged in unfair competition by neglecting to charge sales taxes on books sold over barnesandnoble.com. The gist of the argument was this: Online retailers, like mail-order catalog companies, were not obligated to charge state sales taxes on purchases except when the transactions were with customers who lived in states where the retailer actually had a physical presence. (That's why only residents of the state of Washington are charged state sales tax when they purchase items from Amazon.com.) In its lawsuit, Amazon.com claimed B&N should be required to charge sales taxes to residents of every one of the 48 states where B&N has a store because, the argument went, those stores charge sales taxes. By neglecting to charge those taxes, Amazon.com claimed, Barnes & Noble is "able to charge significantly less than required by law" and is thus obtaining an "unlawful advantage" over Amazon.com.

Thankfully, all that litigious silliness was over by October, when the two sides settled both their lawsuits out of court, with neither admitting any wrongdoing, and neither paying damages. The companies announced they "simply decided that they would rather compete in the marketplace than in the courtroom."

And compete they did. In the fall of 1997, B&N started an Affiliate Network program (a copy of Amazon.com's Associate program) that used commissions and other incentives to enable customers who visit an associate's website to buy books at a discount. B&N announced they had signed up 30 members. By that time, Amazon.com already had 15,000 members in its Associate program, which began in July 1996. "We've been expecting Barnes & Noble to do something like this," sniffed Shawn Haynes, product manager for Amazon.com's Associate program. "We were wondering what was taking them so long."

With B&N flexing its muscles, some in the financial and investment community were preparing for Amazon.com's fall. A lengthy story in *Fortune*'s September 29, 1997, issue was headlined: Why Barnes & Noble May Crush Amazon. Unfortunately, the story showed a fundamental misunderstanding of what it took to be a successful Internet retailer. The author assumed that, "All one needs, it would seem, is a website to present the face that greets customers and takes their orders. Other parties handle the capital-intensive aspects of stocking inventory," and added that "Anything Amazon.com can do on the Internet, so, too, can Barnes & Noble." To which Steve Riggio added: "There was a mystique about how difficult it was to get started on the Web, but it's quickly fading." The article went on to describe how B&N had hired "hot designers from Silicon Valley" to create "a Web shopfront that's just as inviting and useful as Amazon's."

Transcending the websites, *Fortune* said that B&N could get books to customers (a) faster, because it had a greater depth of on-hand inventory as well as long-time direct dealings with publishers, and (b) cheaper, because it gets the best prices from publishers.

Publicly, Bezos was unperturbed. While conceding that Barnesandnoble.com could technically duplicate what Amazon.com had achieved, he felt that the more pertinent question was: "Can Amazon.com establish a world-class brand name before Barnesandnoble.com buys, builds, acquires, or learns the competencies they need to be excellent online retailers?"

Throughout the rest of 1997, B&N kept the pressure on. In October Barnesandnoble.com became the exclusive online bookseller on some of Microsoft's busiest Internet sites—including MSNBC, Expedia, and the Microsoft Investor personal-finance site. Barnesandnoble.com entered into a four-year, $40 million marketing relationship with AOL, which allowed Barnesandnoble.com to place advertising and promotions throughout a myriad of AOL sites, including financial, travel, and entertainment.

But Amazon.com had multiyear exclusive agreements with virtually every heavily trafficked website, including Yahoo!, Excite, Netscape, GeoCities, Alta Vista, @Home, Prodigy, and, most important—for $19 million (more if it exceeded sales quotas)—AOL.com. (Barnes & Noble's agreement was with AOL's proprietary network; not AOL.com.) As a part of the search engines of those portals, when a customer searched for a topic—any topic—the results page would include an Amazon.com logo and suggestions for books on that subject. At the time, Robert Pittman, president of AOL Networks, likened these and other agreements to a "land-grab period and this is Malibu real estate."

Bezos said he didn't have a problem with revenue-sharing: "If we were giving away a large fraction of our revenue, I'd be worried, but we're not." AOL.com was important for Amazon.com to get home users, and Yahoo! and Excite to attract at-work users.

The challenge by Barnes & Noble didn't slow down Amazon.com. By September, the number of customer accounts increased by 54 percent, to 940,000, according to the company's third-quarter financial report. In October 1997, customer Number 1,000,000 was a Japanese consumer who ordered a Windows NT book and a biography of Princess Diana. Bezos, the master of public relations hype, flew to Japan to deliver the books personally. By the end of the year, customer accounts jumped by 738 percent from 180,000 to 1,510,000, on a 838 percent growth in revenue, from $15.7 million to $147.8 million. The losses were almost as impressive, soaring from a piddling $5.8 million to a robust $27.6 million.

B&N wasn't interested in an escalating spending war. Steve Riggio said: "We don't want to win a Pyrrhic victory" by losing money on the online operation.

PUBLISHERS TAKE NOTICE

Publishers, who were in the midst of a two-year downturn in sales and an avalanche of returned books, began noticing that Amazon.com was becoming one of their largest customers, and possibly the solution to their doldrums. At that time, about 38 percent of all books shipped from publishers were eventually returned as unsold merchandise—compared to less than 4 percent returned from Amazon.com.

Amazon.com made a big splash in 1997 at BookExpo America, the annual trade show and convention of the American Booksellers Association. With independent booksellers suing several publishers for alleged antitrust violations, most of the publishers had dropped out of the event. Nevertheless, the independent booksellers made a major stand of supporting the show and putting their muscle behind it. When they arrived at the exhibition hall, they saw that every advertising banner at the end of each aisle had been bought by Amazon.com (for a total of a mere $10,000.) The independents were not pleased that the producers of the show had allowed that kind of exposure for a company that was shaping up as their most serious competitor. To add insult to injury, hordes of Amazonians—led by Bezos himself—each dressed in khakis and logoed red shirts—roamed the aisles as walking advertisements.

Before 1997 was over, almost every major publishing executive had made the pilgrimage from the canyons of Manhattan to the Amazon.com offices, with their coffee-stained carpets, dingy walls, funky door desks and not-so-state-of-the-art warehouse. Michael Lynton, the chief executive of Penguin Putnam, came. So did Alberto Vitale of Random House, Jack Romanos of the consumer group at Simon & Schuster, and John Sargent of St. Martin's Press. Everyone of them realized that Amazon.com could generate steady sales of older titles, midlist, and backlist books; and that its online community could generate word-of-mouth book recommendations. (A portion of that online community showed publishers their literary bent in the summer of 1997, when Amazon.com ran a writing "contest," where users were asked to contribute sentences or paragraphs for use in a murder mystery entitled "Murder Makes the Magazine." Author John Updike wrote the first and last lines, 400,000 people e-mailed contributions to complete it with their own sentences. Each week for six weeks a preliminary winner was selected and earned $1,000 in prize money. A grand prize of $100,000 was given to a winner selected at random. The contest received wonderful publicity in the *New York Times* and other national publications.)

Sargent said his interest was initially piqued when Amazon.com customers wrote rave reviews for a St. Martin's book called *Behind the Scenes at the Museum*, a first novel by British author Kate Atkinson. Those readers increased sales for the paperback version of the novel by 300 percent.

After Michael Lynton toured the Amazon.com facilities, he told the *New York Times* that he could see online commerce "being an enormous benefit to the business because it's not about selling more big, best-selling authors. It's about selling our backlist, and it's very rare that opportunity comes along."

Publishers found that online customers commonly favor older backlist titles and less well known authors rather than traditional besselling authors. Romanos said that in November of 1997, Amazon.com customers purchased at least one copy of 84 percent of Simon & Schuster's 10,000-title backlist, and 90 percent of the Penguin Group's 15,000-book backlist. "It's hugely significant," said Romanos. "It floored me when I saw it. We look at these books sometimes and wonder sometimes why we have them all, and this is really affirmation out there of why we do."

Kent Carroll of the New York publishing house Carroll and Graf saw the impact Amazon.com had when in 1989 he republished the 40th anniversary edition of *Endurance,* Alfred Lansing's telling of Sir Ernest Shackleton's tragic expedition to Antarctica in 1914. One year, *Endurance* sold about 8,100 copies in bookstores, but another 7,100 through Amazon.com. The book continued to sell, thanks to a growing Amazon.com customer base and a growing number of favorable reviews by Amazon customers. Amazon is "not just fulfilling demand, it's creating it," said Carroll.

But publishers were *particularly* interested in all that detailed information on 1 million customers (and their ordering history) that Amazon.com was accumulating. "Amazon is creating a database that doesn't exist anywhere else," said Alberto Vitale. But Bezos was chary of outraging his customers by selling information on them; he knew that such a move would immediately destroy the sense of community that he was assiduously trying to build.

To reduce its reliance on Ingram, Amazon.com began doing more of its own distribution. By enlarging the Seattle warehouse by 70 percent and leasing a 202,000 square foot distribution center in New Castle, Delaware, the company increased its warehouse capacity sixfold, which enabled it to stock 200,000 to 300,000 titles and to buy the bulk of its books direct from publishers, which was a cost savings. With distribution centers on both coasts, Amazon.com could dramatically reduce the time between taking the order and delivery in the customer's mailbox.

To take the reins of the burgeoning distribution system, Amazon.com in August 1997 hired Richard Dalzell, one of the most highly respected people in the business as vice president and chief information officer. For the last seven years, he had worked for Wal-Mart Stores, where he held several management positions, including vice president in the information systems division. Prior to Wal-Mart, he was business development manager for E-Systems, Inc.; seven years before he was a teleprocessing officer in the United States Army.

When a company hires the chief IS guy at Wal-Mart, you know that they have some big plans. "Amazon needed someone whose experience went deep both in the vendor and customer side," said Glenn Fleishman. "They had gotten by with what they had early on. But it didn't conform with the textbook version of retail systems."

Nicholas Lovejoy, who worked directly for Dalzell, said the West Point graduate "brought something to the table that Amazon hadn't seen—which was a manager who trusted his employees to know more about what they did than he knew. He gets more out of his troops because he relies on them. Rick is driven, but he's more driven to do a good job. You don't want to be on the wrong side of Rick because he will win. If you were trying to negotiate a contract with Amazon, you dealt with Rick. He was tough."

Dalzell was certainly a great catch for Amazon.com (and one that would make Wal-Mart Stores stand up and take notice). Another was vice president George T. Aposporos, who was hired in May 1997 to form strategic relationships. Aposporos had been founder and president of Digital Brands, a strategic consulting and interactive marketing firm with a client list that included Starbucks Coffee, Sybase, and American Express.

These moves were all part of Bezos's slow, steady formation of a management team that had the depth and ability to reach the heights that he dreamed of. Some executives who didn't get with the plan were pushed out. Building a strong group was clearly a concern to Bezos, who believed that by the end of 1997 his company had arrived at an "inflection point." Up until then, most of the risk had been external, "where we needed a huge amount of luck to get where we are now," he said. That had changed to where most of the risk was internal "execution risk. . . . Now, all we need is a clear, consistent vision and the ability to execute on it very, very well at high speed." Amazon.com's future success was going to come "from having large numbers of talented employees with lots of executive bandwidth to help guide them. . . . We have built a great management team and a group of people underneath that. And if you look at companies like Microsoft, that's the main way that they've won, too. They don't just have Bill Gates, they have 40 people at the top of that company who are smart and dedicated and hardworking. And if you look down below that incredibly deep executive team, they have more people who are waiting in the wings to take on that responsibility. So we are trying to build that kind of team at Amazon.com."

And as he was building up his management team, Bezos was also creating his public image. As we will see, the selling of Jeff Bezos was another essential element of the Amazon.com strategic plan.

TAKEAWAYS

As Bezos added a new, more experienced layer of management, he, with the help of Chief Financial Officer Joy Covey, mapped out a strategy for taking the company public. Strongly backed by venture capitalists and sought after by other private investors, Amazon.com did not immediately need to have an initial public offering and was able to operate from strength. Bezos was confident enough in Covey to let her take the lead with investment bankers. While all that was going on, Amazon.com was preparing for the onslaught of competition. People continued to join either one of two camps: either you thought Amazon.com was the toast of the town or it was "Amazon.toast."

- Always brace for the competition and be ready to strike back.
- Continually add new, fresh features.
- Work to build an enduring global franchise.
- Use a major portion of investment money to help build that global brand.
- If you have the financial backing, don't be concerned with short-term profitability.
- Strive to make your online business scalable for eventual cost-savings and profits.
- Fight the price war if you've got the financial ammunition.
- Continue to increase your bandwidth of talented managers.

chapter ten

poster child for internet commerce

A leader is a dealer in hope.

—Napoleon Bonaparte

Great leaders are great communicators," said John Doerr. "They have incredible integrity: they're usually the first to recognize problems. They're ruthlessly, absolutely intellectually honest. They are great recruiters: They're always building their network of talented people. And they're great sales executives: They're always selling the value proposition of the enterprise."

Although he wasn't specifically discussing Jeff Bezos, Doerr's words were an apt description of the Amazon.com CEO, particularly when it comes to recruiting and communicating. "One of the things that Jeff understood intuitively, very, very early, was that there were two important things for him to work on: recruiting and press," said Nick Hanauer. "To this day, I think that's what he puts most of his energy into. From the day he opened the doors, Jeff knew what they had to become: *the poster child for Internet commerce.* We used that term a lot. And he knew that the first [well-known Web retailer] would be [the poster child for Internet commerce]. There wouldn't be two; there would be one."

He was correct. The Amazon.com story is a convergence of vision, intelligence, technology, money, and timing, but none of those elements would have mattered without Jeff Bezos's engaging personality, which was sold to the public and the investment community through one of the greatest and cleverest public relations campaigns in modern business history. Ever since the beginning of the company, Bezos masterfully played the public relations tune. Even when the company has had bad press, they've always been able to quickly stop the bleeding. Today, there are plenty of other e-commerce billionaire wunderkinds, who are much more successful—Michael Dell and Steve Case come to mind—but Bezos is probably the best known among the general public. How many people could pick Yahoo! cofounders Jerry Yang and David Filo, Netscape founder Marc Andreessen, or eBay's Meg Whitman out of a lineup?

Here's a sampling of some of the media's glowing descriptions of Bezos:

- "A whiz-kid programmer . . . unassuming." —*Wall Street Journal*
- "Bezos handles success well. A genuinely nice guy who's kept his sense of humor in the face of intense pressure. Also one of the smartest guys in the business." —*Forbes*
- "A personable leader with a penchant for eating a burrito on the run between meetings and working behind a desk." —*Seattle Times*
- "With a genial manner, he seems an unlikely E-commerce mogul. Yet he has made almost no visible missteps since he conceived the idea." —*Business Week*
- "It's almost impossible to be in the same room with Bezos and not have a good time. He's relaxed, he's funny, and he's disarmingly humble." —*Fortune*
- "1998 Digital Man of the Year." —*Time Digital Magazine*
- "Unquestionably, king of cybercommerce." —*Time*

Like many public figures, he has created an alternate persona (a variation on fact) that serves him well. His creation of Jeff Bezos, the self-possessed, self-proclaimed nerd with the manic laugh and the easy smile is an instantly likable character with few pretensions and a seeming absence of ego. The flip side of that is ruthless, competitive Jeff Bezos, the pioneering Sam Walton of the World Wide Web, who can expound upon the intricacies of the business with the clear-eyed calculations of a CPA, and wax poetic about the promise of the future with the passion of a visionary.

Alex Gove, an editor at the *Red Herring*, recalled that the first time he met Bezos was when Jeff was making the rounds of publications to promote his new company. "When companies come in here for the first time, many times they have a PR person who is running interference," said Gove. "You can oftentimes tell how confident a company is by the number of people that it brings with it. The fewer people, the more confident the CEO usually is. Jeff came alone. He didn't have a presentation per se. I think he had printed PowerPoint slides. But he didn't have any theatrics. He was definitely self-possessed. He was just a humble entrepreneur, who nonetheless really believed in what he was doing. I remember thinking, 'Boy, that's an amusing little company.' "

The May 16, 1996, story in the *Wall Street Journal* was just the beginning of the complete media treatment for Bezos and Amazon.com. By the end of that year, the company was the subject of a major feature in *Fortune* magazine under the title: "The Next Big Thing: A Bookstore?" *Time* magazine rated Amazon.com one of the "10 Best Websites of 1996." And that treatment was just an appetizer. By 1998, he was garnering the kind of publicity reserved for luminaries such as Bill Gates (before Microsoft's antitrust trial), Jack Welch of GE, and Michael Dell.

But those people run companies that make money. Jeff Bezos, on the other hand, was creating a company that was deferring profits in an effort to—as he often said—change the world. That's why, when it comes to company finances, he keeps his cards close to his vest. Asked once for an estimate of how much longer he could run the business at a loss while keeping up rapid expansion, he answered: "We don't make external projections about profitability, breakeven, etc.—we don't make any forward-looking projections." He's happier giving answers like this: "Profits are the lifeblood of a company but not the reason to exist. You don't live for your blood, but you couldn't live without it. We were profitable for about an hour in December 1995, but it was probably a big mistake."

That same PR machine was fired up to sell chief financial officer Joy Covey in the first quarter of 1999, when she was criss-crossing the country, selling stock analysts and investors on the Amazon.com strategy, which included big sales and big losses now in exchange for big sales and big profits later. A March 25, 1999, lengthy feature on Covey in the *Wall Street Journal* came out virtually the same day as a business profile/personal feature (with a half-page color photo) in *Forbes*. Six months later, Covey was selected by *Fortune* as the 28th most powerful woman in American business, citing her feat of "convincing Wall Street that a profitless company was worth $22 billion."

Bezos and his advisors realized early on how effective he could be as the company point man. The first proof, Eric Dillon recalled, came after Bezos gave an entertaining interview with a Japanese public television station, and Amazon.com immediately began receiving a spate of orders from Japan. "We said, 'This is powerful. Jeff, you've just become our spokesman.' We had to do this because we're in the consumer branding business. That's why we spent time early on with Wall Street analysts who told media [about Bezos and the company] and Jeff started getting tons of publicity right away," said Dillon.

But he wasn't a natural. Former employee Dana Brown noticed that Bezos's presentation skills become "even smoother as he went through the IPO process. That's when he really became more of a speaker. We saw him learning those skills. He must have gone through a speaking class that told him to pause at particular moments. He would take these long pauses between sentences. He eventually got over that and become more natural at it. He was learning as he went along."

Paul Barton-Davis, employee number two, noted, "Jeff is good at making it sound as if he's bearing his soul, that he's telling you what's really going on. It may sound as if you're being told the honest truth, but this is still all part of the big plan. I don't want to be pejorative. I don't think that what Jeff is doing is necessarily a bad thing. I think everybody does it and it is part of the strategy. He's out there using every tool that he has."

Glenn Fleishman observed that, "There is a Jeff façade that he puts out to the world. The person behind it is not that different. There is a little more steel in his business stance. He is putting all of his energy into the business and what he has left, he tries to reserve something for himself."

Bezos has since become one of the major symbols of the new tycoon. In late 1999, *Forbes* ran an article on the "Burning Man" festival, a testosterone-fueled get-together of engineers, software developers, digital artists, lawyers, and professors in the Nevada desert, which Bezos attended. In a sidebar to the story that compared Burning Man with Bohemian Grove (the long-standing pow-wow of industrialists, politicians, and the like), David Rockefeller was identified as the quintessential Bohemian Grove attendee; for Burning Man it was Jeff Bezos.

An article in *Forbes ASAP* about the best speakers in the tech world singled out for praise both Bezos and Dell, who "may not have the years of experience of Intel's Andy Grove, but they have gained fame speaking their minds on e-commerce and direct selling. Bezos has become famous for his hearty laugh and enlightening speeches."

That laugh; that now-legendary laugh. "Explosive," said *Business Week*; "an infectious, gulp-from-the-throat laugh," wrote *Fortune*; "a long, extended bray, startling the uninitiated," waxed *Wired*; "It's a Tourette-like AHHHH ha ha ha ha bray," wrote *Newsweek*; "A rapid honk that sounds like a flock of Canadian geese on nitrous oxide," trumpeted *Time*. "His laugh is a whole-body noise that his mother says 'starts at his little toe and works its way up,'" said the *Seattle Times*. "In fact, he laughs so frequently it seems trained more to his internal sense of rhythm than to the conversation at hand."

For those of us who have heard it in person, it is a laugh that is disconcerting in its depth and intensity. It is a laugh with its own persona; a laugh so amused by itself that it seems to be laughing at itself, almost apart from Bezos himself.

The laugh quickly became an important symbol in the Amazon.com culture. When employees heard it braying out from Bezos's office, "you knew he was back in town," said Fleishman. "We joked that when we got RealAudio [on the website], the first thing we should put on is Jeff's laugh."

Scott Lipsky, who worked in the office next door to Bezos, said, "There was always a certain comfort in hearing him laugh, especially during the heavy growth phase, which was difficult. It was nice knowing that he was there and that he was as involved as you were. That's part of his being the soul of the company. His laugh is as much the soul as he himself is."

To add to that "nice guy" persona, Bezos takes enjoyment out of poking fun at himself. At the company's Masquerade Ball, he once came dressed as a butler. Holding a trick tray that had empty champagne glasses glued to it, he danced the night away with his wife, Mackenzie, who was dressed, appropriately, as a maid.

Another part of the Bezos mystique is his nerdiness. As proof that he's a nerd, he will point to his wristwatch, which updates itself from the atomic clock 36 times a day. His uniform is always the same: button-down powder blue oxford shirt with tan slacks. The only thing missing is a pocket protector. He and his father, mother, brother, and sister like to pretend to be Navy SEALs by outfitting themselves with small mobile, talk-about radios with ear pieces and lapel microphones, and make a run to the grocery store for a quart of milk as furtive as a night attack on the Vietcong. "It's very, very goofy," said the man who also carries a vibrating e-mail pager, cell phone, ELPH camera, and a state-of-the-art two-inch-thick Swiss Army knife with esoteric features such as a fish scaler, miniscrewdriver to repair sunglasses, and a tiny ballpoint pen.

His tiny glassed-in office in the Second Avenue building was a mishmash of books, a yellow rubber duck, Lego, water machine guns, a carton of bottled water, and a spray-painted sign that read "amazon.com," which Bezos created on the spot as a visual backdrop for a Japanese television video crew. On a PBS *Newshour*, he and economic correspondent Paul Solman amused themselves (and presumably the viewing audience) by throwing sticky rubber objects that were supposed to adhere to the wall, as Bezos's laugh punctuated each toss.

In the most skeptical profile of Amazon.com, writer Peter DeJonge captured Bezos perfectly in the *New York Times Magazine*, calling Bezos a "brilliant, charming, hyper and misleadingly goofy mastermind." DeJonge noted that Bezos understood the value of creating an entrepreneurial mythology that fed into the mystique—the cross-country road trip to Seattle, the creation of the company in a garage. Always mindful of symbolism, his door desk was emblematic of his frugality, and was mentioned in virtually every major media profile. Typical was this assessment by writer Dinesh D'Souza: "Many of today's billionaires seem fanatically determined to appear middle class. Bill Gates likes to be seen in his oversize sweater, Jeffrey Bezos sits at a ramshackle desk he made from an old door."

In the early days the frugality extended to his personal life. When he and Mackenzie moved out of their rented house in Bellevue, they rented a modest 900-square-foot apartment in downtown Seattle's Belltown neighborhood, an easy walk to the company's offices in Seattle. Even after he became a multibillionaire, he continued to drive a Honda Accord.

But beyond the media hype and symbolism, Bezos can back up his grand plan with a brilliant multitasking intellect. "He just shifts gears immediately and he drills right into complex technological issues," said Eric Dillon, who added that Bezos always enjoys himself throughout the process. "He can turn to his right and talk to Shel Kaphan about code; then turn to his left and talk to David Risher about marketing in the Netherlands; and then turn straight ahead and talk to Joy Covey about footnote number 82 in a financial statement. The whole time, there's a laugh on every one of them. It's upbeat."

Although Bezos is a short, slight, balding figure, he does possess what can only be described as (even though I hate the word) *charisma*. He's personable and charming with an engaging intellect and the ability to completely focus in on the person he's talking to. "He could be a cult leader (some might say he already is); he has an aura," said Fleishman. "He doesn't give the impression of dominance, but he has an enormous amount of personal power in every aspect."

As a manager, Bezos is "very focused and determined," said director Tom Alberg. "He is able to make quick decisions and follow through and implement them. He recognizes that if we're going to do it, we've got to do it and do it fast. There's a fair amount of analysis in all this, but very action-oriented. If he has an idea he can force it through." As an example, Alberg cited the decision in July 1998 to add a feature to the book listings that listed the rankings of books (based on sales over the previous 24 hours), which would change every hour. "Everybody thought it was silly. Jeff said, 'We can do it in 48 hours. I want it done. Let's do it,' " said Alberg. The rankings drew a tremendous amount of publicity, particularly op-ed page features in the *Wall Street Journal* and the *New York Times* by authors bemoaning their book's position in the rankings. Today, there is many an author and editor who check the ranking of their book on Amazon.com several times a day.

EUROPEAN EXPANSION

Bezos had always wanted to expand Amazon.com's physical presence beyond the borders of the United States. In 1998, he contemplated expanding into Europe with the help of Bertelsmann AG, the German media colossus. Bertelsmann already had a fledgling online bookselling service called Bertelsmann Online or BOL. Thomas Middlehoff, the CEO of Bertelsmann, was so persistent in his pursuit that he flew Bezos from Turkey (where Jeff and Mackenzie were vacationing) on his corporate jet to Bertelsmann headquarters in Germany. Middlehoff was interested in setting up a deal where each company would have a 50 percent ownership of an online bookselling company. Bezos and Middlehoff ended up meeting four times, but "we just couldn't make it work," said Bezos. Middlehoff believed Bezos backed out because he was "nervous about giving up control." Tom Alberg agreed, saying, ultimately, "Jeff made the decision not to do it, based on thinking we could do it as well on our own."

Not long after Bezos rejected the offer, Bertelsmann announced that it was shelling out $200 million for a 50 percent interest in Barnesandnoble.com. "This venture has one purpose—to compete with Amazon in the U.S.," said Middlehoff.

By that time, Amazon.com had acquired (in April 1998) Bookpages, a British electronic bookstore that provided access to all 1.2 million books in print in Britain, and Telebuch (Telebook) Inc., a major online book store in Germany. Bookpages was founded in late 1996 by Simon Murdoch, a Ph.D. in computer science and a software manager with a British firm. Telebook, which was operated by ABC Bucherdienst, cataloged nearly 400,000 German-language books. The were renamed Amazon.co.uk. and Amazon.co.de respectively, and relaunched in October, complete with all the Amazon.com features and technology, and their own in-country customer-service centers. Distribution centers, which warehoused a large supply of the most popular U.S. titles, were set up in Slough, England, and Regensburg, Germany.

By the end of the 1998, Amazon.co.uk and Amazon.co.de were the leading online booksellers in their respective markets. Of course, they didn't represent particularly big numbers. For example, Amazon's U.K. sales were estimated to be about £60 million, while overall Internet shopping in the U.K. represented less than 0.2 percent of all retail sales, according to a study in the *Financial Times.* At the time, the number of people in the entire continent of Europe connected to the Internet was less than half the number in the United States. Germany, with its 80 million people (and 8 million Internet users), represented a particular challenge because retailers in that country are protected by legislation that prohibits discounting. On the other hand, Amazon.co.de. was a 24/7 operation, while German bricks-and-mortar retailers are forbidden by law to be open on Sundays. (Before the official launch of the website, German consumers were teased by an advertising campaign with lines like "Kama Sutra around the clock.")

Even before its beachheads in Europe, Amazon.com and other online booksellers were threatening the time-honored practice of territorial marketing and publishing rights. Generally, an American publisher will own North American or English-speaking rights for a book and will sell foreign publishing rights to individual publishers in individual countries. But the Internet has no national boundaries. The publication of *Harry Potter and the Chamber of Secrets*, the sequel to the international bestseller, *Harry Potter and the Sorcerer's Stone*, sparked a squabble between Amazon.com and American book publisher, Scholastic Inc., which had paid $100,000 for the rights to publish in the United States the first installment of Harry Potter. The book, written by Scottish author J.K. Rowling, was published in Britain in 1997 by Bloomsbury Children's Books. The U.S. demand was so great for the sequel that customers couldn't wait for the U.S. publication date, which was several months away, so customers ordered the book from Amazon.co.uk. The fires of desire were stoked by the more than 80 rave reader reviews on Amazon's United States website, including instructions on how to order the British version from Amazon.co.uk for less than £14, or about $23, with delivery in less than eight days.

An Amazon.com spokesman said he wouldn't comment about discussions with Scholastic or any publisher, but that it "takes the concerns of publishers seriously and works to try to resolve them."

This poses the question: when a customer in Seattle orders a book published in London, is the transaction taking place in the United States or Britain? Bezos said that he considered that an American buying a book on Amazon.co.uk was "no different than if you go to London on a vacation and pick up a book and take it home in your suitcase. If you do anything that challenges the establishment, you're going to annoy some people."

United States copyright law does bar importing a copyrighted book without permission but it permits an individual to purchase one copy for private use and not for distribution. The law does not address what happens if the customer ordered more than one book, or a bookseller buys multiple copies to resell in the United States. This argument is still taking shape.

Copyright issues aside, these European acquisitions were logical moves because the company had already been doing a brisk international business, shipping books regularly to over 160 different countries, which represented more than 20 percent of total sales.

Some of the most interesting stories in the company culture came out of doing business with international customers, particularly from the Third World and former Soviet bloc countries. "People will go to great lengths because they want access to information and things that help them educate themselves," said Bezos in a 1998 speech, where he related the story of an unusual order from Romania. A customer who didn't have a credit card sent two folded, crisp one-hundred-dollar bills secreted into the sleeve of a floppy disk. He mailed the little package to Amazon.com with a note on the sleeve of the floppy disk that read: "The customs inspectors steal the money, but they don't read English. It's inside the floppy disk."

Amazon.com sold many hard-to-get technical books to overseas customers. Customer-service manager Maire Masco recalled receiving an e-mail from a geologist in Sri Lanka who needed some books that would give him the information he needed to save a hillside from erosion. "He wrote me back and thanked me for getting him these three books that he couldn't order directly from the publisher, who was in

Oxford. They arrived, cheaper than if he had ordered them from the publisher. You hear stories like that and you feel like you're making a difference."

Another memorable order came from an international charity organization that had just received a grant to build a library in Zambia, and had a list of 2,000 books that they wanted to buy. "I grabbed a couple of people in the customer-service department and asked, 'Do you want do a great project?' " said Masco. "Two people, on basically their own time, ordered all these books. We worked it out with the people in the warehouse because the books had to be delivered at a certain time to a cargo airplane at JFK Airport in New York. We weren't supposed to do this because it was totally counterproductive to the business design, but it was just so cool to build this library in Africa."

There were some problems, of course, with overseas shipments. Masco singled out Spain and Portugal as "the black holes of Europe," because a significant amount of shipments would disappear, most likely stolen, and had to be replaced for free. Eventually, of course, Amazon.com added staff who did nothing but investigate fraud, particularly from the former Eastern Bloc and South America. "At some point, they would trace the fraud to certain towns," said Masco. "They would call up people in that town to see if they were legitimate."

The company later formed other subsidiaries in several countries in Europe and Asia, and entered into one of the most extensive global merchant programs on the Internet with Yahoo!. Under the agreement Amazon.com was the premier book merchant throughout many of Yahoo!'s World sites, including Asia, U.K. and Ireland, France, Germany, Denmark, Sweden, Norway, Canada, Australia and New Zealand, Japan and Korea.

Aided by this kind of exposure, a year after its European launches, Amazon.com was the fifty-seventh most valuable brand *worldwide*, above Hilton, Guinness, and Marriott, and just below Pampers, according to a report from a British marketing firm.

EXPANSION AND DIVERSIFICATION

"It was obvious from the beginning that Amazon couldn't stay in books and have margins that anyone would be happy with long term," said Fleishman. This viewpoint became clear as far back as December 1996, when Bezos took all the Amazon.com employees on a corporate retreat to the rustic and high-tech Sleeping Lady resort in Leavenworth, east of the Cascade Mountains in central Washington state.

"The retreat was about going beyond books and how we were going to do it," recalled Maire Masco. "We were already talking about DVDs, CDs, videos. It was the first time we talked about things other than books. We all came to that conclusion ourselves. Whether that was Jeff's intention and he guided it that way, I don't recall. He asked where we were going in the future, and where we thought we were going and what we were going to look like one year out, two years out, three years out, etc. All of us saw diversity in products as the way to go—even before we realized that there was no profit in books because margins were way too small."

Bezos wanted to leverage the company's customer base, competencies, and brand name into products like videos and music, which were obvious extensions. He spelled it out clearly in 1997: "Our strategy is to become an electronic commerce destination. When somebody thinks about buying something online, even if it is something we do not carry, we want them to come to us. We would like to make it easier for people online to find and discover the things they might want to buy online, even if we are not the ones selling them."

In April, at the same time it bought Bookpages and Telebook, Amazon.com made its first foray beyond books, when it acquired Internet Movie Database. IMDB was a British-based comprehensive and authoritative source of information on more than 150,000 movies and entertainment programs and 500,000 cast and crewmembers dating from the birth of film in 1892 to the present. It also represented Amazon.com's first step toward selling videos online.

Music was the next logical expansion move; it had come in second on that original list of products to sell on the Web that Bezos had compiled when he was researching the Internet for D. E. Shaw. Publicly, Bezos bemoaned the fact that Amazon.com's biggest disadvantage in selling music was that it didn't have a First Mover advantage—that belonged to CDNow, N2K's Music Boulevard, and Tower Records. CDNow already had exclusive arrangements with Yahoo and Excite's Web Crawler, and three services—Mr. Showbiz, Celebsite, and Wall of Sound; and N2K was the exclusive music partner for America Online Inc. (through AOL Networks in the United States, Europe, and Japan), Netscape's Netcenter, and the Ticketmaster Group. But privately, he was quietly preparing for a major move into music. In the previous few months, the company had put together an editorial staff of music specialists, and had conducted dozens of focus groups with customers who indicated that they would buy music from Amazon.com, which had already had a small CD business.

"This is critical, category-formation time," Bezos said at the time. "We're investing in technology, in marketing, in brand-building today, in expectation of having a larger company in the future." Because the fixed costs of selling goods over the Internet are high, "it makes sense to amortize that over a larger number of customers." Bezos's expansion strategy was a simple one: leverage the customer base of more than 2.25 million people—greater than any other Internet retailer—and the Amazon.com brand name, "which we've worked very hard to associate with high quality service, low prices, and ease of use (including 1-Click purchasing) and authoritative selection."

On June 10, the company announced its move into music, with an initial stock of about 130,000 titles, which was quickly expanded. Bezos followed the book formula by offering discounts of up to 30 percent on some CDs. (Amazon.com bought the music from a wholesaler and used its warehouse for shipping, so that if a customer bought both books and music, the shipping costs would be lower.) Like the book site, Amazon.com offered customers product information and special features, including excerpts of critic reviews from about a dozen publications, customer critiques and primers for people hoping to learn more about particular types of music or the musicians who play them. More than 225,000 songs could be sampled using RealAudio. Bestseller lists were compiled in a variety of ways, including by artist, genre, or instrument. A user could search for music in 14 genres and 280 sub-genres. For someone interested in finding out about a new type of music, the site listed 10 "essential" CDs that epitomized the style.

Asked whether the "essential" list was subjective, Bezos answered: "Of course it's subjective. But let me tell you something about the online world: If we've chosen poorly—if say, there's a stupid jazz album on our list—we will get so much hate mail within such a short period of time that we'll [use the] feedback, and it will be perfect. That's one of the advantages of being online."

The *New York Times* rated the site's song-title search as the most efficient of any Web music retailer, citing as an example the fact that only on the Amazon.com site did a search on the word "corner" lead to Creedence Clearwater Revival's "Down on the Corner."

Bezos described the site as "not just a store. It's a place where you can learn about music." By the second week in October—120 days later—Amazon.com was the largest online seller of music, and was using the tagline "Books, Music and More" to describe its business. A year later, CDNow and N2K merged into CDNow. Several months after that, Time Warner Inc. and Sony Corp bought CDNow and merged it with their Columbia House music and video direct-marketing joint venture. So much for the First Mover advantage.

While all this was happening, the Amazon.com stock was heading north, from about $40 per share on June 1, to more than $80 three weeks later. It hit $100 on June 24 and $139.50 on July 6, representing a return of *1,450* percent since the May 1997 IPO. Part of the run-up in stock was credited with the move into music. Part of it had to do with a fevered excitement over Internet stocks in general, as typified by the Walt Disney Company's purchase of Infoseek, the online search directory. Investors were all agog, trying to discover the next hot Web-related acquisition.

The run-up even helped a stock like K-tel International, which peddled golden oldies CDs through an 800 number on late-night TV. In June, the stock was selling for $6 a share, but when K-tel announced it was planning to sell those very same CDs on the Web, its stock suddenly rocketed to $65 a share—206 times earnings.

Also contributing to Amazon.com's volatile stock were the growing army of investors who sold the stock "short." Traders that sell short borrow shares and then sell them, betting that the stock will fall. If it falls, the investors buy back the stock at the lower price, return the borrowed shares, and pocket the difference. But that was a losing strategy with Amazon.com stock. When the stock rose, short-sellers were faced with choosing between maintaining a risky bet or buying shares back at the higher price, which was not easy to do because Amazon.com stock had an unusually small "float," i.e., number of shares available for trading. (Most of Amazon.com's shares were held by insiders who did not trade them publicly.) Yet another cause for the high valuation and extreme swings in the stock were "day traders"—inexperienced online investors who buy a stock as it's going up and try to sell it as quickly as possible the moment it starts to go down.

Amazon.com was a fast-moving stock. At one point, the average share was held for a mere seven trading days before being sold. By comparison, Yahoo! was held for eight days and Coca-Cola for 26.4 months.

In August, Amazon.com used that rise in stock to make two separate strategic acquisitions that shocked the Internet community and sent the unmistakable signal that the company was going to be more than just a purveyor of books and music.

The first acquisition was PlanetAll, a Cambridge, Massachusetts–based firm that provided Web-based contact-management services, including self-updating address books, calendars, and reminders for people to stay in contact with friends, relatives, and associates; automatic organization of Web information; and access to more than

100,000 different interest groups. Launched in November 1996, PlanetAll, with 1.5 million members, had achieved a "breakthrough in doing something as fundamental and important as staying in touch," Bezos said at the time. He added that PlanetAll, which was cofounded by Warren Adams and Brian Robertson, was "the most innovative use of the Internet I've seen." It cost nothing to sign up for the service, which asked the user to list his own contact information, as well as the names of friends or contacts he'd like to keep in touch with. PlanetAll also asked those contacts for their permission to supply information such as e-mail and regular-mail addresses to the others in their cohort. All that information is stored in the individual's own database on PlanetAll, which synchronizes the information with the individual's own database at home or work, and automatically updates it. For example, a customer could request that she receive e-mails to remind her of an important occasion that warrants buying a present.

By acquiring a company that amassed personal information on customers, Bezos was beginning the eventual transformation of his company into a personalized one-stop shopping experience, complete with personal tastes, sizes, birthdays and anniversaries, credit card numbers, shipping addresses, etc. PlanetAll cost Amazon.com 800,000 shares of stock. The entire PlanetAll operation and staff was relocated to Seattle in early 1999.

The second acquisition, for 1.6 million shares, was Junglee Corp. of Sunnyvale, California, a search engine that enabled the user to compare prices on an item. Like other similar services, Junglee essentially dispersed intelligent agents or "spiders" to scout out the databases of a range of retailers, and return with prices on virtually any item, from cashmere sweaters to Keith Sweat CDs. Junglee, which was what is referred to as a shopping robot or "bot," promoted four different shopping guides that it powered: Compaq Computer Corp., Lycos's Hotbot, DealFinder, and Snap!, which could scan hundreds of websites in just a few seconds. Junglee made its money through fees paid by vendors for the privilege of being listed in the search, and through advertising on the site. Although Junglee gave Amazon.com a tool for potentially manipulating price comparisons, Bezos told the *Wall Street Journal* that it would be senseless to rig the Junglee database so that Amazon.com prices on books and music were always the best because, Bezos said, "customers would leave." Anyway, he said, customers were more interested in detailed comparisons on *big-ticket* items, such as computers and televisions, rather than the music and books that Amazon sold. (Bezos, of course, didn't mention that his company would be selling big-ticket items some day.) "The long-term vision is a person should be able to come to Amazon.com and find any product they may want to buy," Dave Risher, senior vice president of marketing and product development, said at the time.

A few months later, in early December, Amazon.com unveiled a facelift for Junglee. Gone were the other shopping guides. When a user typed in the Junglee website, she was immediately switched to something new—Amazon.com's "Shop the Web," a service that proclaimed on the screen to be "the place to find anything you want to buy online," including electronics, clothing, travel, computer hardware, toys and other goods, but not books and music. ("Even if someone found a book was 25 cents or 50 cents cheaper at another site, they'd still buy at Amazon.com because of the trust and recognition factors, claimed Bill Curry, an Amazon.com spokesman, in the *Wall Street Journal.*) The service had a link to retailers, such as The Gap for clothing and Cyberian Outpost for computer hardware.

Bezos understood that one of the essentials to uncovering profits on the Web was to be the middleman in the commercial transaction. "Shop the Web" opened up the possibilities of Amazon.com making money on commissions by sending its customers to those other retailers, who would pay Amazon.com a fee for each customer that was hyperlinked to their site. (Amazon.com later took a percentage of each sale.) This move foreshadowed other acquisitions and strategic movies that would be made in the coming years.

At first, Amazon.com tested "Shop the Web" by positioning it in an unobtrusive place on each page, but after the bugs were worked out, the company then set up a "Shop the Web" index tab that was similar to tabs that were already established for books, music, movies, and gifts.

Junglee and PlanetAll gave the Amazon.com website the much-sought-after quality of "stickiness"—multiple features that encourage users to linger at a site. And by adding such strategic and versatile content, Amazon.com made it obvious that it intended to be *the* commerce portal of the World Wide Web. Even before the acquisitions, Amazon.com was the only Internet commerce site that consistently appeared on lists of the busiest U.S. websites, according to the Web ratings firm, Media Metrix. Amazon.com's move also showed people that in order to remain viable, a Web merchant had to continually reinvent itself through both self-criticism and customer comments.

CHOOSE UP SIDES

By September 7, Amazon.com's stock was down 41 percent since peaking in July. At that time, Jonathan Cohen, an analyst for Merrill Lynch, who had just initiated coverage on Amazon.com, recommended that people reduce their holdings, in a report titled: "The World's Leading Internet Commerce Company Is Too Expensive." Cohen wrote, "Amazon.com is not a technology company, it is not a software company, and it should not enjoy a valuation that is even remotely related" to companies that achieve high-profit margins.

Adding to the contrarian chorus was Ron Ploof, of IceGroup, a Wakefield, Massachusetts, electronic commerce consulting company, who singled out the costs that Amazon.com was incurring as it built its brand and dealt with the increasingly complex logistics for order-taking, inventory management, shipping, handling, etc. Taking what he called an "everyman's point of view" to his analysis of Amazon.com's financial situation, he estimated that it cost Amazon.com $55.91 to process an average order, but Amazon took in only $48.76 for that order—in other words, the company incurred a loss of $7.15 for each order it processed.

Nevertheless, the stock began to soar in November. On the tenth of the month, it was trading at 131¾ and a week later, it was up to 148½ on news that the company was expanding into general merchandise, including videos and a holiday gift center, offering a range of products including toys, computer games, and DVDs. That announcement pushed up Bezos's share value by $440 million to about $2.9 billion. By November 20, the shares jumped up again 27⅔ to 180⅝. (The year before, the stock had traded as low as 22⅝) This gave the company a market value of about $9.12 billion. By comparison, Goodyear Tire & Rubber Co., the largest tire maker in the United States, had a market value of $8.71 billion. Amazon.com had third-quarter sales of $153.7 million, compared with $3.2 billion for Goodyear. (By the way, that K-tel International stock, which fell back down to $5 a share in October, rebounded to $39.125 in November when the mania struck again.)

Also that November, Amazon.com began selling VHS and DVD videos. Forty-five days later, it was the number one video retailer on the Web. To those critics who complained that Amazon.com was nowhere near to making a profit, Bezos strongly stated that the company was meeting its basic goal: "Get big fast."

In the midst of all this, in early November, Barnes & Noble announced that it was going to pay $600 million for Ingram Book Company, the country's leading book wholesaler, from whom Amazon.com got about 60 percent of its books. Leonard Riggio, chairman of Barnes & Noble, said the acquisition, which included 11 strategically located distribution centers, "gives us compelling strategic advantages in the Internet business." This announcement came on the heels of Bertelsmann AG, the German media conglomerate, becoming a partner in Barnes & Noble's Internet bookselling unit, Barnesandnoble.com. Under the terms of the deal, the two companies each invested $100 million for 50/50 ownership. Bertelsmann, the world's largest book publisher (whose holdings include Random House Inc., the largest U.S. book publisher), continued to develop its own separate operation, Books Online, in Britain, Germany, France, Spain, and the Netherlands.

The Barnes & Noble/Ingram deal gave Bezos and company the opportunity to further tweak the Riggios. In a press release, Bezos assured Amazon.com customers: "Those who make choices that are genuinely good for customers, authors, and publishers will prevail. Goliath is always in range of a good slingshot."

To which Barnes & Noble, responded with its own statement:

> Barnes & Noble Inc. is amused at Jeff Bezos's quote where he describes himself as an independent bookseller. Well, Mr. Bezos, what with market capitalization of some $6 billion, and more than four million customers, we suppose you know a Goliath when you see one. Your company is now worth more than Barnes & Noble, Borders and all of the independent booksellers combined. Might we suggest that slingshots and potshots should not be part of your arsenal.

Tickled that B&N took the bait, Amazon.com responded with a one-word press release: "Oh."

At the time, Amazon.com expressed surprise at the deal, a position that those in the know would describe as disingenuous. As one well-placed publishing source observed: "Don't think for a moment that Ingram Book Group wasn't offered for sale to Amazon. If Ingram Book Group is put into play by an investment banking firm, they are going to go to any and all potential buyers, including Amazon. Amazon would not have been shocked at hearing of the sale." (As it was, the sale never happened. In the face of a likely challenge from Federal Trade Commission, loud protests of independent booksellers, and threats of a Congressional hearing, B&N dropped the bid for Ingram in September 1999.)

In the middle of all this action in late 1998, another lawsuit was filed against Amazon.com. This one was filed in October by Wal-Mart

Stores, Inc. The Arkansas retailing giant charged that Amazon.com had stolen trade secrets with the 1997 hiring of former Wal-Mart employee Richard Dalzell as Amazon.com's chief information officer. In July 1998, Amazon.com had brought in another Wal-Mart veteran, Jimmy Wright, as vice president and chief of logistics. Wright, who had retired from Wal-Mart in 1998, had spent nine years as vice president of distribution. Wal-Mart charged that in luring Dalzell, Wright, and other Wal-Mart employees, the Seattle company's intention was to learn Wal-Mart's system for tracking sales, merchandising, distribution, inventory, and supplier data. Also named in the suit were Kleiner Perkins Caufield & Byers, Dalzell, and Drugstore.com, a new online drugstore site, which was financed in part by Kleiner Perkins (and later, it would be revealed, by Amazon.com). After several months of countersuits, court appearances, and saber rattling, the two sides settled out of court in April 1999. Under the agreement, Amazon.com reassigned the duties of one unidentified Amazon.com information-systems employee who had worked for Wal-Mart. The employees were limited from working in three key areas of data warehousing, merchandising systems, and distribution.

Meanwhile, back at the stock market, nothing was stopping the Amazon.com stock, which jumped $37⅞ or 21 percent to 218, on November 23, the same day that AOL announced it was acquiring Netscape. With the fabulous run-up in the stock, the battle lines were being drawn between believers and nonbelievers.

In November, in a survey of fund managers, *Barron's* named Amazon.com (along with Microsoft) the most overvalued stock.

On December 15, 1998, Henry Blodget, an obscure 32-year-old analyst with CIBC Oppenheimer, predicted that Amazon.com would hit $400 a share in 12 months, more than double his previous estimate. Blodget wrote in his report: "We continue to believe that Amazon.com is in the early stages of building a global electronic-retailing franchise that could generate $10 billion in revenue and earnings per share of $10 within five years."

A few hours after the start of trading on December 15, the price of one share of Amazon.com stock, which had opened at $243 was selling over $300, but by the end of the day, it dropped back "down" to $259. Nevertheless, Amazon.com's market value had surpassed that of Alcoa, Caterpillar, and International Paper. Less than a month later, on January 11, soon after a three-for-one split, the stock took off on another roller-coaster ride, opening at $158.875 and closing at $160.25, but in between hitting a high of $199.125.

In a July op-ed piece in the *Wall Street Journal*, *Forbes* publisher Rich Karlgaard noted that Yahoo!'s market capitalization was worth more than the New York Times Co., Amazon.com's more than Barnes & Noble and Borders combined, and America Online more than the combination of ABC, CBS, and NBC. All of this prompted Karlgaard to ask: "What really is going on? Are we hearing the trumpets and heralds of the grandly anticipated New Economy? Or is it the carnival bark of a stock-market sucker bet? At the risk of sounding wishy-washy, the answer is resoundingly: both. Yes, Amazon and Yahoo and the like are laughably overvalued. But, yes, Amazon and Yahoo are bullet-proof evidence that we live in a New Economy." And in his own column in *Forbes*, Karlgaard wrote, "Amazon is the first shining ray of the new commercial millennium pure Web play, fleeting as a shooting star, unburdened by any legacy baggage at all. It's the shape of business in the next century."

But Manuel P. Asensio of Asensio & Co., an investment banking firm in New York, told *Forbes*, "Amazon will be the brand name for a tulip someday." He was referring to the tulipmania of 1634 when Dutch speculators ramped up the price of tulip bulbs to extraordinary levels, only to see the market for tulips crash.

"I don't think Amazon will earn enough money to ever justify the stock price," said Sandi Lynne, a fund manager at Hemp Lane Partners, based in Milford, Pennsylvania. "None of the bookstores are fabulous growers or earn enough money for this valuation. That said, I've spoken to 40 investors today about Amazon.com's stock and everyone who doesn't own it is ill," she said. "Hand me my Prozac."

A couple of days after Blodget's $400-a-share blockbuster, Jonathan Cohen, the Merrill Lynch analyst, who thought that Amazon.com was too expensive at $100 a share, told financial reporters on a conference call: "It's fair to say that at this moment, Amazon is probably the single-most expensive publicly traded company in the history of U.S. equity markets." Cohen set Amazon.com at $50 a share, based on the company's estimated 1999 revenue and its long-term operating margins, which he estimated to be between 5 and 7 percent.

On December 17, shares were down 12¼ to 276¾, but by the twenty-first, they were up 32⅙ to a record 318¾, thanks in part to a favorable mention in *Barron's*, which was included in a profile of Mary Meeker, Morgan Stanley Dean Witter's superstar Internet-sector analyst. Meeker said: "The emerging presence of Amazon as a potential online powerhouse reminds us of the early days of America Online—grow, grow, grow, spend, spend, spend, expand, grow, spend more, grow more." On December 28, the stock was up 27⅛ to 351 15/16; on the twenty-ninth, it was down 19⅝ to 332 5/16; and on the thirtieth it was down 11 1/16 to 321¼. Shares were trading at a stratospheric 97.4 times sales (while Wal-Mart traded at 1.6 times sales). Stock options increased in 1998 by 966 percent. No wonder a *Fortune* magazine article about a Manhattan-based psychotherapist who specializes in treating Wall Street types, was titled, "I Hate My Mother . . . Sob! . . . and I Sold Amazon.com at $50."

Thirteen trading days after Blodget's blockbuster prediction—which he would later compare to "throwing gasoline on a bonfire"—Amazon.com's stock, which had just split three-for-one, hit $134, which actually exceeded Blodget's presplit number. As of April 13, 1999, Amazon was trading at $178.38. Adjusting for the January split, that came to $535.13. Virtually overnight, Blodget had become one of the most influential analysts on Wall Street. Soon after, he moved to Merrill Lynch, where he replaced Jonathan Cohen, who had moved on to Wit Capital. In the fall of 1999, Blodget signed a contract with Random House to write a book on the economic impact of the Internet.

"Amazon has shown people how big the Internet can be as an economic phenomenon," said Blodget. "One of the things that's important to understand is that this is a company that initially started growing in a dead industry. The book industry is not growing. All their growth is coming from stealing market share from other people, and perhaps accelerating a little bit the growth of the book market—because one of the great things about Amazon is that it actually increases demand and creates incremental demand. So, in a dead market, they went from 0 to $1 billion in four years. That's one of the things that's missed by a lot of people who just look at these stock prices. There isn't a company out there—with the exception of eBay, which has grown as fast as Amazon."

One of the companies that benefited from the rise in Amazon.com stock was the book wholesaler Baker & Taylor. Both Baker & Taylor and Ingram offer their databases to booksellers, which are in the form of CD-ROMs that are updated monthly. While Ingram's was based on Bowker's Books in Print database, Baker & Taylor's even more extensive database was its own creation. At first, Amazon.com subscribed to the B&T database, for which it paid $1,200—the same price every bookstore paid.

"When Baker & Taylor realized that Amazon was subscribing for $1,200 a year to this incredibly valuable asset, Baker & Taylor told Amazon that that arrangement was not equitable," said a knowledgeable publishing insider. "The Baker & Taylor representatives came out to Seattle and negotiated a commitment from Amazon to pay them $100,000 for the use of their data. The higher-ups at Baker & Taylor said that was a ridiculous figure." In fiscal 1997, Baker & Taylor renegotiated the deal with Amazon.com and entered into a licensing agreement that provided Baker & Taylor with 1,350,000 shares (adjusted for subsequent splits) of common stock of Amazon.com in exchange for providing use of its database, according to a July 23, 1999, filing with the Securities and Exchange

Commission by Baker & Taylor. During fiscal 1999, Baker & Taylor generated $43.7 million in cash proceeds from the sale and settlement of those Amazon.com securities.

THE FIRST INTERNET CHRISTMAS

The Christmas of 1998 will be remembered as the first true Internet Christmas. That holiday season, Internet-sourced retail sales in the United States exceeded $3.5 billion (accounting for 45 percent of total online sales for the year), nearly three times more than the $1.2 billion a year earlier, according to Forrester Research Inc. Not surprisingly, books were the most popular purchase by online customers, followed by computer hardware and accessories, music and video products, and computer software. This performance was boosted by a strong economy, but it also got a boost from the U.S. Senate. In October, the Senate passed the Internet Tax Freedom Act, which mandated a three-year tax moratorium on Internet sales.

It was a spectacular way to finish a remarkable year for Amazon.com, which was the second most visited site on the Web in December, with more than 9 million unique visitors, according to Media Metrix. (Bluemountainarts.com, the online electronic greeting card site, had 12.3 million unique visitors.) The Christmas rush also caught the company shorthanded, but it was able to hire hundreds of temporary workers for the warehouses in Seattle and New Castle, Delaware.

"At Christmases, everybody had to come to the warehouse and work elbow to elbow," said former warehouse employee E. Heath Merriwether. "They would rotate in people from the corporate offices when we didn't have enough staff." It was particularly difficult to gauge staffing levels because there was little history to base them on. "We knew what last year's was and we could generally count on at least doubling it. But you could only hire so many people at a time and suck them into this machine. There would be times when Jeff Bezos, Joy Covey, customer service, vice presidents, and the marketing department would help gift wrap, push boxes, and pick orders. So there was a lot of impromptu training. It did promote a feeling of camaraderie."

Amazon.com gained about 1.7 million new customers between November 17 and December 31, shipping about 7.5 million items during that period, for sales of $252.89 million—a 283 percent increase over the previous year's fourth-quarter sales of $66 million. On the other hand, there was a net loss of $46.43 million, including $22.2 million for acquisitions. The torrent of business so strained the company that it failed to ship some orders to customers in time for Christmas. An apologetic Bezos said: "As the obstetricians say, even one baby dropped on its head is one baby too many."

Amazon.com closed 1998 with book sales of $610 million ($250 million in the fourth quarter), an increase of 313 percent over 1997 sales of $147.8 million. In just three and a half years, Amazon.com became the country's third largest bookseller (virtual or physical), behind Barnes & Noble ($2.7 billion) and Borders ($2.3 billion). The company's sales were equivalent to about 50 book-chain superstores. The number of customers grew more than 300 percent from 1.5 million at the end of 1997 to 6.2 million. But it continued to lose money because of aggressive sales and marketing efforts (accounting for 22 percent of its total revenues), combative pricing, higher costs related to filling orders, and narrower profits on sales of music and videos. For the year, the company lost $124.55 million or 84 cents a share, compared with a loss of $31.02, or 24 cents a share in 1997.

Becoming the second biggest online retailer—trailing only Dell—Amazon.com was succeeding in its quest of getting big fast and, in the process, Jeff Bezos had made Amazon.com the poster child for internet commerce.

But all that he had done up to that point was prologue. Bezos was only getting started. The next chapter in the Amazon.com story will show what he really has in mind for this company, and what it means for all of us.

TAKEAWAYS

The people at Amazon.com knew that only one company was going to be the "poster child of the Internet," and they were determined to make sure that Amazon.com was going to be that company. Their not-so-secret weapon was Jeff Bezos, who quickly became the symbol of the company, much like Bill Gates at Microsoft and Jack Welch at GE.

- Great leaders are great communicators and great recruiters.
- Public relations is a valuable tool—learn how to use it.
- The Amazon.com story is one of vision, intelligence, technology, money and timing, and personality.
- If your CEO has the personality, make him or her the symbol of your company. This is essential in the personality-driven business-media coverage.
- Because the fixed costs of selling goods over the Internet are high, amortize over a larger number of customers.
- Maintain control of your destiny.
- Expand and diversify products and territory.

chapter eleven

get bigger faster

He who can see three days ahead will be rich for three thousand years.

Japanese proverb

If "Get Big Fast" was the mantra for Amazon.com's first three and a half years, the mantra for 1999 and 2000 was "Get Bigger Faster."

Throughout 1999, barely a day went by when there was not a mention of Amazon.com in the *New York Times* or the *Wall Street Journal*, commenting either directly on the company, or referencing it in relation to other .com companies. The company announced a major new initiative or strategic move about every six weeks, as Bezos continued to create an online enterprise that would play several roles: (1) a direct seller of a wide variety of merchandise; (2) a one-stop marketplace for third-parties who can sell virtually anything under the Amazon.com umbrella; and (3) an investor and partner with other online enterprises.

With that in mind, here's how he did it. The following reads like a shopping list because it *is* a shopping list. The company's first major move came in February, when it bought 46 percent of drugstore.com, a Redmond, Washington–based company led by Peter Neupert, a former executive at Microsoft (that other Redmond-based company). The move was in the spirit of the *Keiretsu* approach to interrelated companies fostered by John Doerr, whose firm, Kleiner Perkins Caufield & Byers, brokered the deal. Drugstore.com also had a distinctive Seattle flavor to it, thanks to a jolt of cash from Starbucks Coffee chief executive Howard Schultz's private investment company, Maveron L.L.C. Bezos and Schultz both became directors of the new firm. Immediately following the deal, Amazon.com added to its website an easy-to-find link with drugstore.com. A couple of months later Neupert told a health care conference, not surprising, "Amazon is very effective at delivering us customers." In June 1999, Amazon.com's stake in drugstore.com was reduced to 29 percent when two national chains—Rite Aid, the drugstore company, and General Nutrition Centers, which sells specialty vitamin and mineral supplements—made investments in the new venture.

In March (the same month, a highly critical article in *Barron's* declared the company "Amazon.bomb"), Amazon.com launched its auction site to challenge eBay, the market leader in person-to-person auctions. (eBay, with some 3 million customers at the time, actually made a profit.) Instead of limiting itself to only person-to-person transactions, Amazon.com's auction was positioned as a service that helped people find virtually anything they wanted, whether through individuals or merchants of any size. Amazon.com's commission on sold items ranges from 1.25 to 5 percent, paid by the seller. "We want to build a place where people can come to find and discover anything they might way to buy online," said Bezos. "You realize very quickly that you can't sell everything people might want directly. So instead you need to do that in partnership with thousands and indeed millions of third-party sellers in different ways. To try to do that alone, in strictly a traditional retailing model, isn't practical."

Amazon.com had considered buying an existing auction site, but chose instead to develop its own because it would enable the company to capitalize on its existing customer base, which at that time had grown to 8 million. To minimize the chance of fraud (an occasional problem in online auctions, where buyers and sellers never meet), the company created an Alliance Program, which finds and removes counterfeit merchandise from the site, and it also guaranteed a full refund for any purchase under $250 if the merchandise was not delivered as advertised on the auction site. (eBay already had an insurance program that covered the first $200 of losses due to fraud, with a deductible of $25.)

To make the site more customer-friendly, Amazon.com offered its

1-Click ordering service, competitive fees, and, in its spirit of creating a self-policing online community, asked users to rate buyers and sellers on their reliability. Bezos himself was one of the more active users of the site. In an October 1999 interview with the *Seattle Times*, he mentioned that his fellow bidders/sellers gave him a rating of 4.8 out of 5 stars. (Bezos missed earning a perfect score because one slightly miffed buyer described the transaction as "Slow delivery, but item arrived.")

To publicize the launch, Amazon.com held an auction to benefit the World Wildlife Fund (with all funds going toward the preservation of the Amazon rain forest in South America) by offering, among other things, an Andy Warhol print of the actor James Dean, and Bezos's first door desk. The latter was purchased by Jackie Bezos for $30,100. The company cross-promoted the auctions throughout the rest of the website. If someone was browsing for books on collectible dolls, she also would be shown a listing for dolls that were being auctioned. Memorabilia from the making of the movie *Titanic* was featured on the movie and music pages. Eventually, Amazon.com offered sellers on the collectibles site the opportunity to publicize their sales on the book site. A month later, to improve the site, the company bought LiveBid.com, a Seattle company that uses proprietary Internet technology to connect—*live*—auction houses running traditional auctions to bidders around the globe. (One of the original outside investors in LiveBid was Tom Alberg, the Amazon.com director, and his company, Madrona Investment Group.)

March was a busy month for online auctions, which were becoming the hottest category on the Web. That month, eBay made a $75 million deal with AOL to promote itself to the portal's 20 million customers; Priceline.com, which auctions airline tickets and hotel rooms, went public; Sharper Image, the catalog and retail purveyor of electronics and various gadgets, began offering auctions of new and excess merchandise; Cyberian Outpost, an e-tailer of computer hardware launched its auction site. As the year progressed, the auction business became even more competitive, with pressure from existing companies such as Yahoo!, as well as an alliance of nearly 100 Internet sites, including three of the biggest—Microsoft's MSN, Excite@Home, and Lycos—which was put together by Fairmarket, Inc., a company that sets up and runs auction sites.

Also in March, Amazon.com announced it had bought 50 percent of Pets.com, a small online company, based in Pasadena, California, that specializes in popular and rare pet accessories, products, and food for a variety of animals. The pet category is a $23 billion business in the United States, and, like auctions, has plenty of players, including Petopia.com, Allpets.com, Petsmart.com, and Petstore.com. Although Amazon.com's share had been reduced to 43 percent before Pets.com's initial public offering in December, the company was still Pets.com's largest shareholder, thanks to its investments of nearly $58 million in two rounds of financing, according to the IPO filing.

Sales for the first quarter, which ended March 31, skyrocketed to $293.6 million, a 236 percent increase over 1997's first-quarter sales of $87.4 million, with a pro forma loss $36.4 million. Including the one-time charges associated with all those acquisitions, the company posted a loss of $61.7 million, or 39 cents a diluted share, compared with a loss of $10.4 million the previous year, or 7 cents a diluted share. Despite all that red ink, Amazon.com hit $28 billion in market value on January 8, and at one point during the day, its worth exceeded Merrill Lynch & Co. and Sprint, and was greater than the combined value of JCPenney and Kmart.

The frenzy over Internet stocks was so intense that shares of a company like Zapata, which makes fish oil, jumped 23 percent after it said it would be linked to Amazon.com's website. This was not a big deal; at the time there were 180,000 other associates.

This mania prompted Rick Berry, an analyst with J. P. Turner Co., to characterize the situation as "pretty much the theater of the absurd," and to ask this rhetorical question: "How can you explain this behavior? It is avarice in its most pure form. It's the greater fool theory, which is that someone buys stock in the hope that someone is going to come from behind and buy it for even more."

In late January 1999, Amazon.com decided to raise $500 million though a private offering of subordinated notes that would be convertible into the company's common shares of stock. When the lead underwriter, Morgan Stanley Dean Witter & Co., was deluged with $3 billion in orders within the first few hours of the announcement, Amazon.com promptly hiked the issue to $1.25 billion (at an aggregate principal of 4.75 percent, due in 2009), making it the largest convertible debt offering in U.S. history. The hottest stock on the Internet had simultaneously become the hottest bond.

In June, two months after eBay bought traditional auction house Butterfield & Butterfield Auctioneers, Amazon.com invested about $45 million for a 1.7 percent stake in the 250-year-old international art house Sotheby's Holdings. The two companies formed a joint online auction site, called sothebys.amazon.com, to auction general art, antiques, and collectibles such as coins, stamps, and Hollywood memorabilia. Although the prices on many of those items were too low for Sotheby's to sell in a traditional auction, the venerable auction house was better equipped than Amazon.com to authenticate the merchandise.

Standing in the middle of Sotheby's auction room to make the announcement of the deal, Bezos, dressed in his uniform of powder blue shirt and tan slacks, told the media: "The last time I stood in this room was six years ago. It was the Russian space auction, and I bid on a zero-gravity chess set and a really cool recoilless hammer, but I lost."

When sothebys.amazon.com site was launched in November 1999, in the United States, the U.K., Germany, and Canada, some of the lots included a Marc Chagall print, a gold bar salvaged from the 1857 shipwreck of a Gold Rush treasure ship, and a technocolored Volkswagen Beetle from the movie *Austin Powers.*

In April, Amazon.com paid $200 million, mainly in stock, to acquire e-Niche, Inc., a company that did business as Exchange.com. Exchange.com operated two Web marketplace sites: Bibliofind, for rare, antiquarian, or out-of-print books (its 9 million book listings were twice as big as Amazon.com), and MusicFind for recordings and music memorabilia. The sites provided Internet links for existing used-book dealers and music collectors' shops to make their inventory available online. Exchange.com, based in Cambridge, Massachusetts, had also been pursued by Barnes & Noble.

At the same time, Amazon.com bought two other companies. One of them, Accept.com, based in Redwood City, California, was developing software to simplify person-to-person and business-to-consumer transactions on the Internet. The price tag for Accept.com was Amazon.com stock priced at the time at about $101 million.

The other company was Alexa Internet Co., a fascinating little operation created by a highly regarded Web philosopher named Brewster Kahle. Alexa, which was named after the ancient Egyptian Library of Alexandria, was a Web-navigation service that tracked which sites people visit and was programmed to make suggestions to viewers about other sites they might find interesting. Although the young Alexa had less than $500,000 in annual revenue and zero profit, it was acquired for about $250 million worth of Amazon.com stock. Part of the value of Alexa was its extensive databases—13 terabytes in size (equivalent to 13 million books) that are chock full of "metadata" (information about information)—on the Web activity of millions of people. Based on this treasure trove of details, Amazon.com can discern any individual's patterns of online activity. The goal is to be able to figure out how best to present a customer with a particular product or service, at just the right time when the customer is ready to make that purchase. The purchase of Alexa reinforced the idea that Amazon.com is not just in the merchandise business, it's also in the information business.

This point became apparent toward the end of 1999, when Amazon.com began showing more fully how Alexa fit into its strategic plan. Using technology developed by Alexa, Amazon.com introduced a software application that allowed shoppers to search the Internet for the lowest price on an item—without having to leave the site where they started, whether it was a page on Amazom.com or on any other Web wholesaler or retailer. The application, called zBubbles, searches Alexa's vast database of product information and websites for the best price. Whenever a customer shops at a cybercommerce site that gives comparison information, a gray-hued "Z" icon located on the upper-right corner of the browser changes color to yellow, and a small yellow "Z" pops up next to the products. A click of the "Z" icon produces a bubble that tells the user where to buy the product and provides comments on the products by people who have purchased them. The user is informed that the product can be found on Amazon.com, and it can be automatically purchased from Amazon.com with a few easy tricks. To minimize complaints from its competitors, Amazom.com restricted the planting of zBubbles—which could be downloaded from the Amazon.com and Alexa websites—only to manufacturers' sites and product-review sites, not to direct competitors.

Many observers and privacy advocates are concerned about the multiterabytes of information on mass consumer behavior that Amazon.com is collecting through Alexa. In January 2000, a lawsuit was filed in San Francisco by a man who claimed that Alexa secretly intercepted personal information and sent it to Amazom.com without his consent. Around that same time, Richard M. Smith, an Internet-security consultant, filed a complaint against Amazon.com with the Federal Trade Commission, charging that Amazon.com was collecting more personal information about consumers than the company had made known. The concern over the collection of all this data is shared by Brewster Kahle, the founder of Alexa, who admitted, it "wakes me up in the middle of the night, scared. I'm worried because I know too much." Clearly, this is an issue that Bezos is going to have to deal with if he hopes to maintain the loyalty of his customer base.

One strategy that Bezos picked up from Microsoft was to buy what he couldn't create. He had wanted to acquire Blue Mountain Arts, the online greeting card company, but his advances were rebuffed. It was hard to ignore Blue Mountain, whose 12 million visitors made it the thirteenth most visited site on the Web in March 1999 (Amazon.com was number 15). In April, when its effort to buy Blue Mountain failed, the company added Amazon.com Cards, a free electronic greeting card service with 800 different cards in 45 categories. Copying the Blue Mountain concept, Amazon.com e-mailed the recipient of the card, who could then link onto the site that carried the card. Greeting cards continue to be another hotly competitive spot on the Internet. A few months after Amazon.com's greeting card launch, American Greetings said it would pay AOL $100 million over five years to provide cards through AOL's online websites.

In May, Amazon.com bought 35 percent of HomeGrocer.com, for which it paid $42.5 million in cash. The transaction had been kept quiet for a month because HomeGrocer was afraid that the publicity would have generated so much traffic that the website would crash. That happened to drugstore.com, which had to shut down its site for three days because it couldn't handle the deluge of visitors. Investors in HomeGrocer.com included Tom Alberg, as well as Alberg's former colleague at McCaw Cellular, Jim Barksdale, the former CEO of Netscape.

By July 1999, users who logged onto Amazon.com's "Welcome" page no longer found an online bookstore, but rather an online merchant of books, music, videos, electronic cards, auctioned items, and, the newest additions, toys and consumer electronics (including cameras, digital-music players, and televisions).

Electronics and toys were actually an expansion of the Amazon.com Gift Center, which was launched in November 1998. The Gift Center included a service called Gift-Click, which was the analogue of 1-Click shopping. For a customer who had already registered his credit card number, all he had to do was pick out a gift item, type in the recipient's e-mail address, and hit "go." Amazon.com contacted the recipient and asked where the gift should be sent.

Offering many electronics items at 10 to 20 percent below list price, Amazon.com was hardly the cheapest store on the Web. The company was betting that consumers would pay a bit more for helpful product information, including descriptive reviews written by an in-house staff of 10 copywriters in electronics, and six in toys. One cute feature: Customers could test the noise of a toy to make sure it wasn't objectionable.

Of course, promotional-minded Amazon.com waved some goodies in the virtual face of the customers. Shoppers who visited the toy site were offered $100 gift certificates for helping to construct the site. They were encouraged to give their feedback for product reviews and asked to evaluate toys on the basis of three criteria: entertainment value, educational value, and durability. Amazon.com came up with a contest called Toy Quest, which invited children to submit a 200-word proposal for the design of a new toy, and Amazon.com promised that it would build and sell the top two designs during Christmas 2000, and would pay the designers $10,000 plus 7 percent of royalties.

With the move into toys and electronics, hardly anyone noticed that in July Amazon.com bought 49 percent of Gear.com, an online discount sporting-goods retailer that offers new closeout or overproduced merchandise in its original packaging, at 20 to 90 percent off retail.

The sales continued to go up, as did the losses. For the second quarter ended June 30, the company rang up sales of $314 million, which was up 171 percent from $116 million in the year-earlier period. It had 10.7 million customers, compared with 3.1 million the year before. Excluding acquisition costs and other one-time charges, Amazon.com reported a loss of $82.8 million, or 51 cents a share, compared with a loss of $17 million, or 12 cents a share, in the same period in 1998. Throw in the charges, and Amazon.com turned in a loss of $138 million, or 86 cents a diluted share, compared with $22.6 million, or 15 cents a share. Gross margins shrunk by about 5 percent because of heavy discounting, including offering first-time buyers the opportunity to buy bestselling books for one penny.

In September, in a move to get a piece of the $17-billion-a-year gift-registry business, the company acquired a 20 percent stake in Della &

James, an Internet wedding-gift registry that was changing into an all-purpose gift service. The two companies immediately hitched themselves up with links to each other's website. With its Amazon.com affiliation, Della & James users included books, music, toys, and other Amazon.com products on registries for birthdays or other occasions. After shoppers select these gifts, they are routed directly to the Amazon.com product pages. Amazon.com was part of a group investing $45 million in Della & James, whose other investors included retailers Neiman Marcus Group, Williams-Sonoma, and Crate & Barrel (all existing partners of Della & James), and the venture-capital firms Kleiner Perkins Caufield & Byers and Trinity Ventures.

In October, Amazon.com became the first major retailer to present its wares wirelessly over the Internet through wireless phones, handheld units, and other non-PC devices. (Portals such as Yahoo! and American Online already had specialized sites for handheld devices.) Under the initiative, called "Amazon.com Anywhere," Amazon.com reformatted and simplified the site. The spare graphics and text made for faster downloading and easier navigation for non-PC Internet wireless devices that lacked the power of full-sized personal computers.

Instant gratification fueled this project: "If customers are in the car and they hear a song they like, they can look it up and purchase it," said Warren W. Adams, Amazon.com's director of product development. "In our mind, this is a cash register in every pocket."

Amazon.com Anywhere, which was announced on the same day 3Com Corporation released the newest version of its Palm VII Internet-linked handheld device, enabled people bidding on Amazon.com auctions to be notified if and when they had been outbid on a particular item. (eBay had already offered such a paging service to customers.) Most of the site development and the specialized server software was done by Convergence, a company based in Atlanta, Georgia, which Amazon.com bought in August 1999 for $20 million.

In November 1999, Amazon.com signed a five-year marketing agreement with Nextcard, Inc., an online issuer of credit cards, to deliver cobranded credit card accounts originated on a custom-built website. Nextcard agreed to pay Amazon.com an origination fee for each cobranded credit card account as well as additional compensation, including the renewal fees for each account. Over the terms of the agreement, Nextcard paid $85.0 million to Amazon.com, with the possibility of paying up to another $17.5 million, based on the number of credit card accounts originated. Amazon.com also paid $22.5 million for up to 4.4 million common shares of Nextcard, at a price per share of $39.20, for an 8 percent ownership, according to Nextcard's filing for its initial public offering. The Nextcard deal gave Amazon.com another way to attract revenue from its customer base.

Amazon.com ended the third quarter with a loss of $197 million on sales of $356 million. A year earlier, it had lost $45 million on sales of $154 million. The loss included $111 million in costs for one-time charges related to acquisitions, investments, and stock-based compensation. Excluding these charges, on an operating basis, the company lost 26 cents a share. On the positive side, Amazon.com had 13.1 million customer accounts, nearly triple the total of a year earlier. Repeat customer orders totaled 72 percent of business, up from 70 percent in the second quarter.

ZSHOPS

All of those acquisitions and affiliations set the stage for the company's biggest announcement of the year. On a November day in New York, Jeff Bezos stepped onto the riser at the front of the Versailles room in the Sheraton Hotel. With five television crews recording his every word, he told the assembled: "Sixteen months ago Amazon.com was a place where you could find books. . . . Tomorrow, Amazon.com will be a place where you can find anything, with a capital A."

With that declaration, Bezos introduced zShops, which was Amazon.com's online mall. Joel Spiegel, the vice president and general manager of zShops, said that the name was derived from "z for zero hassle, zero risk, and A-to-Z selection." Virtually anyone—from the Spencer Abbey Trappist monastery selling homemade tea and jam to OfficeMax purveying floppy disks and file cabinets—could establish a store on Amazon.com, and could sell almost anything (except firearms, living creatures, pornography, and tobacco) and gain exposure to the company's 12 million customers. A seller could list as many as 3,000 items on zShops. The company was particularly interested in featuring purveyors of unconventional goods, rather than stuff they could buy anywhere. As an example of an offbeat offering, Bezos held up an edible (presumably) combination of chicken, duck, and turkey with the mellifluous name "turducken."

The price of admission for a seller was a monthly fee of $9.99, plus commissions ranging from 1 to 5 percent. Boldface listings were $2 each; emphasis in a given category, $14.95 per listing, and showcasing on Amazon.com's home page, $99.95 per listing. For another percentage of the sale, any individual or merchant could use Amazon.com's 1-Click shopping service for customers' shipping and credit information stored in the Amazon.com data bank. Amazon.com charged the credit card and then deposited the money directly into the seller account. To facilitate sales between shoppers and merchants who don't accept credit card payments, Amazon.com offered a service called Amazon.com Payments, which was free to shoppers, and cost sellers 60 cents per transaction plus 4.75 percent of the purchase price.

Curiously, the zShop concept was a throwback to the original Amazon.com business model of selling merchandise on the Web without the hassle and expense of carrying inventory. With an online shopping mall stocked with more than 500,000 products—including books, music, toys, electronics, videos—Amazon.com offered four times as many products as traditional bricks-and-mortar mass retail chains such as Kmart Corp. and Target. By opening up a global audience to individuals and small merchants, Amazon.com increased the "stickiness" of its experience; there was plenty of reason to linger at the website.

If a shopper is unable to find what he wants from Amazon.com or any of the zShops, he can find it, at no charge, by combing the Web with Amazon.com's All-Products Search service. Aware that the search engine will often send customers to the competition, Bezos said, "In the categories where we are selling things directly, if we can't be competitive, then we shouldn't be standing in the way of our customers. We don't really care whether we sell something through zShops, or sell something directly ourselves; it is sort of a wash for us. You can't sell everything on your own. You need to band together with third parties."

How does all this affect Amazon's vaunted customer service? By bringing in all those sellers, Amazon.com opened up the potential for harm to its brand name and its reputation for service. Clearly, if the seller—who is responsible for shipping and product quality—is inefficient or dishonest, the customer will surely pin the blame on Amazon.com. Because it does minimal screening of participating zShops, Amazon.com relies on consumer ratings and reviews—posted on the website—to weed out the bad apples. Customers are guaranteed as much as $250 on each transaction made with a zShops merchant; $1,000 if the customer used the Amazon.com Payments credit-processing service.

Like all the other new businesses it entered in 1998 and 1999, the limitless shopping portal business was already crowded and getting more so, with competition that included AOL, Yahoo!, AltaVista, Ebay, Excite@Home's iMall, and dozens of smaller companies forming multistore coalitions. But zShops are more than just about selling stuff; they are also about Amazon.com continuing to gather valuable information on individual shopping habits as well as the most popular products, which Amazon.com could eventually decide to sell itself. With all the data that Amazon.com possesses, and with its far-reaching influence on the Internet, one can envision Amazon.com earning additional revenue from manufacturers who would pay a fee to test-market new products on the Internet.

In November, Amazon.com also added tools, video games, software, and gifts to its product offerings, as well as a cobranded credit card with Nextcard Inc., an alliance that was expected to earn Amazon.com $150 million in fees over five years. Part of the move into tools involved the acquisition of Tool Crib of the North, a large discount mail-order catalog that had its own Internet site. Also that month, Amazon.com expanded into luxury goods when it paid $10 million for a 16.6 percent ownership in Ashford.com, which sells jewelry and leather goods online; and it broadened its toy selection with the acquisition of Back to Basics Toys, Inc., a closely held Internet and mail-order retailer specializing in classic toys.

DISTRIBUTION CENTERS

So where was Amazon.com—a company that insisted on maintaining control of the ordering and shipping process—going to put all this inventory? Speaking in September 1999 at a National Retail Federation conference in Philadelphia, Mary Morouse, Amazon.com's vice president of merchandising, said, "It's very important at this stage of our growth and this stage of the Internet to own the customer experience from start to finish. Our ability to have insight into every step of the process and to give our customers vision into exactly where their package is in our system is very important." She added that Amazon.com didn't want to share resources with another company because during a busy time like the holiday gift-giving season, someone else would be deciding on whose shipment gets priority. So the decision was made to add warehouses all over the country and make them state-of-the-art facilities designed specifically for Internet commerce. After all, that's why Bezos hired Richard Dalzell, Jimmy Wright, and a host of former Wal-Martians.

In January, the company leased a seven-acre, 580,000-square-foot distribution warehouse 30 miles east of Reno in Fernley, Nevada. Amazon.com's third distribution center, it more than doubled the current square footage of the Seattle and Delaware sites combined, and speeded up deliveries to cities in the West and Southwest. Fernley turned out to be the first of several facilities—totaling more than 3 million square feet of warehouse space—that it planned to open in Coffeyville, Kansas; McDonough, Georgia; and Campbellsville and Louisville, Kentucky, at a cost of about $200 million (as well as an additional $300 million for mechanizing shipping operations). Half tongue-in-cheek, Bezos called it "the biggest peacetime buildup" of warehouse and distribution facilities in history; at the very least, it was one of the largest such expansion efforts ever done by one company in a single year. Although Bezos's strategy is risky and expensive, he is gambling it will save money over the long term for Amazon.com, which delivers more than 60 percent of its products through the U.S. Postal Service.

Doesn't the addition of distribution centers go against the original business model? For the original business model, yes. For the business model that changed when Bezos decided to get big fast, no. Amazon.com had always touched the books in its own warehouses, and Bezos believes that by having so much warehouse space—which can accommodate $15 billion in sales—he will be able to maintain customer service as the company gets bigger faster.

BEZOS AS RECRUITER

To handle this incredible expansion, Bezos needed to hire experienced executives who would not be intimidated by the scope of the operation. In order to put together the kind of executive/management bandwidth the operation required, he used his charm, charisma, and power to convince.

In June, Joseph Galli, the former president of Black & Decker's Worldwide Power Tools and Accessories division, had just agreed to become president and chief executive officer at PepsiCo's Frito-Lay North America division. That didn't stop Bezos, who invited Galli to be Amazon's first president and chief operating officer. Although he wasn't interested, Galli did agree to have lunch with Bezos. As Joy Covey would discover, once Jeff Bezos asks you to lunch, it's all over.

"We had an instant chemistry," said Galli. "Sparks were flying. I had a 10-hour conversation with Jeff." Galli called up Frito-Lay and said never mind. "Bezos is such a visionary. [He's] changing the world, making history," says Galli. "I believe I have the most fabulous mentor on earth. To sit at the table with Jeff Bezos and learn about the Internet is incredible."

Galli was also lured by options to buy almost 2 million shares of Amazon.com over the next 20 years (priced at $113.625 a share), and a $5 million bonus for joining the company, according to a filing with the Securities and Exchange Commission. He was eligible for the first $3 million after one year of service, and the remaining $2 million after two years of service. His base salary was $200,000 per year. Amazon.com guaranteed that regardless of what happens with Galli, his option gains during the first 10 years with Amazon.com will not be less than $20 million. If his option exercises don't add up to $20 million, the company will pay him the difference in cash.

In September, Bezos brought in Delta Air Lines' Warren Jenson as senior vice president and chief financial officer. Jenson had been Delta's chief financial officer since April 1998, after working for six years in General Electric's NBC broadcast division. He succeeded Joy Covey, who had been named chief strategy officer in April.

The week before the hire of Jenson, Amazon.com recruited AlliedSignal's Jeffrey Wilke as vice president/general manager for operations, taking over most of the duties of Chief Logistics Officer Jimmy Wright, who retired. Wilke had been directly responsible for AlliedSignal's 15 plants and distribution centers in the United States, Europe, and Asia. The surprise retirement of Wright in September prompted Amazon.com spokesmen to concede that the company was having problems with its expansion plans. "This is complicated stuff. It's challenging. It's all about execution," said an Amazon.com spokesman.

Also joining the company was Ben Slivka, considered by many to be the executive most identified with getting Microsoft to recognize the importance of the Internet. Slivka, a 14-year Microsoft veteran, had served most recently as a general manager in Microsoft's Consumer and Commerce Group, where he worked on Internet

Explorer. At Amazon.com, he became director of information technology, concentrating on improving products and services and helping shape and grow the corporate culture.

Bezos continues to expand Amazon.com's executive bandwidth. But no matter how many people he adds, he remains the most important guy in the place, the heart and soul and brains of the company, with a vision and a personality that drives it forward. The aisles and walls of every company distribution facility are garnished with billboard-sized quotations from Chairman Jeff, such as "Our vision is the world's most customer-centric company. The place where people come to find and discover anything they might want to buy online," and the company's six core values: "customer obsessions, ownership, bias for action, frugality, high hiring bar, and innovation." Because he is so crucial to motivating Amazon.com's far-flung army of almost 5,000 employees, the company's internal radio station, Radio Amazon, plays tapes of his discussions of company plans, and his reiteration of the company motto: "Work Hard, Have Fun, and Make History."

PUBLIC RELATIONS MISCUES

Although Bezos and Amazon.com have been brilliant in manipulating the media, in 1999 the company made some profound mistakes that began to chip away at the carefully crafted notion of an online "community" of book lovers. But each time they got in trouble, the company was able to squelch the problem with tour de force examples of damage control.

The first major faux pas came in February, when Doreen Carvajal, who covers the book publishing industry for the *New York Times*, revealed in a front-page story that Amazon.com was charging publishers up to $10,000 to have their books featured on its home page. For that price, the author would be profiled or interviewed, and afforded "complete Amazon.com editorial review treatment." The company had actually initiated the practice in the summer of 1998 on a more modest scale, when it charged $500 to place a title on the

"What We're Reading" listing for two or three days. At the time, Bezos said, "If Publisher X gives us a better deal [on a new title] than Publisher Y, and we predict the customer is going to like both of these books equally but there's only a slot to show one, let's show the one where we will make more money."

For example, according to internal documents uncovered by Carvajal, Scribner paid $10,000 for Stephen King's novel *Bag of Bones* to gain prominent placement on Amazon.com's "Bestseller" page, along with a profile of the author and a feature in Amazon.com's listing "Destined for Greatness." In addition, the book was featured within its genre listing; a promotional e-mail was sent to people who had already bought King's books from the website; a "Not Yet Published" e-mail notification was sent out before the book was published; a "countdown to launch date" was included on the home page, and an announcement that the book was actually available for purchase was later located on the home page. That kind of prominent placement is commonplace in big bookstores, where publishers pay to have their books featured in in-store displays and cooperative advertising. But Amazon.com, with its "customer-centric," community-oriented, book-lover image, seemed to have held itself up to a higher standard.

When Carvajal questioned Amazon.com about the practice, Mary Morouse, the vice president for purchasing, admitted that the company was worried that "we might have a perception that we're selling placement," but she said that Amazon.com felt it had settled the issue internally by empowering editors who specialize in particular categories to refuse to include books they deemed unworthy. Still, there was no notice to shoppers that placement was paid for. "I think it would be more distracting to have a book tagged," said Morouse. "I think that would clutter it up. The customer experience is really clean and I want to keep it clean."

But after two days of negative press, unfavorable comments from competitors, consumer advocates, and independent booksellers, and e-mailed customer complaints (which was "almost surprising in its intensity," said an Amazon.com spokesman), the company revised its program, promising to disclose when book publishers paid a fee for prominent placement. Bezos was brought out to state the company's position to the press. "We have the largest staff of book editors online or off, and for a book that doesn't meet our standards, there is no amount of money that would cause us to feature it," he said. Showing his expertise for spin, Bezos said that Amazon.com's decision to disclose every paid-for placement was "breaking with standard industry practice" and that "we believe we're the first retailer to list this information for customers, and we hope it will start a trend." He added that Amazon, "as a Web-based store with a real community of book lovers," is "being held to a higher standard than physical stores. And you know what? That's the way it should be." With that statement, he quickly got in front of the issue, turning a "Whoops, we got caught" into "Join our crusade for full disclosure."

Glenn Fleishman, the former catalog manager, said his friends inside Amazon.com were "shocked" by the *New York Times* story. "This was the first time Amazon did something where they said, 'This is what the rest of the industry does, and this is what we're going to do,' instead of doing what they thought was best for the company. Amazon was being blamed because they are an editorial vehicle that people trust. That line was crossed."

Amazon.com crossed another line in August when it introduced a new service called "Purchase Circles." This feature was designed to help purchasers find the 10 hottest products in 3,000 different cities, universities, and various public and private workplaces. (The listings were grouped by organizations; not individuals.) For example, in August 1999, the bestselling book among Walt Disney Comany employees was *Dancing Corndogs in the Night: Reawakening Your Creative Spirit.* Amazon.com came up with the results by cross-indexing the bestselling items with buyers' zip codes and e-mail addresses. The "affinity-grouping" technology was created by PlanetAll, which Amazon.com had purchased in 1998. For some people, it was a chilling reminder of how much data Amazon.com has on the purchasing habits of its 12 million customers.

But Paul Capelli, an Amazon.com spokesman called it "fun. People can see what other people are buying." He added that if companies complained about the inclusion, Amazon.com would remove them from the list. When Deirdre Mulligan, staff counsel of the Center for Democracy and Technology, a civil-liberties group in Washington, D.C., told the *Los Angeles Times*, "This potentially could rightly upset businesses who are concerned about what employee purchases might tell people about them," Capelli responded: "That sounds paranoid to me—that people don't want people to know what videos you want."

But the next day, the company reversed itself, announcing that it would let individuals and companies withhold their data from the anonymous listings. "Privacy is of utmost importance to our customers and to us," said Warren Adams, director of product development. "While the vast majority of feedback from our customers indicates that Purchase Circles have been well received and are extremely valuable . . . some customers have expressed concerns, so we're letting people decide individually."

One of the companies that opted out was IBM. In fact, the request came from IBM chairman Louis Gerstner Jr. himself, who polled his employees on whether they wanted to boycott Amazon.com. Several hours later, 5,000 IBM employees responded to Gerstner: 95 percent of them wanted out of the program. Gerstner later sent Bezos a civil but stern message about privacy: "I'm certainly not telling you how to run your business, but I do urge you to view this as an enormously important issue."

Soon after this flap, *Seattle Weekly* turned the tables on Amazon.com, when it analyzed how Amazon.com employees used the *Weekly*'s website, www.seattleweekly.com. Turns out, the most popular article downloaded from the *Weekly* site by Amazonians was "How I escaped from Amazon.cult," a scathing first-person account by Richard Howard, a short-term customer-service employee at

Amazon.com. Another popular site was the *Weekly*'s "Help Wanted" section.

Although Amazon.com's privacy policy declares that it "does not sell, trade, or rent your personal information to others," it also states: "We may choose to do so in the future with trustworthy third parties, but you can tell us not to by sending a blank e-mail message to never@amazon.com."

The third major public-relations debacle came when the company was sued for federal trademark infringement by Amazon Bookstore Inc., a 2,000-square-foot, feminist cooperative in Minneapolis. Although the store had been doing business under the Amazon name since 1970, it had never registered its name with the U.S. Patent and Trademark Office. But it made the claim under common law rights. Amazon.com's reaction was not atypical of the company. Spokesman Bill Curry said, "Amazon Bookstore sat on its hands for four years while we were building a brand. If there was a problem, they should have said something a lot sooner." (Ironically, at the same time, Amazon.com was suiting a company selling Greek-language books at Amazon.gr and Amazon.com.gr. for trademark infringement.)

The depositions for the case got very ugly. Amazon.com lawyer's initial line of questioning concentrated on whether the co-owner of the little bookstore was a lesbian and was proselytizing a gay agenda. According to the court filing, when the woman asked attorney Paul Weller to clarify his question, he replied: "I'll ask you this, are you gay?" After an objection, he followed up with: "Do you know if any of the women at the bookstore [are] married to a woman?" It went downhill from there.

Curry defended the line of questioning by saying that the owners of Amazon bookstore were attempting to "change their stripes" from catering to a primarily lesbian audience to a more mainstream one. "As part of the litigation, we are trying to get them to confirm their original statements about who owned and operated the store, and what their context was."

With the negative publicity streaming through the industry and the media, Amazon.com worked out a quick out-of-court settlement. Under the agreement, Amazon Bookstore Cooperative assigned the rights to the Amazon name to Amazon.com, and, in turn, licensed the name from Amazon.com.

Amazon.com's attorneys' aggressive questioning about a gay lifestyle was radically different from the company's enlightened position on gay employees, as well as Bezos's libertarian philosophy. "Amazon is supportive of the gay and lesbian community, as well as the diverse communities represented by their clientele," said former employee E. Heath Merriwether, who noted that when an employee is asked to relocate, the company will also pay for moving that employee's domestic partner, regardless of sexual preference.

And then there was the *Mein Kampf* episode. In November 1999, at the time of the tenth anniversary of the fall of the Berlin Wall, the *Washington Post* reported that Amazon.com was shipping a significant number of English translations of Adolf Hitler's racist manifesto to buyers in Germany, where the selling of the book is against the law. With so many people getting their copies from Amazon.com's U.S. site, *Mein Kampf* was listed among the top 10 bestsellers among Amazon.com's German customers.

The company's first response was to say that it believed it wasn't violating German law by shipping English versions, and that it did not want to regulate people's reading habits. But a day or so later, following a complaint by the Simon Wiesenthal Center and an investigation by German authorities as to legality, Amazon.com quickly stopped selling the book to customers in Germany. Barnes & Noble, on the other hand, said it would continue to sell the books to German buyers.

WHAT'S NEXT?

Fueled by strong sales during the 1999 holiday season, Amazon.com, which shipped almost 20 million items, finished its fourth quarter with sales of more than $676 million, 167 percent more than the previous year's $253 million, and far surpassing the $610 million figure for all of 1998. Annual sales were about $1.64 billion. Nevertheless, the company continued to incur huge losses because it spent so much on inventory (particularly toys and electronics), to make sure customers would get what they ordered for Christmas; and marketing/advertising (the company tripled its marketing budget to $90 million) so that the Amazon.com name was constantly in the forefront of the consciousness of e-shoppers. Amazon.com was the top-ranked e-commerce site from November 22 to December 26, with a weekly average of 5,693,000 unique visits, according to Media Metrix. It was the number one holiday shopping destination for an incredible 42 percent of all web shoppers, based on a survey of the accounting firm of Ernst & Young.

In less than four years, Amazon.com went from zero to $2.6 billion-plus in sales. The company went from four people in a renovated garage in Bellevue to a 160,000 square foot renovated former medical center—PacMed Tower on Seattle's Beacon Hill—and more than 7,500 employees in the United States and Europe. The brand is recognized by over 52 percent of adults in the United States and is one of the most familiar brands in the world. Part of that familiarity has come from investing hundreds of millions of dollars in advertising and mass marketing, and part has come from a masterful execution of one-to-one marketing. As book publisher Peter Osnos has said, "Amazon brilliantly, and at great expense, has branded. When people think of ordering a book online, they think of Amazon. It's like Xerox. It's entered the language." So has the word "Bezos." AddAshop.com, a company that sets up online shops for aspiring e-tailers, ran a print advertisement with the headline: "Go from Bozo to Bezos in Just 5 Minutes."

Bezos knows that there will be many, many winners on the Internet, but there will be only a small handful of really big winners. "If I ask you to name tennis-shoe makers, you'll come up with Nike, Adidas, and Reebok, and then it gets harder," said Bezos. "There are a bunch, but it's just not really worth it to your brain to keep track of more than about three brands in an area. But you're willing to keep track of thousands of brand names in total; it's just that they're compartmentalized. I believe you'll see the same phenomenon online."

The Amazon.com brand has become so powerful that in September 1999 the company began selling bags with the Amazon.com logo. Responding to customer demand, the company offered six models, ranging in price from $29.99 to $79.99, including a shoulder tote, messenger bag, backpack, and a monostrap bag, and a computer briefcase.

What will Amazon.com look like five years from now? What will Amazon.com look like a *year* from now? "Jeff wants to have a big impact," said Tom Alberg, the Amazon.com director. "He's always seen a big opportunity and wants to fully capture that opportunity. Certainly, Jeff has the capability of creating a Microsoft, a General Electric, a Wal-Mart."

His friends say Bezos is totally focused on making this vision come true. According to Nick Hanauer, "He's got the discipline to be focused long term, and the discipline to say to himself, the employees, and the shareholders, 'if you're looking for quick returns, don't look here. We're trying to do something extraordinary and we're investing for the future.'" Hanauer called Bezos, "the most single-mindedly focused person I've ever met—to his detriment; it's all he cares about. He lives, eats, breathes Amazon.com. It occupies virtually his every waking moment. He is maniacally focused. I worry about his health. I worry about what he's going to be like when he's 50."

The bigger question: Is the Amazon.com model even working?

At the beginning of the year 2000, Amazon.com was having problems with every new category it had entered. eBay was still by far the dominant auction, and eToys tenaciously held the same position in the toy category. Blue Mountain Arts was still the leader, by far, in greeting cards. Pure-play electronic retailers spent an enormous amount of money on expanding their customer base. Amazon.com spends about 26 cents per dollar of revenue on marketing to bring in new customers—compared to 4 cents per dollar for traditional retailers.

The competition for selling stuff is fierce. Researchers at the University of Notre Dame have found that any two randomly selected pages on the World Wide Web are on average only 19 clicks away from each other. Thanks to intelligent software agents called shopping bots, consumers can instantly compare prices among vendors. One website, Buy.com, which sells books, videos, and music, is programmed to scan Amazon.com's prices and automatically undercut them. And, of course, looming over the horizon is Wal-Mart, which would like nothing better than to crush the upstart from Seattle.

In the meantime, Amazon.com continues to look for even more businesses to get into. In January 2000, the company spent $60 million to acquire a 23 percent stake in Kozmo.com Inc., a company that delivers video and digital video disk movies, snacks, and other items purchased over the Internet, usually within 60 minutes of receiving the order. (The move could be a hedge against all the distribution centers Amazon.com has built.) Also in January, the company agreed to acquire 5 percent of the outstanding shares of Greenlight.com, an online car-buyng company that is supported by a network of car dealers. Greenlight has the financial backing of Kleiner Perkins Caufield & Byers.

At the same time, Amazon.com began to modify its revenue focus by leveraging its 16-plus million customers and the value of its real estate. Amazon.com began selling placement on one of its home page tabs—the most prominent positions on the website—to other e-tailers. Greenlight agreed to pay $82.5 million over five years. Drugstore.com committed to paying $105 million over three years. At the same time, Amazon.com agreed to invest an additional $30 million in drugstore.com, giving it an almost 28 percent ownership. In February, the company entered into a similar alliance with Living.com, Inc., an online merchant of beds, sofas, pillows, linens and other home furnishings. Under the agreement, Living.com agreed to pay Amazon.com $145 million over five years for a tab position. For an undisclosed sum, amazon.com also bought an 18 percent stake in Living.com with warrants for an additional 9 percent. With these and other moves, Amazon.com had become as much an e-shopping mall landlord as well as a powerhouse retailer.

Clearly, Bezos does intend to sell everything to everybody. To reinforce the comprehensiveness of its selection, the company tweaked its logo in January 2000. Amazon.com replaced the downward curve underlining the company name with an upward curve that started at the letter *A* and ended with a dimple under the letter *Z*, forming a smile, and underlining the point that the company offers customers any product from A to Z.

"The further we go into this, the more we find new things to do. We think it would be really foolish to slavishly commit to plans we made in the past." But he has also said that the biggest challenge the company faces is "making sure that we continue to provide this kind of service level, even under the constraints of this growth," said Bezos.

Will the model work? Modern retailing has historically seen an ebb and flow between specialty stores and general-merchandise stores, between discount-happy category killers (such as Toys "R" Us) and warehouse stores such as Costco. Will people interested in buying a lot of things log onto Amazon.com, which will help them find anything they need? Or if those people are looking for a specific item—a Barbie doll or a power saw—will they go to a specialist or a general store? Will they join an online buying club? Will they buy what they need at an auction? Will they haggle over the price?

So, then, what is Amazon.com? Essentially it's a work in progress that could become a titanic portal to rival Yahoo. Bezos has said that he wants to build something the world has never seen. Although he is often asked if Amazon.com aspires to be "the Wal-Mart of the Web," he told *Fortune* that the company "is not trying to be the Anything of the Web. We're genetically pioneers. . . . Everybody here wants to do something completely new. I wake up every morning trying to make sure I can confound journalists and pundits who try to encapsulate us in an eight-second sound bite." He has said that one of the ways he defines success is "how well we defy easy analogy."

By the time you read this book, Amazon.com will have changed in some profound way. When you look again, it will change again.

Predictions? I think that there is a future for both virtual stores and brick-and-mortar stores, and that the real winners will be the so-called "clicks-and-mortar" retailers that combine a physical presence with a virtual presence. After all, Wal-Mart, Sears, and Nordstrom have been in the distribution and logistics business for more than a hundred years—for both retail and mail-order sales. They deal with picky customers every day. They have discernable cultures. The future belongs to these multichannel operations who sell merchandise in many ways at many price points.

A preview of retailing's future came at the end of 1999, when Wal-Mart announced a strategic partnership with American Online. AOL granted the retail giant permission to use AOL's CompuServe division for low-cost Internet access, while Wal-Mart agreed to promote CompuServe and AOL both in its stores and its television advertising. AOL, in turn, agreed to promote Wal-Mart's Internet site to AOL's 19 million users. At the same time, Yahoo! teamed up with Kmart, and Microsoft forged separate "clicks-and-mortar" alliances with Tandy Corp. (owner of the Radio Shack chain), the Best Buy Co. retail chain, and Simon Property Group, the nation's biggest shopping mall owner. And what will the merger of AOL and Time Warner mean to Amazon.com? Stay tuned.

One day, we will eventually see Amazon.com in the physical world, either with stores or kiosks. That proposition sounds crazy, but stranger things have happened in the world of retail. Brick-and-mortar obviously goes against Amazon.com's business model, but Bezos has been tweaking that model since Day One.

One thing is certain: even if Amazon.com went out of business tomorrow, it will have made an enormous impact on how business has changed at the end of the twentieth century and the beginning of the twenty-first. Virtually every company, regardless of size, has changed its thinking because of Amazon.com. For example, when General Motors

Corp. announced its formation of a new Internet-oriented business group called e-GM in August 1999, President and Chief Operating Officer G. Richard Wagoner Jr. said that the move was prompted by the sheer number of people using the Internet every single day. "We look at companies like Amazon.com, which we hadn't heard of three or four years ago and look at the impact they've had, and we say, this is something that we need to get our arms around," said Wagoner. "We want to play aggressively in this business and we want to win."

Surely when General Motors gets around to getting its e-commerce act together, you know that something revolutionary is going on. Whatever you think about Amazon.com, it is the prime spark for that revolution.

Time magazine certainly agreed when in chose Bezos as its Person of the Year for 1999. At the age of 35, he was the fourth youngest person ever picked for that honor, trailing only 25-year-old Charles Lindbergh in 1927, 26-year-old Queen Elizabeth II in 1952, and 34-year-old Martin Luther King Jr. in 1963. The magazine described Jeff simply as "unquestionably, the king of cybercommerce . . ." and an individual who has "helped build the foundation of our future."

Will Amazon.com be everything Bezos expects it to be, or will it be, as he often warns his people—with some hyperbole, perhaps—a footnote in Internet history? At the end of 1999, it was rated the best website for books, music, and videos; for toys and games; and for general merchandise; and drugstore.com was tops in health, according to Forrester Research. But how soon will it be before the next Amazon.com comes along, to depose the king? (To put Internet time in perspective, the *New York Times*, in November 1999, described the company as "the granddaddy of book sites.")

An astute student of business, Bezos is keenly aware that the pioneers are not always the survivors. "I tell people around here to wake up petrified and afraid every morning," he said. "I know we can lose it all. It's not a fear. It's a fact."

Be that as it may, I would not bet against Jeff Bezos.

TAKEAWAYS

Jeff Bezos pressed his foot to the gas pedal to make sure that Amazon.com would "Get Bigger Faster." He spent a good portion of 1999 creating a company that would have virtually everything for everybody. He took advantage of the company's lofty stock price to buy what he could not create. Along the way, his company made several public relations gaffes that showed that the company had to combat its own arrogance and sense of rightness.

- Get Bigger Faster to stay ahead of the competition.
- Buy what you can't create internally.
- When you get bad press, kill the negative news as quickly as possible with a firm decision and a dollop of spin.
- Bring in the type of management that can take you to the next level.
- Work every day to create a long-lasting company.
- "Work Hard, Have Fun and Make History."

notes

INTRODUCTION

page

xxii "In the knowledge sector . . . Jeff Bezos's brain." *New York Times Magazine*, April 12, 1999.

CHAPTER ONE: WHO IS JEFFREY BEZOS?

page

3 "But the reality . . . made me cry." *Wired,* March 1999.

5 "There was always . . . any bigger." *Seattle Times,* September 19, 1999.

5 "One of the things . . . opportunities." *Seattle Times,* September 19, 1999.

CHAPTER TWO: I'LL TAKE MANHATTAN

page

15 "Outside of Bill Gates . . . tactical instincts." *Red Herring* July 1997.

15 Minor recalled . . . "his own company." *Independent*, May 12, 1998.

18 "I didn't . . . on blind dates." *60 Minutes II*, February 3, 1999.

18 "professional dater" . . . "aren't resourceful." *Wired,* March 1999.

23 "the Rosetta stone of the Internet." *Architects of the Web,* Robert H. Reid; John Wiley & Sons, Inc., 1997.

24 "Shaw would later claim . . . on Shaw's dime. *New York Times Magazine*, April 12, 1999.

27 "With that huge diversity . . . customers value selection." Speech to Association of American Publishers, Washington, D.C., March 19, 1999.

30 "That was actually" . . . "another 48 hours." Speech to Association of American Publishers, Washington, D.C., March 19, 1999.

30 " 'a regret-minimization . . . make that decision." Speech at Lake Forest College, Lake Forest, Illinois, February 26, 1998.

CHAPTER THREE: SEATTLE

page

33 "When something is . . . your most valuable asset." Speech at Lake Forest College, February 26, 1998.

35 "This is a car . . . for *free*." Speech to Association of American Publishers, Washington, D.C., March 18, 1999.

35 He later said . . . "out to be Seattle." Speech at Lake Forest College, February 26, 1998.

37 He was looking . . . "the perfect person." Speech to Association of American Publishers, Washington, D.C., March 18, 1999.

CHAPTER FIVE: OUT TO LAUNCH

page

66 "Fortunately, though . . . in advance." Harvard Business School Study, 1997.

67 "I don't know . . . incredibly optimistic." Lake Forest College, February 26, 1998.

67 "We had very low" . . . "exercise our systems." Lake Forest College, February 26, 1998.

68 "Before 1995 . . . what the Internet was." *Washington Post*, July 20, 1998.

68 "Turns out that" . . . "this lichen book." Lake Forest College, February 26, 1998.

68 "We didn't invest" . . . "invested in Jeff." *Time,* December 27, 1999.

72 "It is very exciting" . . . " 'know this person?" Lake Forest College, February 26, 1998.

73 "He said we" . . . "'Yeah, let's do it." Lake Forest College, February 26, 1998.

74 "Our business plan" . . . "try new things." Speech to American Association of Publishers, Washington, D.C., March 18, 1999.

75 "I've been staring at it in horrified fascination for days." Conference call with stock analysts, July 21, 1999.

75 "We were trying" . . . "dramatically improved things." Speech at Lake Forest College, February 26, 1998.

82 "We have a strong focus" . . . "matter to customers." *Business 2.0,* April 1999.

CHAPTER SIX: GET BIG FAST

page

84 To illustrate that confidence. . . "littered with corpses." *Web Week,* October 1995.

91 "Despite this primitive, infant technology" . . . "this very quickly." Speech to Lake Forest College, February 26, 1998.

94 Although that was still. . . " 'what's going on here.' " Speech to Association of American Publishers, Washington, D.C., March 18, 1999.

96 Marc Andreessen . . . "Just plain wins." *Architects of the Web,* 1997.

98 "If we treated them right" . . . "their credit cards." *Seattle Times,* January 5, 1997.

99 "the avatar of the Web." *Fast Company,* February 1997.

99 "*Keiretsu* are rooted . . . work with partners." *Red Herring,* February 1998.

100 "We joked that we were going to have to change our voice-mail system to say, 'If you're a customer, press one. If you're a VC, press two.' " *New Yorker,* August 11, 1997.

101 "We had to compete" . . . "for Amazon.' " *Fast Company,* February 1997.

103 "Kleiner and John . . . on prime real estate." *New Yorker,* August 11, 1997.

CHAPTER SEVEN: RAISE THE BAR

page

105 "We're the only start-up company I know that started in a garage." *Web Week*, August 19, 1996.

106 "In the world today . . . building a great team." *Fast Company*, February 1997.

106 From the very beginning . . . "sort of the meta-interview." *Wall Street Journal*, May 4, 1999.

107 He told the *Wall Street Journal* that managers . . . "are interesting and fun to be with." *Wall Street Journal*, May 4, 1999.

107 David Risher, who . . . "find out what they need." *Wall Street Journal,* May 4, 1999.

108 "I'm looking for people" . . . "for their actions." *New York Times Magazine*, March 14, 1999.

110 "Competitors can never copy a culture" . . . " 'not intense.' " Speech at Lake Forest College, February 26, 1998.

111 "I think they recruit" . . . "in their own right." *Seattle Times,* July 27, 1998.

112 He estimated that . . . "change a corporate culture." *Seattle Times,* July 27, 1998.

113 "That's either poor planning . . . every four months." Videotape of moving day, November 1996.

118 "I had interviewed with" . . . "Peninsula." Harvard Business School Study, 1997.

119 "She said there" . . . "impress each other." *Wall Street Journal,* March 25, 1999.

119 "I couldn't sleep" . . . "part of the team." Harvard Business School Study, 1997.

CHAPTER EIGHT: "ANAL-RETENTIVE" ABOUT CUSTOMER SERVICE

page

127 "When people ask . . . a better service." Speech at Lake Forest College, February 26, 1998.

127 "that we were going to obsess . . . over them." Speech at Lake Forest College, February 26, 1998.

127 "The Internet is this" . . . "is the customers." *Business Week,* September 27, 1999.

127 He considered that the . . . "going too far." Speech to Association of American Publishers, Washington, D.C., March 18, 1999.

128 The value proposition "that you" . . . "primitive, infant technology." Speech at Lake Forest College, February 26, 1998.

129 "We will never make" . . . "an engaging and fun one." Speech at Lake Forest College, February 26, 1998.

130 "I abide by the theory" . . . "they'll like that." *Washington Post,* July 20, 1998.

131 "If you spend" . . . "for a purchase decision," *New York Times* magazine, March 14, 1999.

131 "People don't buy books" . . . "trying to capture that." *Wall Street Journal,* May 16, 1996.

132 When publishers and authors asked Bezos . . . "with the customer reviews." Speech at Lake Forest College, February 26, 1998.

138 "I don't think anybody could predict" . . . "as we go." *Seattle Times,* January 5, 1997.

143 "When we did focus groups" . . . " 'it really was that easy.' " Speech at Lake Forest College, February 26, 1998.

148 "It's a Tupperware party" . . . "of the Internet." *Bloomberg News,* September 10, 1999.

150 "means that if you order . . . to your customers." Harvard Business School Study, 1997.

154 The company received an e-mail. . . "do something about this?" Speech to Association of American Publishers, Washington, D.C., March 18, 1999.

154 In another instance. . . "I assure you." Speech at Lake Forest College, February 26, 1998.

156 "helping people make purchase" . . . "a customer company." *Business Week,* September 16, 1999.

CHAPTER NINE: TOAST OF THE TOWN . . . OR AMAZON.TOAST?

160 "We definitely think" . . . "had some competition." *Wall Street Journal*, January 28, 1997.

161 "Barnes & Noble isn't doing . . . just a fact." *New York Times Magazine*, April 12, 1999.

161 "as soon as it was ready." Harvard Business School Study, 1997.

162 "While Jeff and I . . . a no-brainer." *Ibid.*

162 "we were committed" . . . "enduring global franchise." *Ibid.*

162 "This is not yet an official bakeoff" . . . "distribution, and analyst quality." *Ibid.*

163 "the CFO should be the CEO of the going-public process." *Ibid.*

163 "We decided that we liked" . . . "have their full attention." *Ibid.*

164 "as just another step" . . . "to build our brand." *Ibid.*

164 "We hoped these" . . . "economies of scale." *Ibid.*

164 "decided to remain true . . . a significant problem." *Ibid.*

166 "the confidentiality of many" . . . "underpinnings to our business model." *Ibid.*

166 "really a relief to me" . . . "right choices for your long-term strategy.' " *Ibid.*

167 "designed as the preeminent . . . worldwide," *Wall Street Journal*, May 13, 1997.

168 "When we first started . . . can be anything." *Business Week,* September 16, 1999.

169 "We've always offered" . . . "in terms of purchasing power." *Wall Street Journal*, January 28, 1997.

170 "First of all" . . . "concerned about two guys in a garage." *Entrepreneurial Edge*, Volume 2 (Spring) 1997.

172 "Can Amazon.com establish . . . excellent online retailers?" *Fortune*, September 29, 1997.

172 "If we were giving away" . . . at-work users. *The Wall Street Journal*, January 28, 1997.

173 "We don't want to win a Pyrrhic victory" by losing money on the online operation. *Fortune*, September 29, 1997.

174 "being an enormous benefit . . . that opportunity comes along." *New York Times*, January 5, 1998.

175 "It's hugely significant" . . . "of why we do." *Ibid.*

175 "not just fulfilling demand, it's creating it," *Washington Post*, July 20, 1998.

CHAPTER TEN: POSTER CHILD FOR INTERNET COMMERCE

179 "Great leaders are" . . . "value proposition of the enterprise." *Fast Company*, February 1997.

181 "We don't make external projections about profitability, breakeven, etc.—we don't make any forward-looking projections." *Upside Today*, June 8, 1999.

181 "Profits are the lifeblood . . . a big mistake." *Business 2.0*, August 1999.

184 "It's very very goofy." *60 Minutes II* , February 3, 1999.

185 "Many of today's billionaires . . . an old door." *Forbes*, October 11, 1999.

187 "we just couldn't make it work," *Fortune,* November 9, 1998.

187 "nervous about giving up control." *Ibid.*

189 "no different than . . . annoy some people." *New York Times*, April 1, 1999.

189 "People will go" . . . "inside the floppy disk." Speech at Lake Forest College, February 26, 1998.

191 "Our strategy is to . . . the ones selling them." *Independent*, May 12, 1998.

193 "Of course it's subjective . . . of being online." *Upside Today,* June 8, 1999.

194 Amazon.com was a fast-moving stock . . . Coca-Cola for 26.4 months. *Business Week*, September [illegible]3, 1999.

198 "Get big fast." *New York Times*, M[illegible] 9, 1998.

201 "Amazon will be the brand name for a tulip someday." *Forbes*, December 28, 1998.

201 "I don't think Amazon will earn" . . . "my Prozac." *Bloomberg*, December 17, 1998.

205 "As the obstetricians say, even one baby dropped on its head is one baby too many." *Seattle Times*, January 19, 1999.

CHAPTER ELEVEN: GET BIGGER FASTER

208 "We want to build" . . . "model, isn't practical." *Business Week*, May 31, 1999.

209 his fellow bidders/sellers. . . "but item arrived.") *Seattle Times*, September 19, 1999.

210 This mania prompted Rick Berry . . . "for even more." *New York Times*, January 11, 1999.

213 "wakes me up . . . I know too much," *Forbes*, January 24, 2000.

216 "If customers are in" . . . "a cash register in every pocket." *New York Times*, October 4, 1999.

219 "In the categories . . . band together with third parties." *Bloomberg*, September 29, 1999.

221 "We had an instant chemistry" . . . "the Internet is incredible." *Fortune*, November 8, 1999.

222 "This is complicated stuff . . . all about execution." *Seattle Weekly*, October 21, 1999.

224 "If Publisher X gives us . . . more money." *Washington Post*, July 20, 1998.

225 "breaking with standard industry" . . . "the way it should be." *Seattle Times*, February 9, 1999.

226 "This potentially could rightly upset . . . what videos you want." *Los Angeles Times*, August 26, 1999.

226 "Privacy is of utmost importance" . . . "letting people decide individually." Associated Press, August 27, 1999.

227 "Amazon Bookstore sat . . . something a lot sooner." *Wall Street Journal*, September 9, 1999.

227 "As part of the litigation . . . their context was." *Ibid.*

229 "Amazon brilliantly . . . entered the language." *Washington Post*, July 20, 1998.

229 "If I ask you to name" . . . "same phenomenon online." *Wall Street Journal*, July 12, 1999.

230 26 cents per dollar of revenue on marketing. *Business Week*, November 15, 1999.

232 "is not trying to be the Anything of the Web" . . . "defy easy analogy." *Business Week*, September 15, 1999, and *Fortune*, November 8, 1999.

234 "granddaddy of book sites." *New York Times*, November 18, 1999.

234 "I tell people around here to wake up petrified" . . . "It's a fact." *60 Minutes II*, February 4, 1999.

index